The Cinematic ImagiNation

The Cinematic ImagiNation

Indian Popular Films as Social History

JYOTIKA VIRDI

RUTGERS UNIVERSITY PRESS
New Brunswick, New Jersey, and London

Library of Congress Cataloging-in-Publication Data

Virdi, Jyotika, 1962–
  The cinematic ImagiNation [sic] : Indian popular films as social history / by Jyotika Virdi.
    p. cm
  Includes bibliographical references and index.
  ISBN 0-8135-3190-X (cloth : alk. paper) — ISBN 0-8135-3191-8 (pbk. : alk. paper)
  1. Motion pictures—India. 2. Motion pictures—Social aspects—India. I. Title.

PN1993.5.I8 V57 2003
791.43'0954—dc21   2002024836

British Cataloging-in-Publication information is available from the British Library.

Manufactured in the United States of America

For Julia and Jogin
my teachers in the academy . . . in politics

Contents

Preface

A SCANDAL IN cinema studies of the last few decades has been the lack of attention paid to Indian popular cinema, the world's largest film industry. At a recent Society for Cinema Studies' plenary a panelist's speculations about the vanishing 1970s' style energy in film studies initiated an animated debate.[1] The discussion failed to acknowledge that underlying this stagnation is the field's saturation with Hollywood and western cinema—that film studies stands at the brink of a sea change if we "unthink" Eurocentricism, decenter Hollywood/western cinema, and explore nonwestern film cultures, and that multicultural comparative film studies curricula will provide the sorely needed disciplinary reinvigoration.[2] Though attention to national cinema is an index of growing interest in "other" cinema literatures, it is still light years from dislodging Hollywood's centrality in film studies.

It is therefore appropriate to caution against the current rush to declare the internationalization of cultural studies still under Euro-Anglian hegemony. Such premature proclamations at best signal a desire to include diverse cultural economies in media studies.[3] However, demanding an international approach to cultural studies and a place for Indian national cinema is not meant to invoke a simple-minded national-imperial opposition, indict the west's homogenizing influence, or valorize a national claim to cultural sovereignty.

Rather, I contend that Hindi cinema's particular hybrid form reveals nationalism itself as a contradictory force: the handmaiden of a dominant elite discourse, reinventing imperial metropolitan culture on the one hand and bringing regional/oppositional strains to heel on the other.[4] It enjoys popular mass investment in the hegemonic ideal while claiming to resist acculturation. Understanding nationalism bound within religio-ethnic identity—not new to the Indian experience or other parts of the world—has gained new urgency in global geopolitics after the events of September 11, 2001. Feting the cultural "other" that gained currency in cultural studies requires careful reconsideration. The thin line between nationalism and fascism, insurgent freedom fighters and "terrorists," calls for a case by case judgment of the genealogy, cause, class, and bloc such movements represent.

Postcolonial studies, the officially authorized enclave for studying the Third/First World dynamics in the academy, privileges the literary text. Produced by a narrow class of intellectuals, consumed by an elite reading public in the ex-colonies, and satisfying the growing taste for such texts in the First World, the literary text falls squarely within the high culture zones of a transnational bourgeoisie. Its stranglehold—marked, for instance, by the growing popularity of Indians writing in English, and celebrated by such publications as *Granta* and the *New Yorker*—must also allow room for "plebeian" cultural forms, such as popular Hindi cinema.[5]

In India, fifty years after independence, the literary text barely constitutes the fringe of cultural consumption; the attention it receives far exceeds its reach or impact. Hindi cinema's popularity and importance rivals—or more likely outstrips—the literary text. The imperialism of literature that has been canonized as "writing back" to the empire even eludes Edward Said, who calls for careful attention to the media yet nevertheless falls back on the salutary effects of the literary text.[6] Said's book *Orientalism* launched postcolonial criticism, a corpus that has expanded over the last two decades.[7] Yet its preoccupation with literary work lacks the cultural immediacy that bell hooks or Cornel West bring to bear on African American studies when they engage, for instance, with rap music's place in the mosaic of that culture.

As slogans of multiculturalism and diversity take hold in campus politics and terms like "postcolonial" and "postcoloniality" forge their way from English departments to the more diffusely housed body of work called cultural studies, they get reconstituted as a hazy mix of theoretical claims—or, more controversially, as "area studies" tied to a generalized history, politics, and culture of colonialism.[8] Global reconfiguration (due to increasing Euro-American cultural domination and ethnic transmigration) demands a new understanding of cultural politics, diverse epistemologies, and a shift in postcolonial studies' exclusive devotion to the written word—particularly given nonwestern cultures' predominantly oral traditions.

The drive to internationalize media studies and dethrone the Indian literary text in favor of popular cinema is fueled by my interest in foregrounding class politics within the cosmopolitanized local/global context. In deconstructing national cinema, rather than valorizing its claims to "Indian culture" I steer clear of a binary opposition between a "low," popular, resistant Hindi cinema and a hegemonic "high" literary text culture. Cultural critics' cautionary tales of global concentration of media conglomerates at the close of the twentieth century call for reconsidering fantastic readings of resistance in popular texts.[9] I view popular cinema as both furthering and challenging reigning hegemonic discourses. Discursive conflicts, a prominent feature of popular culture, rarely provoke radical ruptures in dominant discourse. Rather, they deflect or reconstitute hegemony, or induce change—both reform and backlash—visible only when we take a longer view of history.

Positioning this book in the interstices between postcolonial, film, and cultural studies, I approach Hindi cinema here through several theoretical frames: the specter of globalization, the internationalization of cultural studies, considerations of the nation embedded in national cinema or postcoloniality, popular culture as a legitimate slate for reading social history, and the place of gender, sexuality, class, caste, and religious community in shaping that history. In this interdisciplinary spirit I offer something to a broad spectrum of academic and nonacademic readers: literary and cultural critics engaged with film, media, postcolonial, and women's studies, cultural and South Asian historians, political theorists engaged with nationalism, western and nonwestern "Indophiles" and "filmphiles," and the growing Indian reading public.

I am keen to demonstrate to film scholars and students that Hindi cinema redeploys familiar classical Hollywood cinematic strategies, yet is novel in the way it marshals its own distinctive aesthetics and poetics to address the nation and (de)colonization. Postcolonial literary critics preoccupied with the Indo-Anglian literary text have inevitably focused on the twin processes of colonialism and nationalism to engage with the shorthand used by Hindi cinema to deal with identical issues. Elite educational institutions sustain English, a colonial language with tremendous symbolic and material power the vernaculars lack, reproducing cultural and material stratification. And, the English print media's supercilious attitude toward Hindi cinema capitalizes on caricaturing Hindi cinema. A new critical approach to Hindi films, therefore, can replace such disdain with an appreciation for Hindi cinema's importance in Indian cultural politics.

I am also invested in using Hindi cinema to illustrate to political theorists, historians, and sociologists how arcane theories of the citizen-subject and nation attributed to modernization are negotiated in the popular imagination. Cultural critics who examine Indian modernity through television, advertising, fast food, and consumer culture declare that it has not completely subsumed India's feudal structures. My intent is to show how popular Hindi cinema keeps that elusive modernization process center-stage and I claim a place for film in the domain of South Asian cultural history—along with the arts, architecture, literature, and religion.

Serious intellectual attention is paid to Indian popular cinema in a growing number of essays and general overviews.[10] In the 1990s three books in particular, Sumita Chakravarty's *National Identity in Indian Popular Cinema: 1947–87*, Rachel Dwyer's *All You Want Is Money, All You Need Is Love: Sex and Romance in Modern India*, Vijay Mishra's *Bollywood Cinema: Temples of Desire*, and Madhava Prasad's *Ideology of the Hindi Film: A Historical Construction* were welcome additions examining popular and art films. While I share their eclectic methodology, which draws on film, feminist, and Marxist-cultural theories, this book stands in contrast to theirs' in several ways. My film selection is less free-wheeling; I concentrate on popular cinema, a prodigious body of work with distinctive aesthetic features, idiom, iconicity, system of production, and modes of consumption.

Rachel Dwyer's work, for instance, combines a few critical films, pulp fiction, and film journalism (only an aspect of this book's focus) as key textual sources to understanding the contested space of Indian middle class values filtered through notions of erotic and romantic love. I take a longer historical view of post-independence Hindi cinema, as well as dealing with sexual politics. Madhava Prasad's premise is that Hindi films (particularly between 1950 and 1970) are based on the same template, and in Vijay Mishra's view, in Bombay cinema, dharma presides over what is "primarily a sentimental melodramatic romance."[11] Change in postindependence Hindi films is central to my project, which I trace through shifts in its discursive history. I do not suggest a prescriptive model to analyze Hindi films; rather, I track the ways in which the nation implants itself in the popular imaginary. Multiple discourses crisscross, merge, or contradict one another as controversial public events, laws, social movements, and personalities influence the nation's history. While theorizing a body of texts is the critic's *raison d'être*, my framework is open and flexible enough to absorb alternative readings.[12]

Finally, my work is driven by the central preoccupation in Hindi films: the nation. Sumita Chakravarty does identify a unique "national identity" in Indian cinema by drawing on Hindu philosophical principles in her investigation of cinema as "imperso-nation" and "masquerade."[13] I analyze how this "nation" plays out as a prominent trope along the terrain of gender, sexuality, family, and community. Far from trying to validate or reify Hindi films' "Indianness" or national identity, I point to the flaws, the fundamental untenability of the same in Hindi films.

If we consider how "the modern history of literary study has been bound up with the development of cultural nationalism, whose aim was first to distinguish the national canon, then to maintain its eminence, authority, and aesthetic autonomy," then we must be wary of cultural nationalism that creeps into our methodology, and hold suspect assertions for distinct indigenous theories and apparatuses.[14] Chakravarty takes the Indian nation as a given and Nehru's *Discovery of India* as the master text of its history. For her, Indian films, through specific historical and mythological genres, bear out this unique cultural history.[15] In this book, instead, I deconstruct the nation, its content, form, history, and theories by revealing how artifacts like Indian popular cinema work to naturalize it. While I acknowledge that history narrativizes the nation, and that master texts are vital to the architecture of the nation and national identity, I also show how these bulwarks deploy rhetorical tropes to manage illogical and contradictory strains, anxiously deflecting imminent breakdown.

Hindi cinema constitutes and is constituted by a shifting discourse that constantly reimagines the nation: it is important that we view "India" as a political, contingent, developing, unfixed framework, without a forced coincidence between nation and territory or chronology, ethnicity, community and religion.[16] Hindi films are deeply imbricated in social transformation, and documenting that transformation is the object of this book.

Acknowledgments

I AM INCALCULABLY indebted to: Juia Lesage, mentor and pioneer in the field for her unfailing support; Gina Marchetti for her careful review, probing insights, and thought-provoking engagement with the manuscript; Ellen Seiter, whose encouragement has meant more than she can imagine; Antoinette Burton for generously giving her time and shoulder to lean on; Meg Greene and Brian Greenberg for their time, warmth, and hospitality at a moment's notice; Linda Williams for putting me on the road to film studies; and Leslie Mitchner for faith in my project.

Several colleagues have helped at crucial moments: Bill Cadbury, Mary Gold, Lalitha Gopalan, Linda Kintz, Bob Kolker, Barbara Miller, Dan Moshenberg, and Rajeswari Sunder Rajan. I thank the staff at the National Film Archives of India in Pune: Suresh Chabria, Mr. John, Arti Karkhanis, Ms. Lakshmi, and Ms. Shinde; Mickey Dutta, Tom Fuerth, Chris Laskey, and Tory James for technical support at the University of Windsor; and the AIIS (American Institute of Indian Studies) for a fellowship that helped initiate this project. I am extremely grateful to Anne Sanow for her meticulous editing. I also thank Marilyn Campbell for seeing the book through production. The publishers apologize for the poor picture quality of some of the frame grabs from videotapes and DVDs in this book. They were the best available, and we felt that it was important to include them as illustrations regardless of quality.

Sections of chapters 2 and 5 have been published in slightly different versions and I wish to thank the journals for permission to reprint them here. "*Mr. and Mrs.55*: The Comedy of Gender, Law, and Nation" appeared in *Jump Cut* 43 (2000): 76–84; "Reverence, Rape—and then Revenge: Popular Hindi Cinema's 'Woman's Film' Genre" in *Screen* 40:1 Spring (1999): 17–37; and "Comic Woman, Victim Woman: Pushing the Boundaries of Gender and Genre in Popular Hindi Cinema" was published in *Visual Anthropology*, Vol. 11 no.4 (1998): 355–372.

My eternal gratitude goes to my mother, Raj, a feminist long before it became acceptable, who gave us her sense of independence; and my father, Tej, whose stance on gender equity sets him apart from his generation. My sister, Malika, who dares to follow her dreams, and my brother, Ranjit, who inherited all the "mellow genes," have come through in various crises for which I remain permanently indebted.

Arvind Rajagopal, a skeptic, Rakesh Shukla a cynic, and Usha Zacharias, who combines both with humor, all sustain me with their friendship. Thanks also to friends now scattered all over the world: Shobha Aggarwal, Bishakha Dé Sarkar, Gaurav Dutt, Vrinda Grover, Charu Gupta, Indrani and Shreekant Gupta, Manisha Gupte, Anand and Sujata Jagota, Sanjay Kalra, Jyotsna Kapur, Deepti Mehrotra, Sidhartha Mohanty, Laxmi Murthy, Nandini Ooman, Ranjana Padhi, Mira Sadgopal, Shobha Sadgopan, Sathyamala, Jogin Sengupta, Mukul Sharma, Shalini Sinha, Bharat Shekhar and his father Rajinder Shekhar, Aseem Shrivastava, Shree Rao Seshadri, Sudhi Seshadri (my hero), Kanta Subbarao, Emmanuel Theophilus, Vasantha Venkaswamy, and the Saheli collective in Delhi.

Finally, words fail to express my debt to Anand Swamy for his loving support through our long friendship, his indefatigable generosity, compassion, endurance through the highs and lows of this project—and our life together. In part I dedicate this book to him.

The Cinematic ImagiNation

Introduction

POPULAR HINDI CINEMA provides a fascinating account of Indian history and cultural politics. Hindi cinema's own agenda—imagining a unified nation—is the organizing principle of my project. In Hindi films the image of the nation as a mythical community—a family—collapses under the weight of its own contradictions. Gender, heterosexuality, class, and religious communities crosshatch the nation, and each of these disrupt the nationalist narration in Hindi cinema to reveal a different history.

Films have fascinated and entertained the Indian public for a hundred years since the Lumière brothers first exhibited this craft in 1895. Yet serious intellectual attention to commercial cinema, the popular form dominated by Hindi films, has only just begun.[1] This book's scope concentrates on popular films of the Nehruvian era and its decline, the past fifty-odd years since India's independence from British Rule in 1947. I use independence as a dividing line, a watershed in contemporary Indian history. (Hindi films from this point on, not coincidentally, are shot through with a fascination with the "new nation," its present, past and future.)

Hindi cinema is the largest film industry in the world with the most prolific rate of production—a staggering 800 films a year—screened for approximately fifteen million people a day. It is *the* dominant cultural institution and product in India, providing affordable entertainment to audiences drawn primarily (though not exclusively) from the working class in urban centers. Though Hindi is a regional northern language, Hindi cinema's audience transcends lingual-regional boundaries within the nation, making it fit the national cinema billing like no other. Beyond national boundaries its aesthetic and affective mode attracts nonwestern audiences in Africa, Eastern Europe, Russia, and the Middle East. It resonates powerfully with the Indian diaspora, often becoming their only connection with the homeland and the main intergenerational culture diasporic families share while located in places as far-flung as Australia, Africa, Britain, Canada, the Caribbean islands, Southeast Asia, and the United States.

The pleasures the commercial film offers, and the desires it creates, make it a vital part of popular culture and a critical site of cultural interpretation. Despite its permeating Indian culture, Hindi cinema's stylistic conventions are paradoxically in complete disjunction from everyday reality: the films use dialogues instead of speech, costumes rather than clothes, sets and exotic settings, and lavish song and dance routines—hardly everyday familiar surroundings. Within the mise-en-scène, this nonspecificity of address distances Hindi films from "authentic" portrayals of Indian life. Regional markers of costume, dress, and culture are either erased or deployed arbitrarily, and elements from different regions are mixed to figure as signs of cosmopolitan culture that account for a particular type of kitsch, the insignia of Hindi films. Even though they abide by other realist conventions, such as cause-and-effect linear narratives, continuity editing, and spatial/temporal unity, the films show scant regard for looking "authentic" or bearing a similitude to realism.

This is perhaps why the popular film has been condemned and ridiculed by India's literati, who see only that it is replete with hackneyed plots, unchanging themes, and trite messages. Critical attention to Indian popular films is recent, but measured against the sheer number of films and their history, serious exegesis is very limited.[2] Conventional wisdom about popular cinema is that it is entirely transparent and that any tools of analysis are in excess of the task in hand.

Theoretical Location

To classify Hindi films I skirt several conventional approaches: the mythological, the "social," and the chronological decade-to-decade historical account. Neither time period nor stars, nor auteurs, is the axis against which I plot a historical narrative. (Indian films have often been historicized in terms of the rise of specific popular stars, their styles, and personae read as an index of important social undercurrents.[3]) Nor are Hindi films interpreted here as a throwback to foundational myths contained within Hindu epics, the *Ramayana* and the *Mahabahrata*; the limited critical work done on Hindi films and cinematic narratives tends to fall back on Indian mythology and posits the figures that appear in these classic epics as archetypes in Indian cinema.[4] In a postcolonial society suffering from the ravages of colonial dislocation, such a critical move carries the appeal of an antiwestern, anti-imperialist epistemology—of posing an alternative indigenous knowledge. It assumes that a kernel of pure, untouched Indian culture exists somewhere that has defended itself against the modernist onslaught. Though I empathize with the sentiment that motivates such a strategy, I do not adopt it as part of my own critical approach.[5] In part, my response stems from an unease with the dangers of "reactive indigenism" that lurk behind it.[6]

The fact is that western ideology, theory, and training are part of the condition Indian intellectuals and cultural workers live in.[7] I claim a cultural studies approach, which in the Euro-American academy is invested in new social movements around race, class, gender, and sexuality, forging an interdisciplinary arena with distinct or overlapping methodologies drawn from anthropology, communication, history, literature, and sociology.[8] However, this cultural studies approach becomes thoroughly inadequate when it deals with the particularities of the postcolonial nation. Cultural theories used to study western texts do not deal with the complexities of decolonization, a process that marks the form and content of Indian cultural texts. I focus on how the films play out the politics of caste, class, community, gender, and sexuality, all bearing traces of a specific Indian social and historical context.

The colonial encounter left its trace on every aspect of Indian polity and culture. Contrary to conventional wisdom about the "east" and "west"—and never the twain shall meet—an osmosis did occur in Indian cultural forms, creating new hybrids.[9] These changes demand an epistemological shift in theories applied to postcolonial cultures like India. For instance, social psychologist Ashis Nandy, a proponent of an "indigenous sensibility," views Hindi cinema's peculiar hybrid nature as a deliberate refusal of "authenticity" and "realism" of the kind expected by a western audience. He reads this as a symptom of protest and resilience against an alien culture of modernization.[10] If such a view—specific to the postcolonial situation—reveals resistance to imperial pressure on the one hand, it is culpable of "indigenous chauvinism" on the other.

The failure of conventional cultural and film theory to grasp—much less account for—the particularities of decolonized nations and their hybrid national culture has given way to the emergence of postcoloniality. As a distinct area study, postcolonial theory deals with the complexities of decolonization occluded by cultural studies; I locate this project at their intersection.[11] While the term "postcolonial" accurately reflects the gesture of ceding political control (or more precisely self-government) to the ex-colony, in the era of multinational corporations and financial oligopolies the term becomes emptied of real significance as new forms of imperial control replace old ones. In the 1990s India opened its doors to transnational corporations, abandoning the lip service it once gave to the idea of a mixed socialist economy during the Nehruvian era. Free market proponents who view state socialism as a thing of the past are gleefully writing that era's obituary.

Indian media workers and intellectuals have felt an overpowering sense of optimism and elation about these cultural changes. The pressure on the tightly controlled state-owned media system has forced it to open its channels to a proliferation of ideas and voices now competing for a place within the media marketplace.[12] A revolution is taking place on the air waves and in televisual space, and its effect on film cannot be discounted since television and film have never functioned as altogether discrete media.[13]

The present moment of flux has unleashed intense confusion and debates between intellectuals on the left and right as to whether these changes signal opportunities for growth or whether they further consolidate entrenched hierarchies. What these changes bode for colonial relationships is uncertain; however, they raise unsettling doubts about colonialism remaining a thing of the past. Despite these problems—and the resonance the term "postcolonial" has with "postmodernism," in keeping with academic fashion—we do have a useful body of literature subsumed under the rubric of postcolonial studies that deals with pertinent issues related to colonialism, culture, and politics.[14] Notwithstanding the ambiguities contained within the term, I find it useful to subsume a study of Hindi cinema within postcolonial studies because of other concerns central to its discourse, namely the making of a "new nation."

As a preliminary attempt within literary theory, Fredric Jameson has speculated about "third world" texts and their preoccupation with a social imaginary bound within and by the idea of the "nation."[15] His 1986 essay sparked off a debate among theorists traveling between the U.S. and Indian academy.[16] Aijaz Ahmad is one among the many "titans" of postcolonial cultural studies and his response is worth going over quickly to identify key issues within the tangled web of theories about "third" world fiction, particularly since many of the critics use the "Indian case" as a springboard for their theories.

Jameson argues that the nation is a dominant trope in all third-world literature and fiction, and that the entire world of arts can be encompassed within the national allegory. Aijaz Ahmad hotly contests this, protesting first about tidy categories such as first, second, and third world, and then arguing that Indian writings have been preoccupied by "other things" such as women's emancipation and education.[17] Feminist research points to the most serious failure in this debate: the elision of gender and sexuality, categories deeply embedded in imagining the nation. Ahmad implies that women's "things" are radically separate, "other," rather than deeply intertwined with the nation. Women and feminine values are in fact "code words for national values and identity. . . . The figure of women and feminine values have [always] been . . . deeply implicated in and utilized by national discourses."[18] Furthermore, the sexual exploitation and oppression imbricated within the domestic sphere remain unattended to by both nationalist discourse and Marxist theories privileging class, to which both Jameson and Ahmad subscribe.[19] The task at hand is to foreground the issues of women and minority movements along with anti-imperial discourse, without sublimating or allegorizing any one of them.

Nationalism and Cinema

In *Waving the Flag*, Andrew Higson argues that "a nation does not express itself through culture: it is culture that produces the nation."[20] Yet despite relentless attempts to define the nation, it remains hopelessly elusive. Benedict Anderson, Ernest Gellner, E. J. Hobsbawm, Tom Nairn, and Hugh Seton-Watson have all appraised it: a product of capitalism, underdevelopment as well as development, and tensions between modernity and atavism, the nation drives mass movements and uprisings, determining the center of gravity and destiny of not only politics and economics but also the citizen-subjects' sense of identity.[21] Indeed, nationalism displaces the stranglehold of a medieval theocracy in its modern-day secular version of citizen subjecthood. In part this is because nationalism is perceived as "natural" rather than constructed—at once tenacious, adaptable, and resilient. Yet for all its force and continually changing guise, nationalism is still a relatively unexplored, or rather sporadically explored, phenomenon.

Tom Nairn revisited this topic three decades after his first treatise on nationalism, *The Break-Up of Britain.*[22] The west's "semi-hysterical response" to demonized eastern ethnic nationalism after 1989, Nairn argues, is "tribalism" disguised as uneven economic development. Living in the United States and working in Canada, as I do, with my passport and work permit carefully scrutinized by both border patrols, the irony of viewing resurgent nationalism as a peculiar form of East European, African, or third-world ethnic tribalism is never lost on me. The fact is that nationalism has never receded anywhere in the world, and in this "globalized" era it exerts a powerful influence on everything from geopolitics to the acutely private space of psychic identity.

Recent interest in national cinemas coincides with global eruptions of ethnic nationalism, which either signal the last gasps of resistance against globalization or the sublimation of the socialist enterprise in the post-Cold War culture. Nationalism might be the single most important twenty-first century political challenge: channeling resistance against the unfettered power of transnational corporations (TNCs), even as both nations and TNCs divide rather than unite the international working class. Media scholars have shown interest in Benedict Anderson's explanation of the nation's origin, the nineteenth-century imagined community attributed to the spread of print media capitalism. In India, however, where literacy rates are low, nonprint media are far more important, and Hindi cinema's influence is even more profound than that of state-controlled radio and television.[23] Though cinema offers a palimpsest to study the imagined Indian nation, it has been neglected by literary-critical scholars as well as by historians, political theorists, sociologists, and anthropologists.

The emerging national cinema literature mentions this common elision of cinema's role in creating the imagined community, the nation. British and Latin American cinema chroniclers are hard-put to even claim a national cinema status, given the extent to which these cinemas interact with international forces of production, labor, finance, distribution, and consumption.[24] Even the themes and preoccupations in British and Latin American films make them indistinguishable from Hollywood productions. Popular Indian cinema, however, is a national cinema proper not only because it is produced and consumed predominantly within national boundaries, but also because of other factors that identify a national film industry: inheriting and circulating notions of national identity, negotiating conflicts experienced by the imagined community, producing new representations of the nation, and constructing a collective consciousness of nationhood through special cultural referents.[25]

Hindi cinema is unique in using the family as the primary trope to negotiate caste, class, community, and gender divisions, making for complex but decipherable hieroglyphics through which it configures the nation and constructs a nationalist imaginary. Deploying an affective mode of address, Hindi cinema is an emotional register and therefore a virtual teleprompter for reading the script called "nation." Furthermore, the postmodernist interrogation of binary divisions (such as the private/public dichotomy under capitalism) animates my search for the links between the enduring private elements of family, marriage, and heterosexuality, the accompanying discourses on masculinity/femininity, and the public discourse of nationalism. In short, my work shows how Hindi cinema projects the imagined nation on the terrain of family, heterosexuality, and community through contestations that throw into relief its social structures and realignments.

The nation's capacity for both infinite fission and consolidation has attracted intellectual curiosity.[26] David Lloyd argues that nationalism occurs in conjunction—not congruence—with several social movements, and the ruptures among them are preempted by the "superordination of the state form . . . structured according to the ideology of the

hegemonic elites created by colonialism."[27] I show how cultural artifacts and the nonprint media such as film and the arts facilitate elite
hegemony and precede that superordination by the state—particularly
since the nation is constantly reinventing itself.[28]

The Nation in Hindi Cinema

There are key institutions and discourses in contemporary Indian history that legitimize multiple social hierarchies. The period 1950 to the
present, coinciding with roughly fifty years of independence, is predominantly marked by Nehru's vision, his quasi-socialist "mixed economy."[29]
The films I have selected in this study are those that have been popular box office successes during this time.

There are difficulties involved in defining whether a film is "popular." First, box office hits are calculated as national aggregates, and such
a calculation conceals variations in the success of a film in different
regions and over a period of time.[30] The notion that Hindi films follow a formula is also an issue. In an industry driven by the profit principle, all successful films spawn a series of clones. Yet not all commercial
films supposedly following a formula are successful as business ventures,
and more than eighty percent of films produced each year fail at the
box office. The films included in this book are only those that captured
the public's imagination—an outcome not easy to replicate. Popularity
is a matter of contingency, and success depends on a combination of
factors such as historical context, publicity, and the formal aspects of
the film: acting, style, script, star quality, and production values. Popularity cannot be explained away as something dependent on the formulaic, since the "formula" is infinitely changeable. This book does not
explore the mystery of what makes a film popular; rather, it offers a post
facto analysis of films that have already been popular.

While I contest the idea of a formula in Hindi cinema, there are
unquestionably a range of elements that get repeatedly strung together
and reshuffled, accounting for change in the films. This is of central
interest in this book. I have selected approximately thirty popular films
over the last five decades and locate the connections between them. I
track the ways in which the films interlock, weave, loop around, or respond to each other, creating patterns and making visible strands popu-

lar in the national imaginary. Popular films touch a major nerve in the nation's body politic, address common anxieties and social tensions, and articulate vexed problems that are ultimately resolved by presenting mythical solutions to restore an utopian world.[31] The situation, complication, action, and resolution in all popular film narratives both creates and is created by a collective social imagination.

The concept of nation subtends that imagination in Hindi films, and centers its moral universe. All ethical dilemmas revolve around the nation; good and bad, heroes and villains are divided by their patriotism and antipatriotism. Because of its reach and appeal, popular Hindi cinema enjoys the privileged position of a national cinema. In it, the nation appears not as a melting pot of diverse cultures but rather as a dominant, generic north Indian culture prevalent in the Hindi-speaking belt. This combination of features lends itself especially well to situating the study of these films at the intersection of cultural and postcolonial studies.

My point of inquiry is the construction of the nation: the postcolonial "new" nation, and the national imaginary Hindi cinema constitutes and reflects. The nation is constructed in Hindi cinema through a complex apparatus of metaphors, discourses, and modes of address. It is imagined through a stock set of tropes, symbols, characters, and narratives that are meant to first air, and then resolve, contemporary anxieties and difficulties. The films iron out tensions among various constituencies in the nation and play out utopian ideals—ideals embraced by audiences from diverse linguistic and cultural backgrounds. It is this that gives Hindi cinema a special status, its national-popular acceptance.

"National" as related to Hindi cinema bears all its varied meanings: as pertaining to the nation, as imbued with emotional fervor for the nation shared by varied constituencies, and as a Pan-Indian phenomenon. The term "popular" also needs elucidation here, especially in combination with other terms such as "popular culture" and "national-popular." Though the films I discuss here are commercially successful, Hindi cinema on the whole is clearly marked as "popular" culture— with all its connotations of trivial, inferior, "low" culture, entertainment meant to please the masses, and distinct from elite, "high" culture.[32] It is useful, however, to bear in mind the reminder that aspects of high and low culture move up and down the hierarchy over time making it difficult to maintain a radical distinction between them.[33]

As for the "national-popular," Antonio Gramsci's exposition is useful. In Italy, it was necessary to establish working-class hegemony based on a broad alliance between different class interests, as a bulwark against fascism—a task in which Italian intellectuals had historically fallen short in the interwar years due to their social distance from the regionally and linguistically divided masses. The national-popular was adopted as the left intelligentsia's mandate after World War II in their use of progressive and socialist realism in various art forms, including film and literature.[34] Gramsci's ideas on the national-popular bear tremendous significance for the Indian context, and the Italian left's reception of his ideas in the 1950s vividly parallels Indian popular cinema of the same period—especially the genre referred to as the "social," and the presence of Indian Peoples' Theatre Association (IPTA) and other leftist screenwriters, artists, and personnel in the Bombay film industry.

While a more detailed study of the period is necessary to trace the origin, extent, eclipse, and finally extinction of these influences, it is clear that the 1950s Hindi cinema, poised as national-popular culture, passed over into commercial interests with little or no connection with the left and instead began faithfully serving the interest of the bourgeoisie. This cinema represents bourgeois hegemony successfully, straddling an alliance with the working class. In this it reverses Gramsci's aforementioned aspiration for a "national-popular"—even though it still constitutes the national popular, which for Gramsci "designates not a cultural content but, . . . the possibility of an alliance of interests and feelings between social agents which varies according to the structure of each national society."[35]

Thus while the industry faithfully articulates the interests and values of the bourgeoisie, all classes, especially working-class audiences, identify with it.[36] David Forgacs argues that "'Culture' in Gramsci is the sphere in which ideologies are diffused and organized, in which hegemony is constructed and can be broken and reconstructed. . . . Gramsci's notes on the national-popular reveal the extent to which cosmopolitan traditions of the Italian intellectuals have impeded the molecular ideological activity by which such a reformation could be brought about."[37] In India, too, it is not the cosmopolitan intellectual class as much as Hindi cinema that performs the function of building a national-popular culture, sustaining the notion of an "Indian" nation against diverse regional, linguistic, class, and city-country disparities, maintaining the hegemony of the bourgeoisie that passed from a colonial empire to a bourgeois democratic state.

While Hindi cinema strains to build a powerfully imagined nation, cracks and fissures within a postcolonial genealogy constantly threaten to rupture this cinema's favored myth. Differences of caste, class, community, and gender inevitably interrupt the "official" narration. For instance, animosities among religious communities, primarily Hindus and Muslims (referred to as "communalism" or "communal politics"), manifest themselves in overt and covert ways. Interconnections and contradictions among social groups are sometimes unwittingly revealed in the cinematic discourse. I am most interested in examining how social hierarchies cut across, shift, diverge, and converge in different political alliances. Shifting alliances struggle, coexist uneasily, or realign themselves to reveal postcolonial culture's topography. For instance, women's emancipation can join with anti-imperialism to consolidate national identity and mean one thing, but as a sign of community identity in the context of fundamentalist electoral politics, it can mean quite another.

Conflicts arising from social hierarchy are generally located in narratives about the family—the most important trope which Hindi films mobilize to build the idea of nation. The family is the perfect locus for melodrama, since it draws upon intense affective relationships shared among its members. By drawing parallels between family and nation, the same affect becomes transposed on the nation; familial ties suggest a common "genesis narrative." We speak of the "mother tongue," the "fatherland" or "motherland," or "the family of nations."[38] In India, early nationalist leaders are referred to as forefathers (as are the founders of the U.S. Constitution).[39]

While a host of family members related to the protagonist appear in film narratives, some relationships are privileged in the level of their intensity and passion: the mother-son bond is one such relationship. As family stories go, "lost and found" narratives also enjoy popularity. In these narratives, typically the protagonist's family is scattered in his early childhood only to reunite at the end through chance events and

after enduring a series of ordeals. These films can be read psychoana-
lytically as rehearsing "separation and loss" from the mother with a
promise of return and fusion.[40] But these stories are also important from
the perspective of India's rapid pace of country-to-city migration. In a
nation too poor to provide institutional guarantees of welfare and social security, for immigrants the city signifies hope for upward mobility
but also risk, uncertainty, and fear of failure if there is no family support. Films often depict the protagonist's changing fortunes when he is
separated from the family—only to rediscover his rich father or brother
in the denouement, thus regaining both family and wealth. Here family and class divisions are enclosed in the same frame, sharpening dramatic conflict by positioning wealth and poverty side by side, even
within the same family.

But the family does not just provide a site of affective support and
nurturance. It has depended on the sharp hierarchy of institutionalized
gender inequality, which places men at the top and subordinates other
family members to patriarchal authority. The family as a source of
nurturance and love is plagued by other difficulties. Gender trouble creates tensions, revealing cracks not only in heterosexual relations but
also in national politics. The roles of hero and heroine, pivotal in all
popular film, are central to ideas about femininity and masculinity in
the making of the Indian nation. Plotting gender against the axes of
heterosexuality, family, class, community, and nation is a useful hermeneutic device. By decoding gender signification in the symbolic realm—
in the imaginary—gender inequalities are exposed that somehow
congealed during the nation formation process. Despite the rhetoric of
women's emancipation, these inequalities became further entrenched.
Male economic advantage in the public sphere continued in the private sphere, while discriminatory laws against women's rights in the family were enshrined in the new constitution.

The divisions between gender, community, and nation are not in
"splendid isolation from each other; nor can they simply be yoked together. . . . Rather, they come into existence *in and through* relation to
each other."[41] As the growing body of literature compiled by feminists
has begun to show, nation and nationalism as envisioned by male im-
perialists and anti-imperialists alike are deeply ingrained with categories of gender.[42] Unequal power and essentialized notions of male

potency/agency and female victimhood/passivity cut across narrative accounts of the nation, class, community and, of course, heterosexual romance.

In Indian history and cinema the woman figure is an embattled one, a site on which colonial and communal conflicts have been fought through the nineteenth and twentieth centuries. Women's emancipation (outlawing *sati* and child-marriage, and legalizing widow-remarriage) was at the forefront of the contentious nineteenth-century social reform movement in colonial India. It succeeded in drawing women into the public sphere to some extent, but it imploded with the growth of the national movement by the turn of the twentieth century. In the private sphere, however, women lost the battle fought through the 1930s and 1940s to inscribe equal rights in the Constitution. By the late 1970s, and particularly through the 1980s, women's discontent around unresolved "private" matters erupted in the public sphere, forcing litigation and legislation on dowry, rape, and domestic violence—once again raising the intractable differences over Hindu and Muslim approaches to "personal law" in the Constitution.

Gender was mobilized as a sign to unify the "Indian" against the "western" in the anti-imperial agon of the nineteenth-century reform movement and also to mobilize different religious communities, who were divided over the role of women in mid-twentieth-century Constitutional debates. These debates erupted again in the mid–1980s with a growing demand for governing the "personal" sphere through religious laws, keeping intact Hindu and Muslim patriarchal control over their respective community, identity, and women. Hindi cinema overlays such differences with a benign idea of a unified nation, and the woman as its idealized insignia. In fundamental ways this history affects how women are represented in postcolonial Indian culture. Gender politics have been in play again since the 1990s; in this post-Nehruvian era of "structural adjustments" to globalization, individual agency is cast as (bourgeois) feminist opposition to the neotraditional revival. The male figure in cultural representations is typically granted agency and is capable of performing the requisite actions to effect change and social justice.

The family in Hindi films functions as a site where several contests are dramatized. Romantic love, for instance, confronts and transcends class hierarchies or patriarchal authority. Film plots conceive this strictly in heterosexual terms, yet they also acknowledge difficulties in man-woman relationships, even if only unwittingly. Hindi films centering on the nation push vital differences to the margins of the frame. In tracking the marginalized and recessed figures it is interesting to see how they struggle against, accommodate, and reconstitute one another—as well as figures at the center of the narrative—to tell the nation's history. The complex interaction between gender and sexuality in seemingly simple narratives inform us about contemporary culture.

Focusing more specifically on class, Hindi films have been extraordinarily sensitive to its politics.[43] In India, as in many other countries in Latin America, Africa, and Asia, the "springtime" heralded by the liberation movement's revolutionary fervor ended in unmitigated difficulties as the new nations failed to meet basic human needs for food, health, housing, and education. Just as gender inequality was institutionalized, so were the poorer classes divorced from access to the nation's resources.[44] Discrimination—contrary to the guarantees enshrined in the Constitution—and few educational and economic opportunities led to sustained violence, arson, and riots directed against minority Muslims and lower-caste Hindus (the latter putatively the beneficiaries of affirmative action).[45] When state capitalism failed to deliver the nation from the lingering effects of colonial ravages, minority Muslims, women, and lower castes were made scapegoats. The promise of the new nation belied real liberation and egalitarianism.

Hindi films openly address class conflict. The films depict avaricious industrialists, middlemen, moneylenders, traders, and landlords as exploiting workers, the landless, and the underprivileged. Class issues were articulated in K. A. Abbas's scripts for Raj Kapoor's productions in the 1950s. But the placatory tone in these films was replaced by the recognition that class conflict was intractable in Indian public life. In the 1950s Nehru's "tryst with destiny" held promise, even if the future seemed daunting. But by the 1970s uneven development, overpopulated cities, false electoral promises, and worker-peasant-student unrest resulted in the nefarious nineteen-month "Emergency." In 1975 Indira Gandhi exploited this constitutional provision to suspend civil rights, snuff out political opposition, and temporarily overturn democratic processes. During this time the screenwriter duo known as "Salim-Javed"

(Salim Khan and Javed Akhtar) created the figure of the angry man—the working-class hero. It was a role that became Amitabh Bachchan's insignia and catapulted him to superstardom. Several Hindi films which reveal sensitivity to class are discussed later in this book, and I probe different ways in which class conflict is staged and resolved.

But what does a filmic rendition that elicits sympathy for the underclass mean in a nation-state where socialist rhetoric has always been part of the official stated policy? Comparing films made in the first fifty years of independence (the Nehruvian era) to those being made today and in the future might tell if these are merely a sign of decaying socialist idealism. Before the 1970s, and the arrival of the "angry young man," class was represented with a permeable boundary, easily crossed over by heterosexual love. This is a far cry from how class actually operates, with its ironclad apparatus built into minutely differentiated hierarchies of social, economic, and cultural capital. In a society extraordinarily conscious of class, caste, and ethnic identity, cinema carefully sustains heterosexual romance, which itself is largely a figment of Hindi films' imagination. In reality most marital alliances occur within an elaborately coded structure of "arranged marriages." Caste rules are an important aspect of this institution and are openly observed by the "educated" middle class, notwithstanding the official rhetoric and the fact that it is constitutionally outlawed. Yet there is no mention of this in popular Hindi films.[46] I therefore read caste and religious divisions as a subtext buried within class distinctions.

As a powerful source of social conflict, class is pertinent in Indian politics. Yet its representation attenuated in the 1980s. The "revival of romance" in this period is no longer told as a story of class transgression. There are two possibilities that might account for this shift. First, the expansion of the middle class in the late 1980s seems to open opportunities for upward mobility. The heroes and heroines of the 1980s' films generally share similar class origins (with some differences of access and mobility within the same class). This moment of economic opportunity is reminiscent of the 1950s, when stars dislocated by the experience of Partition arrived in Bombay to try their luck in the film industry.[47] Some of them created their own empires. Family connections, however, continue to play an important role in the film industry and today the children of these stars often obtain easy entry due to their privileged status. Feudalism, far from being displaced, coexists with capital formation in the film industry. The other possible explanation for the revival of romantic love films in the 1980s is that "romance" shifted its target. The new enemy was the authoritarian patriarch, a response to the consciousness spread by the women's movement.

The Hindi film is a register on which different tensions and conflicts leave their trace. At times the film narratives focus on these conflicts, openly confessing them as "problems" within the nation. At other times these conflicts are repressed within the subtext or remain in the margins, and have to be retrieved against the dominant narrative.

Cinema as National History

If the nation is a discursive construct produced by culture and history, the historical narrative is the chief architect of that discourse. Conventional or "manifest history" marks the passage of time with landmark events that obliquely influence peoples' ordinary life experiences.[48] Thus, the repression of the peasant rebellion in the 1950s, famines, shortages, and the Green Revolution in the 1960s, the rise of workers, women, and ecological movements in the 1970s and 1980s, the rise of Hindu fundamentalism, the intensification of caste wars and regional separatist movements in the 1980s and 1990s, economic liberalization in the 1990s, the Indo-Pak Kargil war, and nuclear testing by these two countries at the close of the twentieth century—all are part of manifest Indian history. But reference to these and their impact on Hindi cinema is elliptical.

In film literature, historical films bear the onus of "authentic" representation and are inevitably suspect for blurring boundaries with fiction—particularly since their narrative strategies are replete with situation, conflict, and resolution, scenarios that are told with a beginning, middle, and end. But what of films that do not profess history, films that are documents from past historical moments?[49] Both kinds of films are important; historiography and fiction are "narrative refigurations of time."[50] In this book I trace India's postindependence social history through avowedly nonhistorical films.

However, history itself is a contentious matter, and currently under postmodernist interrogation for its grand master narratives of progress, historical paradigms, and historiography based on secular, imperious, western chronology, implicit in officially archived sources that discount unofficial resources: folklore, legends, myths, ballads, and rumors, the stuff of "subaltern history," history from below, espoused by some historians working on the Indian subcontinent.[51] Given recent right-wing machinations around the Indian Council of Historical Research (ICHR) and the revision of history textbooks, expanding the archive source and historiographic method to include popular film texts could well become an extension of the subaltern history project.[52] As Pierre Sorlin states,

> Born from the crisis of grand, all-encompassing theories, postmodernism postulates that it is the task of historians neither to "interpret" the past nor to explain how and why events occurred. . . . Postmodernism looks for symbols, or representation that takes place in the head of individuals but which, while being private thoughts or images, could also be common to many people. It starts from the fragmented, the very simple acts performed daily.[53]

Hindi films provide records of the barely perceptible changes in people's daily experiences, rather than landmark events or "manifest history." A nonlinear discursive social history may be mapped through repetitive themes, narratives, conflicts, resolutions, and evasions that at different moments reveal gradual social reconfigurations—or a sharp break with what went before. Or, in Tony Barta's words, "history can only be 'seen' as a conceptual web, as an infinitely complex set of relations which we simplify by categorizing and connecting . . . the patterns of relations by which we make meaning . . . from the record of the past."[54]

The Hindi in Film

India has a complex political history surrounding Hindi's adoption as a national language. Since Pakistan was created by the nation's Partition, in the postindependence period Urdu (the primary language of Muslims in South Asia, used in literature and the arts, and once the language of administration) was denied official recognition despite its popularity in the north and south. Urdu was supplanted by the movement for Hindi in the second half of the nineteenth century.[55] As Indian films have remained silent about this conflict for about forty years, I look elsewhere for tell-tale signs. The politics of language—that is, the use of Urdu subsumed by Hindi's hegemony—indicates a revealing metanarrative.

Hindi was declared a national language after independence, even though it is native to only five northern states among twenty-two. Apart from conflict between supporters of Hindi as a national language and regionalists who resist this coercive imposition, other pressures constantly bear upon Hindi from proponents of its elite versus its popular form, the classical versus the common—but most importantly, from the tug of war between the influence of Urdu and Sanskritized Hindi favored by orthodox Hindus.

Mahatma Gandhi's attempts at developing a common lingua franca (Hindustani, a Hindi-Urdu admix) based on the unity produced by the national movement to prevent a wedge between the Hindu and Muslim variations in the language were defeated by the *Hindi Sahitya Sammelan* (Hindi Literary Society) that gained control of the Indian Congress in the 1930s. This pro-Hindu, anti-Muslim group was able to standardize Hindi and create an array of institutional apparatii to support and promote it: secondary- and college-level diplomas were devised for teaching purposes; the "Board of Scientific Terminology" was established in 1950 to extend Hindi vocabulary; and an Encyclopedia of Hindi was inaugurated in 1956.[56]

As far as the use of language in literary production goes, Hindi novels were usually translations, and Hindi was merely a "cause" to uphold. Hindi readers tended to read short stories, and Urdu was the dominant literary language. Hindi novels only became popular in the early twentieth century, while regional-language fiction had taken root a century earlier. Differences in the strength of the middle class, the spread of nationalism, and the development of educational opportunity account for this regional variation. Hindi translations first promoted by Bharatendu in the latter half of the nineteenth century and later by Devakinandan Khatri expanded Hindi readership in an unprecedented way. Khatri used a mix of Urdu and Hindi—a language of common speech. But in the early nationalist phase there was a concern for the development of Hindi as a language separate from Urdu and the development of Hindu identity around a language. The idea of India as a nation became synonymous in North India with those speaking Hindi.[57]

The Hindi used in popular Hindi films has an awkward relationship with the genesis of the nation and its language politics. It is buffeted by tensions among social and ideological players embattled in the process of nation-making. Even if we accept that the same language assumes different modes in different institutional settings—education, administration, the court, or the street—the language of popular cinema bares contradictory dynamics. Ostensibly it uses the state's language, imposed from above. But, in fact, it acts as a complicating and even countervailing force to the state-controlled language. For instance, the Hindi used in administration is a classical and elite version, while popular film Hindi has always had a penchant for the common, the plebeian.

However, the Hindi used in popular films has never been fixed. To the contrary, it registers shifts, and reveals change and traces left by the uneven successes of different contestants—Urdu and Sanskrit being the most dominant. But what is important and unmistakable is Hindi cinema's paradoxical lack of identification with—even inimical relation to—a coercive state apparatus. It circulates "the" national language, although it always distances itself from Hindi's classical, literary, and official forms. Leftists, separatists, regionalist, and linguistic chauvinists notwithstanding, the Hindi used in Hindi cinema is accessible to all categories.[58]

Pointing to the significant contestation between Hindi and Urdu within the locus of Hindi cinema, Mukul Kesavan notes that popular Hindi film is the last "stronghold" of Urdu in India. Kesavan traces Urdu's presence in cinema to its immediate ancestral heritage: Parsi theater. In the eighteenth and nineteenth centuries Urdu and not Hindi was the cultivated elite's language. Like any other literary language, it "reveled in its difficulty and conscious artifice." Urdu was particularly well disposed to "stylized melodrama," and Kesavan cites Sohrab Modi's *Sikander*, performed by Prithviraj Kapoor, as the quintessence of this. Although many have pointed to Hindi cinema's ancestry in Parsi theater, Kesavan pinpoints its influence to the song and dance sequences, its "fine disregard for the unities of time and place," its "metaphoric extravagance" and lack of "sobriety" or "authenticity." In contrast, "high-minded Hindi drama failed to strike roots . . . [and] remained stillborn" with no audience to sustain it.[59]

This linguistic division continues in contemporary films. Art cinema, with its penchant for realism, excises song, dance or any kind of frivolity, and tends to use Sanskritized Hindi. Titles like *Ankur* (Seed), *Bhumika* (Role), and *Ardhsatya* (Half-truth), have assumed a mantle of seriousness that appears to express a deeper anxiety—to distance itself from the common (*bazaari*) Urdu. On the other hand, Urdu has a resonance that its equivalent in Hindi cannot match. Urdu is often used in film titles, screenplay, lyrics, the language of love, war, and martyrdom. Titles of films include *Awaara* (Vagabond), *Sahib, Bibi aur Ghulam* (The Lord, his Wife and the Slave) in the 1950s; *Safar* (Journey), *Bawarchi* (Cook), and *Khamoshi* (Silence) in the 1970s; and *Tawaif* (Courtesan) and *Tezaab* (Acid) in the 1980s. Words like *watan* (motherland), and *shaheed* (martyr/sacrifice), resonate with patriotism and in the language of love *dil* (heart), *khoon* (blood), and *kismat* (destiny) invoke emotions in a way that their Hindi equivalents, *hridaya* (heart), *rakt* (blood), and *bhagya* (destiny) do not.[60]

I would add to this argument that the extent of Urdu used in commercial Hindi cinema has not been stable either. If we examine the Urdu used in films like *Sikander*, we can find no equivalent for it in later or contemporary times. Urdu did not receive the state patronage that Hindi did; and, further, Hindi was made a compulsory language taught within the educational system. It was later foisted as the language to conduct administrative business, and thus Hindi's use led to Urdu's steady erosion. The generation educated in northern India before independence learned Urdu in the school system, and this made Hindi comprehensible to them. Although the shift was gradual and two generations communicated with each other through a blend of Urdu and Hindi, known as Hindustani, the ultimate victory of Hindi in the official sphere has been more or less complete.

This decline of Urdu is mirrored in Hindi films. It is not easy for many schooled in the postindependence era to follow some 1950s films, merely because of the extent of Urdu idiom and expression used. It is true that many Urdu words have survived and become part of Hindi cinema's popular vocabulary. But that is as far as it goes. The fact is, for the most part popular Hindi cinema has forsaken the florid Urdu that was part of its extravagance and retained a "residual" Urdu, affected by an aggressive state policy that promoted a Sanskritized version of Hindi as the national language. Today Hindi films are much more inclined to substitute Urdu words with Hindi ones, perhaps because of the preparation by the extensive state-controlled national radio and television. Still, the Sanskritized version of Hindi promoted by the state-controlled radio and television has little to do with "the rhetorical and emotional registers of Hindi cinema."[61]

The Bombay Film Industry

A word should be said about the film industry and its place in India's public sphere. Although the Bombay film industry has always presented itself as being in a state of siege, today it is threatened as never before. In addition to the censorship and taxation that it has complained bitterly against since the 1950s, the industry faced a set-back in the 1980s with the arrival of video technology and its attendant problem of video piracy. The proliferation of cable television is making a further dent in theater attendance. In addition, the high-tech visual effects of Hollywood films pose a new challenge. Dubbing Steven Spielberg's *Jurassic Park* into Hindi raked in previously untapped revenue. Although the Hindi film industry has never had the wherewithal to compete with Hollywood-style visual effects, the Indian English press coined a neologism, "Bollywood," to refer to the Bombay film industry. This awkward misnomer is weighed with innuendoes about Hindi film as a mere Hollywood mimic.

Though Hindi films embrace Hollywood-style elements of linear narrative, with closure and a strong hero who affects that closure, they are adapted to a local sensibility, are topical, and, most important, are connected with an indigenous star system and genre expectations from the Indian audience that will always exclude Hollywood.[62] I am not so much making assertions about Hindi cinema's cultural sovereignty as pointing to tenacious indigenous cultural forms at home which shape that cinema. These could, methodologically speaking, become the entry point for identifying the "national" features of Hindi films.

In terms of the larger market available, Hindi cinema's potential competitor is not so much Hollywood as the Tamil and Malayalam language regional cinema. When successful, regional cinema has influenced Hindi cinema. But in Hindi cinema's relation to both Hollywood and regional cinema, a limited influence is all we can discern. For Hindi cinema always substantially transliterates the original and adapts new elements carefully and in accordance with audience expectations it has developed over the years. Developments in the early 1990s briefly threatened the hegemony of Hindi films. It appeared that Hindi film would have to cede its leading position to regional cinema—Tamil cinema, for instance—while regional production in Malayalam also bid for a national audience. These shifts affected aesthetics and form; they also cross-fertilized ideas and influences.[63] Several seemingly disjunctive media realigned by the mid–1990s, revealing a greater degree of mutual influence than ever before. The idea of segmenting the audience and creating new markets also began to take hold. New production ventures and investor collaboration have taken place among different regional cinemas as well.

Cinema, a Public Discourse

Hindi cinema's imbrication in public discourse, as an object of contention, intensified with the growth of the right wing's influence in the 1980s. With cinema's refraction of national events, its polarization of public discourse increased further in the 1990s as several Hindi films became flashpoints for lawsuits against censors, street clashes, and even death threats. Like Salman Rushdie's *Satanic Verses*, a literary transgression in the 1980s that drew world-wide attention to concerns over artistic license, the place of state edicts in culture, and religion in politics, the Hindi film repeatedly became a site for culture wars.[64] Representations of sexuality, gender, caste, religious minorities, and the state were battlegrounds to define the national. For example, theaters exhibiting Deepa Mehta's *Fire* (1996), a film exploring a lesbian relationship in an extended Indian family, were vandalized by right-wing extremists. Media discussion and electronic chat groups wrangled over whether homosexuality was a "foreign affliction" or rooted in Indian "tradition."

Fluctuations in representations of the state have caused their own problems. Mahesh Bhatt clashed with the censor board for exposing the erosion of secularism within the Indian police force in *Zakhm* (Wound, 1998).[65] In 1977 *Kissa Kursi Ka* (Story of the Chair), allegedly about state excesses during the 1975–1977 Emergency, was destroyed, while J. P. Dutta's *Border* (1997), anticipating the 1999 Kargil debacle in its fictional Indo-Pak war depiction, was valorized.[66] Eulogizing patriotism and martyrdom, *Border*'s music flooded the airwaves and gory full-page photo features produced during the war uncannily replicated its visuals.[67]

Bombay (Mani Ratnam, 1995) and *Bandit Queen* (Shekhar Kapur, 1994) were controversial for challenging the Hindu upper caste's ultra-nationalist tyranny over the Muslim minority and lower castes. Bal Thackerey, the right-wing party chief, refused to allow *Bombay*'s screening in the city until some parts of the film were excised. An attempt was even made to assassinate its director. Shekhar Kapur's *Bandit Queen*, woven around the axes of gender and caste politics in India, became mired in litigation. The film documents the life of Phoolan Devi, a *dalit* (oppressed lower caste), and depicts the woman's savage treatment by upper-caste aggressors, her transformation into a bandit, and the retaliatory terror she unleashed until she laid down her arms in 1982. After a twelve-year incarceration she embarked upon a career in politics.[68]

The consolidation of "backward" castes and dalits in North India over the last two decades signals a turning point in Indian politics.[69] The dalits, no longer an electoral appendage of the dominant Congress Party, are an important countervailing force against growing Hindu fundamentalism. Their success in the two northern states of Uttar Pradesh (U.P.) and Bihar, notorious for the worst caste wars, is more than symbolic. The appearance of *Bandit Queen* or *Bombay* at this political conjuncture is no accident of history; rather, it is intrinsically tied to contemporary politics.

It is clear that Hindi films are sites which intersect political life and spill into its social text.[70] They address issues that trouble the nation. The interplay between the texts and their social context entails contests among different lobbies affecting contemporary culture. Popular commercial films deal with the same political and cultural issues using a constellation of myths, utopias, wishes, escapism, and fantasies. The most popular elements of these myths and archetypes that recur within popular film narratives are part of what I examine in this book.

Gender politics, the representation of masculinity and femininity, and the transaction between them in heterosexual romance and the family are all important elements of Hindi popular cinema and its screening of the nation's social history and cultural politics. In the chapters to come I unravel the utopian myths and analyze the dynamic interplay among different hierarchical constituencies that rewrite the official history popular films.

First, I take up films that celebrate the new independent nation and the euphoria of ending colonial rule—films that imagine the nation in terms of a successful bourgeois revolution. I show how faith in traditional male heroes fades over the decades and is displaced by an alternative figure. In chapter 2 I illustrate how the idealized female figure is embedded in the national imaginary as the insignia of the nation. A repository of "Indian" tradition, distinct from her European counterpart, this idealization of Indian womanhood has serious implications for national debates on women's place in the family, the private sphere.

If the woman is the idealized nation, the ideal male hero rescues the nation from imminent danger. In chapter 3 I examine the past five decades to trace the ways in which the nation is constructed not only along the topos of the family, anti-imperial rhetoric, and invocations of the grandeur of antiquity, but also through the dangers represented by the figure of the villain. Villains, the opposite of ideal masculinity, are fashioned by a changing public discourse on what imperils the nation. This changeable face of villainy in cinematic discourse is vital to the discursive history of the nation.

Next I take up landmark films that air the impact of women's positioning in culture and law and the crisis it precipitates in the private sphere, in representations of love, and the field of heterosexual romance. Chapter 4 explores the normative duties pitted against women's subjective desires in the form of romance triangles, interrupting the heterosexual economy prescribed by the restrictive patriarchal-nationalist rhetoric of the 1950s and 60s. This discourse is central to Hindi cinema's "women's films," in which female protagonists wrestle with various aspects of patriarchal culture.

In chapter 5 I map the changing discourse of gender politics, which by the 1980s had developed into a more open antipatriarchal stance. The new "avenging heroine" became a prominent feature in films, in tandem with the emerging women's movement in India. This figure to an extent replaces the "angry man" of the 1970s, as well as the idealized male hero.

Finally, in chapter 6 I take note of the "revival of romance" in the late 1980s and throughout the 1990s, this time with the patriarchal father figure as the new enemy. Signaling the end of the Nehruvian era and inaugurating economic "liberalization," romance occurs against a backdrop of the excesses of new commodity culture and opulence. Compared to earlier heterosexual romance films that explore and challenge social hierarchies in Indian culture, the narrative and form in these later films endorse—and even embrace—the values of globalization.

Chapter 1	Nation and Its Discontents

To say that Hindi cinema is a national cinema at once begs several questions: What is a nation? What are the criteria by which we designate a cinema "national"? We also need to ask what the basis is for designating Hindi cinema a national cinema, or the "national-popular." And in a multilingual nation like India, film raises questions about the role of language in the nation's formation.

The popularity of Hindi cinema has to do with its unique regime of narrative and theme, tradition of spectacle, and its aesthetics and stylistic conventions. It is a cinematic apparatus that draws upon the literary and nonliterary creative imagination, both contemporary and historical. This imagination is also intrinsically tied to—in fact constructs—the nation, a political formation that arrived in India at about the same time as film technology. Here I discuss the nation Hindi cinema imagines and popularizes, film's place within the national-popular, and the extent to which films are constituted by other forms that service the nation-making process.

The Nation, in Theory

Nation and nationalism are particularly troubled concepts for historians and political theorists alike. It is a constantly shifting entity that first emerged in the eighteenth century; it offers a primary form of identification, yet it is difficult to establish the criteria on which it is based: "All . . . objective definitions have failed."[1] Nation is an abstract notion, a myth that cannot be scientifically defined.[2] Neither race, geography, nor language are sufficient to determine the nation's essence. Yet people are willing to die, fight wars, or write fiction on its behalf. Human consciousness invents a nation where such a thing does not exist.[3]

Nationalism arguably emerged in Europe as a powerful ideology in the late seventeenth century, arising within a specific social formation and sustained by culture, a force at once cohesive and fractious. The concept of "nation" spread globally, and it continues to this day in full strength as a prime player in contemporary geopolitics. Fictional and mythic representations construct nations in art and literature, spurring nationalist sentiments, while nations popularize and favor particular myths and fantasies.

Benedict Anderson has argued that the "dawn of nationalism at the end of the eighteenth century coincided with the dusk of religious modes of thought."[4] Nationalism is a mode of thinking that has impacted our social, political, literary, and fictional imagination, even our deepest psychological being—our very sense of personal identity. The nation is the most resilient form of community imagined, and the devotion it elicits from followers is next only to the intensity religion evokes.[5] Nationalism, in fact, effectively replaced religion in seventeenth-century Europe.[6]

The development of nations in the nineteenth and twentieth centuries is integrally bound to capitalist development, and the modern world economy is shaped by its link to national economies. Nation states protect contracts and the accumulation of wealth; in the nineteenth century, national economy implied protectionism.[7] Ernest Gellner's theory is that "the economy needs both the new type of central culture and the central state; the culture needs the state; and the state probably needs the homogeneous cultural branding of the flock."[8] The Indian case, however, falls right through the cracks in this theory of centralized homogeneity. India's most striking aspect is the flexibility with which it accommodates diverse cultural units under its umbrella of nation. However, a sense of unity is derived from various other factors: a state-imposed unified system of law, language, and education; the constitution; one monetary currency; and the creation of a national imaginary. The latter, I contend, is sustained in no small part by the visionary nature of Hindi cinema.

Nationalism took root in India among a small, westernized elite at the beginning of the nineteenth century. Inspired by the French Revolution, the American War of Independence, and the Enlightenment ideals of freedom, liberty, and the right to self-determination (which ran counter to political subjugation and economic exploitation), Indian politics moved toward imagining a nation marshaled by cultural revivalism and historical reinterpretation. Throughout the nineteenth and early twentieth centuries the nationalist movement coalesced into a process ridden with paradoxes: it invented "Indian" traditions to distinguish itself from the white colonizer. Like other anti-imperialist struggles (but distinct from western nationalism), Indian nationalism adapted "ancient" culture and tradition into a modern concept of "nation."[9] Paralleling bourgeois democratic revolutions in Europe, where a powerful mercantile class displaced monarchical and ecclesiastical authority, in India the nation was an intangible ideal, a chimera, fought for and won against British imperialism.

The Indian nation is a political entity, its state dominated by a class of people extending their power over a determinate geographic boundary. It was power won and sustained through a discursive apparatus deploying various modes of dissemination—through the fictional and literary imagination and the writing of history, enabled by print, communication, and an educational system. No single institution is the harbinger of the nation without also being shaped by it. Cinema, with its preeminence in the world of visual images, has been seriously underrepresented and underestimated as a locus of both imagining the nation and creating a national imaginary. Particularly in India, film supplanted a long-standing oral tradition and assumed the status of the "national-popular." Hindi film draws on all the elements of the discursive nation-making apparatus while constituting one in its own right.

The Creative ImagiNation

Fiction, history, print, and telecommunication—common discursive modes imbricated in nation-making strategies—have all had effects on Hindi cinema. It has been said that nations "are imaginary constructs that depend for their existence on an apparatus of cultural fiction in which imaginative literature plays a decisive role."[10] And Timothy Brennan has argued that in third world fiction after World War II,

> the uses of "nation" and "nationalism" are most pronounced. The nation is precisely what Foucault has called a "discursive formation"—not simply an allegory or imaginative vision, but a gestative political structure which the Third World artist is either consciously building or suffering the lack of. The literary act and the institution of literary production, are not only part of the nation-forming process, but are its realization. . . . The rise of modern nation-states in Europe in the late eighteenth and early nineteenth century is inseparable from the form and subject of imaginative literature.[11]

Nations, therefore, are nothing more than the fictional fancies of their creators. Brennan goes on to quote Victoria Glendinning, who comments specifically about the case of the Indian subcontinent. Pakistan, she says, is a nation "insufficiently imagined . . . India was a fiction invented by the British in 1947. Even the British had never ruled over more than sixty percent of India. But it was a dream that everyone agreed to dream. And now I think there is actually a country called India."[12]

There are two movements that explain, in literary terms, the development of the national in fiction. The first is a search for a common history, what has been called an "anti-death process": it pinpoints a movement of origin, a beginning, an irreversible continuity that is the birth. The second movement strives to delimit the nation within an enclosed space.[13] Several factors contribute to nation making, but the first one is often considered the most important: providing a sense of the past, a historic association with the current state. Territorial nation-states search the past for a common history, often inverting contemporary events to explain it. As Ernest Gellner puts it, writing history is a form of narration that effects a fusion of "will, culture and polity."[14] Hugh Seton-Watson says that "various governments invent tradition to give permanence and solidity to a transient political form."[15] The past, or tradition, becomes what E. J. Hobsbawm calls a "usable past," a way of "creating a people." And the origin of European nationalism is patterned on Judeo-Christian principles: "'the idea of a chosen people, emphasis on common stock of memory of the past and hopes for the future, and finally national messianism.'"[16]

Sudipta Kaviraj points to the discursive nature of the writing of history that constructs the "Imaginary Institution of India." He argues that "India" is the effect of a narrative that performs the political function of imposing cohesion among a number of groups that otherwise do not share a common political identity.[17] Quoting Antonio Gramsci's writings about the eminent falsity of a unilinear history, Kaviraj says that "history was political propaganda, it aimed to create national unity—that is, the nation. . . . It was a wish, not a move based on already existing conditions."[18] He goes on to explain that in societies where tradition is the only legitimizing criterion, the nation attempts to disguise the past in order to pass off its modernity, which it justifies through a falsified version of antiquity. In the case of India:

> The naming of the Indian nation, I wish to suggest, happens in part through a narrative contract. To write a history of India beginning with a civilization of the Indus valley is marked by impropriety. An India internally defined, an India of a national community, simply did not exist before the nineteenth century; there is therefore, an inevitable element of "fraudulence" . . . in all such constructions. "The history of India" is the mark of an ideological construct.[19]

This powerful force of nationalist ideology permeates every institution and discourse, and is marshaled to build the "imagined community." Print media, for example, enables an "ideological insemination" by which "people . . . begin to think of themselves as a nation." People can read a novel alone, knowing that millions of others are doing the same. The novel brings together readers from both "high" and "low" cultures and from different ethnic and regional groups.[20] The narratives—whether they adopt the disciplinary mantle of history, literature, general pulp, the novel, or newspaper—all contribute to shaping the imagined nation and the national imaginary, and each of these rely on print technology.

What role does language play in all this? In India, Hindi, a regional language among many others, was ascribed the status of a national language in the course of the nation-making process. Yet the coercion a national language implies, an aspect of nation-making strategies, is not associated with Hindi cinema. Unlike other regional-language cinemas, Hindi cinema appeals to and is embraced by people from all linguistic regions in the country. Consequently, Hindi cinema is one of the constitutive forces in popularizing the national.

That the nation pervades every institution, mechanism, discourse, and discipline, and in turn is constituted by these, leaves little doubt about the extent of its influence in public life. The question at hand is this: To what extent does the nation influence cultural forms that carry its imaginative figuration? And what are the mechanics of its configuration in Hindi cinema?

Theorizing National Cinema

Focusing on the sense viewers make of films, and demarcating and defining the scope of "national cinema," Andrew Higson applies the term to films identified by a common site of production and consumption. Such a classification includes where the films are made, by whom, and under whose ownership. It simultaneously enables a text-based approach that examines the content, style, world-view, "projections of a national character," and construction of the nation in the films. To attribute national identity to a range of industrial and textual practices implies that audiences and producers have expectations of that cinema's coherence, unity, unique identity, and "stable set of meanings."[21]

Hindi cinema derives its coherence from the many creative forms it draws upon.[22] In the late nineteenth century, as the nationalist movement gained momentum and intensified cultural revivalism, art forms were regenerated and deployed through new interpretations. Cinema of course deploys a unique apparatus that relies heavily on the other cultural forms imbricated in the nation-making process. Hindi film's visual aesthetic, narrative form, and audio style have been influenced by nineteenth-century Parsi and Urdu theatrical traditions, with an emphasis on song and dance, disregard for unity of time and space, and an emphasis on "frontality" in painting; and by literary forms such as the epic and the romance, as well as the novel.[23]

If the novel is a recent western art form, film is of course even more recent.[24] Notwithstanding the "high" and "low" distinctions within the reading public, the novel is, relatively speaking, an elitist form—especially compared to television, film, song, and poetry. Timothy Brennan notes that the novel "has been the form through which a thin, foreign educated stratum . . . has communicated to metropolitan reading publics, often in translation. It has been . . . allowed to play a national role . . . in an international arena."[25] Popular Hindi films, in contrast, are consumed almost entirely by the indigenous public, although viewership in nonwestern cultures and among the Indian diaspora is growing.[26] Structurally, Hindi film adopts elements of both the epic and romance—although it has a greater penchant for sagas, plots with a multitude of events, rather than a focus on character interiority. If the novel is a form that represents and is produced by bourgeois individualism, Hindi films focus not so much on individual characters but on complex plots and events—what happens, and how.

The novel did have an unmistakable impact on Hindi films, however, and many novelists wrote screenplays for films in the 1950s. The novel in India was not a simple British legacy; it arose from a complex cultural development. Several factors led to the novel's emergence, notably the growth of the bourgeoisie and modern capitalism. The novel is "a genre generated and sustained by the middle class . . . against the feudal values of the epic or romance."[27] Hindi films have adopted a peculiar hybrid form with elements of the epic and the novel.

At the heart of all Hindi films lies the "fictional nation." Serious tensions that threaten to fracture the nation are obsessively manifested in film as moral conflicts or ethical dilemmas. Resolution of these dilemmas is the central goal of the "national fiction," the Hindi film. Form and style in the films are streamlined to meet the narrative demand of the fictional nation, which requires nonparticularized references to time and place. Thus Hindi films tend to be general in description, scrupulously nonspecific, and parsimonious in detail, providing a deft but sketchy idea of the setting. For example, a rich or poor house, urban or rural, feudal-aristocratic, western or traditional setting is suggested with minimal elaboration.

Indian writers were slow to develop interest in the perceptible physical reality of their surroundings. While stylized descriptions of the landscape or physical beauty of the heroine are easy to come by, "a realistic presentation of actual people or objects, interiors or buildings, [is] either absent or rare."[28] Likewise, films absorbed the didactic tenor assumed by early novels in India, with the great divide between good and evil mapped in favor of patriotism against treason, democratic against feudal, and indigenous against foreign.

The most striking feature of the nation is homogeneity among heterogeneous ideological strains, interests, and groups. They consent to share a common identity and accept the hegemony of the privileged class. It is important to examine the "process by which cultural hegemony is achieved" in and through cinematic representations. A coherent national identity comes about by naturalizing a particular cultural formation; nationhood and film histories are produced by repressing internal differences among groups criss-crossed by hierarchical relationships—in terms of gender, ethnicity, community, religion and class. Nations are not a "given" but something that is "gained," and cinema is one of the means by which this happens. By constructing an imaginary homogeneity, film represents the interests of one group while marginalizing others. It has been argued that national cinema is a form of "internal colonization," offering up a contradictory unity and privileging a limited range of subject positions.[29]

In postcolonial territories the nation had to subsume class disparities. The neocolonial writer had to create an "aura of a national community," even through forms of cultural expression significantly eroded by imperial culture. A new indigenous dominant elite used the colonial legacy and continually renewed its identity to establish legitimacy. Brennan, invoking Horace Davis, says that "'State and nation build each other'. . . . the state *predates* or precedes nationalist sentiments, which are then called in after the fact, so to speak."[30] In India, literary production musters nationalist sentiment, which provides a cultural imagination to support, service, and uphold the state.

Hindi cinema, a catalyst in the nation's homogenizing mission, appeals to the underprivileged by building faith in the nation-state's protective beneficence. Differences—economic and cultural—are repressed as the nation positions itself as representing the common unity and interests of all groups.[31] Nationalism faces the difficult challenge of maintaining the allegiance of the uprooted and alienated rural population as it migrates to urban shantytown ghettoes. As critics we bear the burden of explaining how Hindi cinema secures the nation—privileging a few—while attaining mass popularity. This calls for unraveling the process by which pleasure in hegemony works. This means understanding how cinematic narratives successfully repress and conceal contradictions among differentially privileged groups, offering audiences unity and universal identification.

A number of films narrate the "nation and/as family," troubled by conflicts yet repeatedly rescued by adopting a devotional stance to the fiction called nation.[32] These films directly or indirectly address the onerous task of nation-building: the continuous process of preserving and protecting it from potential ruptures caused by linguistic differences, regionalism, communalism, the opposition of ethnic minorities to nationalism, and the struggle of reactionary feudalism against democracy. The tropes of masculinity and femininity incessantly deployed in Hindi cinema are the compass I use to negotiate and deconstruct the topos of the nation.

Nation and Its Embodiments

I begin with *Henna* (1991), among the first popular films to openly acknowledge the birth of two nations from one. On August 15, 1947, the Indian subcontinent was declared independent of its two hundred years of British rule. Two nations, India and Pakistan, came into being with Hindu and Muslim majorities respectively. Large-scale violence erupted as migrants crossed the new border in either direction. Literature from the 1950s is filled with despair about the senseless Partition, but open mention of it in popular culture is more or less completely repressed.

More than forty years later, *Henna* harks back to the originary moment of the Indian nation, arbitrarily divided by and contained within imaginary "boundary" lines. In lieu of veiled references to the "enemy" across the border, the film candidly refers to the twin nation, Pakistan. *Henna* was Hindi cinema's great master Raj Kapoor's grand finale, completed by his son Randhir Kapoor after his father's sudden death. The film is an appeal for unity and Hindu/Muslim amity within the nation. It is also ostensibly an antiwar film, promoting peace between India and Pakistan. Yet the text's rhetoric and narrative strategy reveals an uneasy fit between the two levels of appeal, pointing to a fault line in the imagined nation.

The film's protagonist, Chander Prakash (played by Rishi Kapoor) runs a lumber industry in Srinagar, Kashmir. His impending marriage to his girlfriend, Chandini, is thwarted by an accident: his jeep rolls into the Jhelum river and he is presumed dead. But Chander's body, swept along by the river, is discovered in a hamlet on the other side of the nation's border, in Pakistan. Khan (Saeed Jaffery), his daughter Henna (Zeba), and widow friend Gul *Chaachi* (Farida Jalal) nurse him back to health against the admonitions of Khan's son, Ashraf. Ashraf fears Shahbaaz Khan (Kiran Kumar), the notorious local army officer, who terrorizes the villagers and patrols the border for spies sent by the Indian army.

Chander regains consciousness but suffers a complete loss of memory. Henna falls in love with him and they are about to be married when Chander regains his memory during the frenzied wedding festivities. Khan's plan to help Chander cross the border and return home is foiled by Shahbaaz Khan, who demands Henna in marriage as the price for ensuring Chander's safe passage. After several reversals, Henna successfully helps Chander cross the border, but dies in the crossfire between the two border armies. Chander reunites with his former fiancée, Chandini, who faithfully awaits his return.

The film is prefaced with a slow pan of a river flowing through a picturesque valley, over which the narration tells us: "This story is set on the bank of the Jhelum river, which begins in India and flows through Pakistan. On one side, Hindus worship it, praying to the rising sun, and on the other side Muslims offer prayers to their Allah at sunset. The water doesn't make distinctions between different human beings. Then why do people observe difference in their hearts?" Nature and culture are invoked together, and the film unequivocally asserts that "difference" is a cultural construct. After Chander's accident, a simple physical map marking the India-Pakistan border, and Captain Shahbaaz Khan's exposition on torturing "spies" who infiltrate these borders, become loaded with meaning.

Khan ruminates about man-made, lifeless lines drawn on paper that erase "God-given love in peoples' hearts." His words echo the film's theme: it is absurd to make difference a source of strife. The Captain responds: "These are not personal matters. These are matters of the state you don't understand." Khan's poignant and ironic answer rings through the remaining text: "Yes, humane people will not understand state politics." At the end of the film, Chander stands over Henna's dead body, making an impassioned speech for a world without borders, without war games, and for lasting peace. Yet despite the film's appeal to secular principles and Hindu-Muslim amity, the narrative as a whole belies this message, pointing instead to the impossibility of Hindu-Muslim romantic love, permitted only briefly in a moment of amnesia.

Romantic love in Hindi films has transgressed divisions between all endogamous groups and communities except the Hindu and Muslim communities. This was true until Mani Ratnam's 1995 film *Bombay*, originally made in Tamil (also released in Telegu) and dubbed for the national audience in Hindi.[33] Manmohan Desai's *Amar, Akbar, Anthony* (1977) is more typical of Hindi cinema's style of secularism, where references to the nation and appeal for communal amity remain oblique. In *Amar, Akbar, Anthony*, a family of three boys and their parents are separated on August 15 (Independence Day). Each boy meets a different fate: the oldest, Amar (Vinod Khanna) is raised by a Hindu police officer; the middle child, Anthony Gonsalves (Amitabh Bachchan) is adopted by a Catholic priest; and the youngest is adopted by a Muslim man and grows up to be a *qawali* singer, Akbar Allahbadi (Rishi Kapoor). Twenty-two years later, the brothers and their parents reunite. Meanwhile each son has found his life partner—miraculously, all women of their own community. Amar, the Hindu, marries Laksmi (Shabana Azmi); Akbar, raised as a Muslim, is with Salma (Neetu Singh); and Anthony finds Jenny (Parveen Babi). The nation and its fragments—the three brothers—unite to fight the villainous Robert, the man behind the family's (read: nation's) disintegration.

These films are testimonials to the limits of the Nehruvian secular nationalism practiced by all classes and communities in Indian society, scrupulously mindful of religious, ethnic, and caste identity—distinctions observed even by those who pay lip service to secular principles. Films such as *Henna* and *Amar, Akbar, Anthony* trace the religious divide between communities that is central to national politics—a schism that constantly threatens stability. Hindi cinema's appeal for secular unity, a plea to break through the confining communal animus, is accompanied by terrible uneasiness and a fear of violating rules of communal endogamy—even though the films violate every other social norm that divides the rich from the poor, the upper from the lower caste, the rural from the urban, and the virgin from the whore.

Although community identity and differential treatment of religious groups is central to the political agenda of the Right, which has gained significant ground since the late 1980s, there are many other tensions that keep the nation in a state of perpetual instability. Actor-director Manoj Kumar's films *Upkaar* (Benefaction, 1967) and *Roti, Kapada aur Makaan* (Food, Clothes and Shelter, 1974) are inflected by contemporary political turmoil that seized the nation's attention. *Upkaar* articulates the great rural-urban divide and is a legitimate protest against the urban bias in development planning.[34] Made on the heels of the Indo-Pakistan war in 1965, it turned into a propagandist film, drumming up patriotic sentiments at a critical moment among viewers facing food shortages and a war-torn economy. *Jai jawaan, jai kisaan* (Hail soldier, hail peasant) was the national slogan of the late 1960s, coined to forge an expedient alliance between two key constituencies called upon to serve the nation in its hour of need. The state demanded sacrifice while venerating the soldier and the peasant.

Upkaar is the story of two brothers, Bharat (Manoj Kumar) and Puran (Prem Chopra). In the course of a family feud their evil uncle, Charandas, kills their father, leaving Bharat, the older brother, to head the family. Bharat, a peasant, works hard on the land, while Puran, sent to the city to study, learns the ways of decadent westernized urban life. Buying into the slander Charandas and the village moneylender/trader, Lalaji, spread to drive a wedge between the two brothers, Puran suspects that Bharat reaps a major profit from the land and demands to see the accounts. Bharat places the entire land in the name of Puran's future children, leaves the village, and joins the Indian army in its war effort.

Puran, Charandas, and Lalaji use the war for personal profiteering and are caught by the police. When Puran learns his partners lied to him about Bharat, he returns home. Bharat returns home, too, wounded in action, hanging between life and death. In the end, as the family reunites, Puran marries the girl from the village, engaged to him since childhood, and Bharat marries Kavita, a doctor from the city who chooses to practice medicine in the village clinic.

Apart from being stylistically well-crafted, *Upkaar's* real success lies in the powerful signifiers it uses to imagine the nation: *dharti* (land), *mitti* (soil), *dharti maata* (mother earth), *khoon* (blood), *paseena* (sweat), *hul* (plough), *bandook* (gun), and *tiranga jhanda* (tricolor flag). These symbols are strung together in a semiotic chain to invoke powerful patriotic sentiments. Earth, soil, and mother conjoin to become mother earth, cultivated with the peasant's plough and sweat and protected with the gun by the soldier willing to sacrifice his life for the nation. The peasant and soldier are strategically honored subject-citizens whose sacrifices virtually equal a sacred act.

When Puran demands to divide the land, Bharat replies, "The land is our mother. We don't divide our mother." Later, when he gives Puran the land, an emotionally overwrought Bharat pontificates: the land bears their mother's tears, their ancestors' sweat, and the wealth of coming generations. To protect it is their *dharma* (religion/lifestyle); to work it with the plough, their duty. Therefore, they must promise never to turn away from the land. The mix of metaphors here is deliberate—a peasant's capital, his land, is purposefully made interchangeable with national territory, a semiological stroke that equates it with "motherland." When Bharat seeks employment from an army captain, he argues that the plough and the gun are related to the soil, and later when he prepares to go to the front after war is declared, he explains this connection to his mother. He asks for her blessing to protect Mother India, which until then he's served as a peasant.

Service to the nation becomes service to the mother, naturalizing it like the family, a trope for nation. Family relationships are central to constructing the nation in film narratives. The men are split between the good and bad son or brother; another tack is for the essentially good son to turn bad by succumbing to the underworld, only to return to the point of origin, suitably chastened.

In *Roti Kapada aur Makaan* three brothers, Bharat (Manoj Kumar), Vijay (Amitabh Bachchan) and Deepak (Kiran Kumar) graduate from college against terrible financial odds. Bharat, the oldest brother, is extraordinarily patriotic but unemployed for years on end. When Vijay agrees to make money by becoming a henchman for some unseen mafia man, stirring up trouble on university campuses, Bharat castigates him severely. Vijay leaves home and promises to return only if he makes something of his life.

Meanwhile, Bharat's travails are never-ending. He loses his girl-friend Sheetal (Zeenat Aman) to a wealthy businessman, Mohan (Shashi Kapoor), for whom she works as a secretary. Bharat's odyssey in the workplace introduces him to the honest worker Harnam Singh (Prem Nath), and the appalling corruption and sexual exploitation the local trader, Lala Dhaniram, and his cronies inflict on Tulsi (Moushimi Chatterjee), a laborer. When Bharat is abruptly laid off and his father dies because of unaffordable medical care, he caves in and accepts a job with the corrupt Seth Murli Ram, a businessman-trader-cum-mafiosi.

Meanwhile, Vijay joins the army and loses his arm in action at the front. The youngest brother, Deepak, joins the police force, discovers Bharat's involvement with the mafia, and is determined to arrest him. Vijay, however, who returns to the family now a war hero, is certain of Bharat's innocence and helps him expose the mafia. Together they subvert the mafia's plan to detonate a bomb under a train carrying food supplies. In the end, the mafia is pitted against an unbeatable patriotic force: Bharat, Vijay the soldier, Deepak the police officer, Harnaam Singh, Bharat's working-class friend, and Mohan, an honorable businessman.

Roti Kapada aur Makaan reflects a dark cynical 1970s' mood in a nation troubled by increasing unemployment, a dismal future, student unrest, and the loss of hope—a continuing existentialist crisis with no respite in sight. From the opening sequence that establishes society's failure to meet the most basic human needs—food, clothing, and shelter—the film repeatedly refers to student unrest provoked by their bleak future. In the film's prologue, before the opening credits, shadowy figures walk through labyrinthine bureaucratic offices. One man declares angrily, "If these jobs are promised to people who are well connected, then why bother calling us for the interview. Bharat, nothing is going to come of hanging on to a degree and waiting quietly in the sidelines." A youth rises to face the camera and tosses a stone, shattering a glass door.

An exchange between Bharat, Vijay, and their father demonstrates the sea change in the younger generation's perception of education as a vehicle for upward mobility. Surprised that Vijay's college is closed every other day, the father says,

> In my time, colleges were like temples.
>
> BHARAT: It was a time when a student knew he was assured of a job when he completed his education. Today a student is in the dark, uncertain of finding a job after he gets a college degree.
>
> VIJAY: That is the bitter truth. Yet no one understands this. Quite to the contrary, they point fingers at students, say they have got out of hand.
>
>   Do you remember father, last year a friend of mine after years of hard work, passed his exams, and when it came time to graduate, he went all dressed to the hall. But when he received the degree, he tore it and threw it away. It was probably painful.
>
> FATHER: What did he lose? It's his parents, who struggled to pay for his education that lost everything.
>
> VIJAY: His parents spent twenty to twenty-five thousand rupees, but he lost twenty to twenty-five years of his life. And twenty-five years of a youth's life is worth much more than twenty-five thousand rupees!
>
> FATHER (TO BHARAT): What's come over him?
>
> BHARAT: It isn't just him. This is the voice of every youth that's wandering in the dark.

A sense of futility and overwhelming cynicism pervades the mise-en-scène as well as the script. Light strains through the lattice work on one side of the dark veranda, casting its shadow on the opposite wall. Bharat's silhouette, set against that wall, unequivocally conveys his sense of imprisonment by forces beyond his control. His words represent the "voice of every youth."

Roti Kapada aur Makaan, in keeping with the growing disenchantment overtaking the country in the 1970s, displaces an earlier spirit of hope to build a nation. In choosing representatives of various constituencies in the nation—the soldier, police officer, worker, entrepreneur, trader, student—frequently conjoined in the narrative through kinship ties, the family is likened to the nation. Petty traders and moneylend-

1. Vijay trapped by social forces. *Roti, Kapada, aur Makaan* (Food, Clothes, and Shelter), Manoj Kumar, 1974.

ers are villains. Tulsi, the working-class woman, literally and figuratively represents all labor, raped by big business.

In narrative forms like the epic, the form of classical Sanskrit drama, the hero's fate is linked to that of the community; in romance the hero follows a "heroic or chivalric code," while in the novel, the protagonist's choices are "his own."[35] Romance uses archetypes; that is, "stylized figures which expand into psychological archetypes."[36] The creation of characters that are like "real people" requires the acceptance of "subjective individualism," in which characters do not merely represent class, caste, or a social role. Realist fiction, however, has not been a dominant form of narration in India. Indian novels reflect this central dilemma—as does Hindi cinema—with its predilection for sagas and elaborate plot lines motivated by chance events and coincidences.[37] Fiction and film minimally etch character psychology or the interior working of the mind; generally, male and female protagonists are fixed archetypes. Conflicts arising from their circumstances cause them to stray temporarily from their position, only to return to this original point in the course of narrative resolution.

Characters in Hindi cinema inevitably stand in for specific classes, groups, and professions, brought together through kinship ties. The family and family ties figure prominently in nearly every Hindi film. The centrality of the family in Hindi cinema may be ascribed to migration from rural to urban centers, the attendant dislocation, and the need to give concrete shape to the "faceless authority of the state." The citizen-subject's relationship with the nation is modeled on filial relationships and, by implication, the state is cast as the idealized parental authority figure. In effect, family and state power is fused.[38]

Social institutions such as family and state are ubiquitous in both city and country. Rather than an interchange or fusion of authority, the authority inscribed within them represents a concatenation of power to which individual subjects become accustomed. The family in Hindi film is often a metonym for the nation. The emotional force associated with it makes it the site for dramatic emotional conflict. This is projected on the nation, and becomes the most immediate and effective way of enabling identification and eliciting the subjects' loyalty. For example, the father/judge character dispenses justice in the case of the protagonist/son/outlaw, or the brother/police officer brings to book the protagonist/brother/ outlaw.

Along the topos of familial conflicts the central confrontation is between good and evil, which are mapped onto national and antinational opposition. The principal purpose for staging this contest is to rescue the always endangered imagined community, the nation. The nation and its discontent are central to almost all Hindi films, which relentlessly focus on problems of disunity, poverty, white-collar crime, corruption in high places, regionalism, communalism, modernity, tradition, and feudalism.

As a means of arousing patriotism and consolidating the nation against another nation, an unidentified "enemy" hovers at the margin of the screen. In *Henna*, perhaps for the first time ever, the "enemy," Pakistan, is given a face—even a humane one. The film makes a distinction between the state's subjects' spirit of love and peace and the Pakistani state's hostility, embodied in the diabolical Pakistani army officer, Shahbaaz Khan. References to war—the 1965 Indo-Pakistan war in *Upkaar* and the 1971 war for an independent Bangladesh in *Roti Kapada aur Makaan*—are invoked to evince a nationalist spirit. These films vary in the intensity of their critique of war with all its machinery, propaganda, and loss of innocent lives.

If *Henna* is unequivocally antiwar in spirit, *Upkaar* reflects confusion in its simultaneously nationalist and antiwar sensibility. Bharat's relentless homilies about serving the nation as a soldier and peasant legitimize jingoist sentiments that build consensus for war, death, and killing. Madan Chaacha (Pran), the wise village old-man figure, makes an impassioned speech toward the end of the film destabilizing the earlier prowar, pronationalist rhetoric. Bharat, severely wounded, limps back to his burnt-down village and pleads for a drink of water. But the water Madan pulls out of the well is bloodied, leaving Bharat's thirst unquenched. Looking upward at the dark sky, Madan demands an answer from the warmongers whose thirst for blood is insatiable

Pleasure and Terror of the Feminine

In other films in which the nation is central, it is metonymically figured as a fascinating but horrific woman who is at once terrorized, terrifying, dreadful, and pleasurable. Mehboob Khan's *Aan* (Oncoming, 1952), Bimal Roy's *Madhumati* (1958), and N. Chandra's *Pratighaat* (Retribution, 1987) are films in which the woman signifies the nation in sharp—even contradictory—ways to air dilemmas that plague India's postcolonial

2. Madan draws water, but it's bloodied. *Upkaar* (Benefaction), Manoj Kumar, 1967.

life. Specifically, these films expose contradictions between feudalism and democracy, the marginalization and virtual genocide of ethnic tribes, and the general escalation of corruption and violence in public life.

I begin with *Aan*, made by Mehboob, an avowed nationalist who shared Nehru's vision of India's socialist future. Mehboob's studio logo, the hammer and sickle, valorizes the worker-peasant alliance as the backbone of the nation, yet the film accommodates an "Indian" faith in destiny. The voiceover narrates alongside the logo: "Only what's acceptable to god happens." This opening is followed by an homage to the "peasant-cum-soldier" on the audio track: "This is the peasant who through the ages has seared the earth for food, and during war, turned his plough into a sword to protect the kingdom." The film is dedicated to the serf, exploited uniformly over centuries, notwithstanding political upheaval and changing monarchs.

Aan dramatizes the revolutionary moment in history when feudal forces fought to retain authoritarian control against the sweeping force of democracy and the rule of law. Textually, it is easy to read the film's depiction of feudalism as an unspoken reference to colonialism. This slippage is significant because of the curious silence Hindi cinema maintains about colonialism and the elaborate subterfuge it uses to refer to it.[39] The semiology of signs mobilized in the film coincides with a general social euphoria about a new independent state and its constitution. These signs make the text susceptible to a more open reading, allowing a critique of feudal aristocracy to stand for a critique of colonial rule.

Perhaps the level of abstraction demanded by the political theory invoked in *Aan* tailors a rather unusual narrative; set in a nonspecific time and place, the narrative resembles a "once upon a time" fairy tale. Members of the aristocracy—the king, the prince, and princess—literally represent the last anguished gasps of the feudal-monarchical order dismantled after independence. Figuratively, they are symbols—standins for British rulers. The aptly named heroine, Raj (Nadira)—a word that means "rule"—is an autocratic, repressed princess who wants to continue her family's totalitarian rule over its subjects.[40] In this effort her corrupt brother (Prem Nath) supports her; but a commoner, the hero Jai (Dilip Kumar)—a name meaning "victory"—and his village friend, Mangla, challenge Raj.

Narrative tension centers around the contest between the feudal and democratic forces, and the powerful heterosexual attraction/repulsion between which Raj vacillates in her relation to Jai. The storyline culminates in Jai taming the shrew and sealing his victory over her. The density and layered meaning embedded in this seemingly simple, fairy-tale-like text derive from the ingenious mapping of political concepts onto the topos of gender and sexuality. The film is instructive because of the transparency with which it plots embattled political conflicts on the body of the woman: Raj battles to contain her repressed libidinal energy and maintain her aura of stern authority and distance. She fails because of the overpowering force of her attraction and passion for Jai. The analogy here is clearly not the unlikely love interest between feudalism and democracy, but the coupling of female tyranny with narcissistic feudal aristocracy and the gentle, firm, but powerful male with the liberal, progressive, and ultimately successful forces of democracy.

Clearly, two parallel strains run throughout the film: Raj and Jai's hostilities that conceal feelings of romantic love, and feudalism's inimical relation to democracy, which will completely overrun the former. When Raj insists on holding on to her ancestors' traditions, her father, the benign king, reminds her that rulers who use force must remember that victims of injustice are more powerful than its perpetrators. No authority can trample the awakening of the subjects. This ode to democracy—faith in the might of the ruled—parallels the unequivocal celebration of ending authoritarian aristocracy and the demise of colonial authority, the British Raj. At the end, when the king, assumed to be dead, is found, the crowds animatedly shout, "Victory to the king—no, no, victory to the subjects!"

The domestication of Raj serves as an exorbitant metaphor for subduing and controlling feudalism, read here as routing colonialism. The female protagonist is mobilized as a sign not of the colonized nation but of the colonizer: a neurotic masculinized figure, the antonym of all things considered essentially feminine—harsh, arrogant, fractious, rebellious, intractable. As the film proceeds, the viewer enjoys witnessing the intensity of the passion and tensions engendered by Jai and Raj's contest for power. Raj's character signifies sadomasochistic feudal power assailed, broken down, and ultimately conquered by Jai.

The contest's stage is set when Jai makes a sexual advance to Raj.

3. Jai, Mangala, and Raj. *Aan* (Oncoming), Mehboob, 1952.

She responds, disingenuously as we soon find out, by threatening to have him lashed in public. He then threatens to teach her to live like and love the common people she despises. "I will make you Mangla," he warns elliptically, referring to her status as a common woman and potentially his wife.

Politically, Jai is the harbinger of the rule of law—one law before which all, rulers and ruled alike, are equal. His victory is complete when the masculinized Raj, dressed in a western pants suit ("warrior clothing," as Jai's mother describes it), is slowly transformed. She succumbs to heterosexual passion and accepts her feminine role signified by the bridal attire she finally wears.

Raj's western attire constitutes part of a chain of signs that let us read the film as Mehboob's attack on colonial rule. This can also be inferred from other signifiers of modernization (old-fashioned cars and guns) that frame the narrative within a more specific period. Even more significant is the moment when the king abdicates his throne, announcing that he is not leaving his kingdom to his heirs, the prince and princess, but to his subjects, the *praja*. A close-up reveals the words of the decree being penned: "Rights, social and political to one and all, discrimination against religious. . . . " Access to the rest of the declaration is obscured by the hand that moves the pen to inscribe it. If indeed this is a metonym for the nation and the declaration of its constitution, by inadvertently concealing a critical aspect—the status of religion—the declaration speaks volumes about the ambiguous space religion occupies in the new nation.

On the other hand, what the film sustains is its use of woman as insignia of colonial rule. Raj's body registers excitement, pain, and sadomasochistic pleasure when she attacks Jai. Initially unable to aim the gun at him, she fires a shot in the air. Soon after, when he is injured, her body betrays her feelings. As she heaves, flinches, and winces when Jai is in pain, we become aware of Raj losing control over her repressed sexual energy, leaving her vulnerable before a common man. The heterosexual male's charisma is equated here to democratic forces, before which a tough woman, even a feudal aristocrat, becomes weak-kneed.

Democracy's irrepressible victory (and thus tyrannical feudalism/colonialism's defeat) is complete. Although rarely cast as an insignia of the colonizer, always metonymic of the Indian nation, the Indian woman character is also marked by the universal split between Madonna and whore. It appears impossible to mobilize her in the cultural imaginary as anything beyond these two incarnates. Representing Raj as the raj (British rule) justifies the pleasure in seeing the woman—a symbol of threat and power—domesticated. Her taming is performed literally in a montage sequence where she painfully learns arduous housework—pounds grain, lights the stove, makes bread, fetches water, sews clothes—and inhabits the domestic space Mangla would have. *Aan* projects a gender economy that reverses the traditional coupling of woman with victim/nation, hinging her instead on the demonized figuration of colonial tyranny. She is not the powerless creature who needs rescuing, but a titan who has to be contained. The male hero enjoys agency to stage the requisite action—taming instead of rescuing the victim. This feature recurs in other narrative scenarios as well.

In Bimal Roy's *Madhumati* (1958) gender is again the central axis on which the narrative turns. If one film must be singled out as narrating the contest between several constituencies in the nation-making process *Madhumati* would be it—because it unwittingly tells that story. The central narrative is told as a flashback, a remembering of life from

the past, a narrative within the metanarrative. The metanarrative is
depicted in the prologue and epilogue, but its connection with the narrative—kept a surprise for the audience—is made in the last scene.

The film begins with two professional gentlemen traveling in a
chauffeur-driven car through inclement weather and a treacherous
mountainous terrain. They are hurrying to the train station where the
protagonist is to meet his wife, Radha, and their child, to whom he is
exceptionally devoted. Suddenly stranded by a mudslide, the two men
take shelter in a large *haveli* (mansion) while the chauffeur fetches help
from a nearby village.

When the men enter the decrepit haveli, a gaunt caretaker wel-
comes them; an intense sense of déjà vu grips the protagonist, Deven
(Dilip Kumar). Everything about the place is familiar—its gothic ar-
chitecture, wide staircase, imposing columns, and arched doorways lead-
ing to long winding hallways. He has an intimate yet inexplicable
knowledge of its topography: the walls, the windows, the lake outside.
He even recognizes spaces where pictures are missing from the walls.
As the caretaker confirms his intuition, everyone is overcome by surprise.
The caretaker explains that many years ago the haveli belonged to Ugra
Narain Singh, the last *zamindar* (landlord), king of the area.

The men retire for the night, but Deven is unable to sleep. A
woman's scream awakens him; her sobs and a strange noise beckon him
to explore the mansion. Deven stumbles and struggles to overcome his
initial inability to remember clearly. As the montage of images—the
flying curtain, a chandelier, a man on horseback, the long shot of a
woman—swirl across his face, he begins to remember his past association with the place. The central narrative begins, and the curtain veil-
ing his memory lifts to reveal, in flashback, the past.

Anand *babu* (also played by Dilip Kumar) arrives in a beautiful
mountainous region, its pristine glory untouched by modernization. He
is there to assume his position as the manager of the lumber estate,
owned by the young scion of the princely state, Ugra Narain Singh.
Anand *babu* (a term used derisively by the British, and also used by the
underclass to address those with authority) represents the new breed of
white-collar professionals who relocate according to their job demands,
a burgeoning modern national professional class—a new middle class—
produced by education and technical training rather than any ethnic

or regional identification. It is from Anand's perspective as an outsider that we learn about local politics, territorial conflict, and longstanding local feuds.

The "company" is owned by the feudal aristocracy, which is both morally corrupt and exploitative. Feudal and capitalist relations are conflated in the film and treated with equal contempt. The logic of aggressive extortionist policies culminates in the aristocratic estate grabbing land from the indigenous population and using it for the lucrative tree-felling and lumber business, thereby stripping the forest's resources. The local tribe (the traditional landowners) are pushed back into the mountainous terrain where Paan Raja, once the tribal king and owner of these lands, lives with his daughter Madhumati. In an uprising led by Paan Raja's son against the company-inspired atrocities, the son was killed by Ugra Narain Singh's henchman, Veer Singh. Since then, no passage into each other's territory is granted by either the company or the local tribe. It is Anand's faithful servant, Charan Das (Johnny Walker) who provides him—and the audience—with this expository information.

An artist, Anand spends his after-work hours sketching pictures of the landscape. He meets and falls in love with Madhumati (Vyjayanthimala), a woman whose radiance, "childlike innocence," and simplicity appeal to him. She introduces him to her people, culture, beliefs, customs, and festivals. Paan Raja, initially suspicious of Anand, an outsider, accepts the young professional when he agrees to marry Madhumati—a sign of his willingness to embrace the community. But Ugra Narain has designs on Madhumati and traps her while Paan Raja and Anand are away. The film does not disclose the outcome of the tussle between Ugra Narain and Madhumati when she tries to flee the haveli. Later, Paan Raja and Anand find a piece of her clothing on a tree and conclude she is dead.

Overcome by grief and unable to forget Madhumati, Anand languishes in the woods, gazes at a sketch of her, and is tormented by seeing her apparition time and again. Then one day Madhumati's double appears, dressed in urban, middle-class clothes. Anand approaches her assuming she is Madhumati. The woman resists his advances, insisting that her name is Madhavi, not Madhumati. Anand's persistence terrifies her and it is not until her family and friends, picnicking nearby in

the woods, come to her rescue that Anand realizes his mistake. But
Madhavi discovers Madhumati's sketch; struck by its similarity to herself, she becomes intensely sympathetic to Anand's predicament. When
Madhavi visits him to return the sketch she agrees to assist Anand in
getting conclusive evidence to have Ugra Narain Singh arrested.

Dressed like the tribal hill-woman Madhumati, Madhavi appears
in Ugra Narain Singh's haveli. Terrorized by the "resurrection" Ugra
Narain panics, and recounts what really happened to Madhumati. In
her scuffle with Ugra Narain Singh she fled and fell off the haveli's roof.
The charade over, Ugra Narain Singh's confession enables the police
to arrest him. Meanwhile, Anand, possessed again by Madhumati's spirit,
follows her apparition, falls off the haveli's roof, and dies at the same site.

The flashback ends here and the film returns to the metanarrative.
Deven announces that he was never united with Madhumati in his previous life, but with his wife Radha he has found love again. It is the
early hours of the morning and the chauffeur returns to the haveli to
drive the two men to the train station. In the last shot we see Deven's
wife emerge from the train. It is none other than Madhumati, the urbane Madhavi.

Stylistically, the film adopts a combination of Bimal Roy's brilliant

4. Madhumati confronts her killer. *Madhumati* (Bimal Roy, 1958).

adaptation of film noir and Gothic romance, interrupted now and then by the bright openness of an enchanting landscape. Noir lighting and sharp contrast of darkness and light alternate to depict Madhumati's bright spirit or the sinister haveli, the site of her murder. The haveli is a physical structure bearing testimony to years of feudal tyranny. Madhumati's spirit continues to wander, shrieking and sobbing, trapped within the decrepit haveli's Gothic architecture. Her former lover returns to tell this tale at the beginning of the film.

Sharp lighting contrast also signals climactic moments of danger and suspense. The entire misty landscape, once an embodiment of Madhumati's free spirit, becomes dark and desolate after her death, pierced occasionally by a shaft of light. Her apparition appearing within the darkened landscape, illumined only by a waterfall, makes for an ingenious adaptation of noir-like features to connote otherworldliness. The narrative's predilection for supernatural elements is effectively supported by the camerawork as well as the soundtrack, with ambient sounds of the forest. There are of course other extraordinary production values: the superb pace, a perfect balance of narrative movement in telling or delaying the exposition of important events; excellent editing; Salil Choudhury's memorable music; Shailendra's evocative lyrics; and performances by a talented cast, including Johnny Walker's comic role as Charan Das.

The story resonates with folklore from the mountainous terrain of north India—or elsewhere in India, anywhere distant from "modern" development. Narratives abound in such distant regions about gods and goddesses of local origin, spirits propitiated because they are known to haunt particular sites—rocks, caves, forests, mountain peaks, and the like. For instance, the howling noise the wind makes as it travels through dark forests may be construed as voices, words, or lingering spirits. The source of these local myths remains unknown; they are part of peoples' faith. They live in the collective memory attached to a place, sites made sacred by the experience of loss of a loved one, and rituals associated with it that are passed from one generation to the next. To what extent this lore is based on "true events" is hard to say. But the process by which these narratives come to stay is of special interest today to anthropologists who seek out myths, folk tales, and other ritual forms as central devices for accessing cultural belief systems.

Madhumati is written by none other than Ritwik Ghatak—a superb filmmaker in his own right—from whom many believe Satyajit Ray undeservingly stole the spotlight and title of "the master" of Indian cinema. Ghatak spins folklore and mixes its mythic quality with contemporary realism, melodrama, historical materialism, and Hindu faith in life before birth and after death. The film uses fictional license to create a story in which memory permeates the division between life and death. It suggests a plausible, uncanny similarity in the appearance of two unrelated individuals, yet the film strains to remain within the boundaries of realism, as opposed to magic or surrealism.

For the most part, the film meticulously observes a cause and effect strategy. The appearance of Madhumati's spirit after her death builds on Indian faith in the endless cycle of life. Despite the artistic license used to make the spirit of the dead visible, the narration never transgresses boundaries that would make it inconsistent with popular spiritual notions. For instance, the dead cannot be incorporated into the lives of the living except as ghosts or spirits. Death alone makes reunion with the spirit possible. Madhumati appears and speaks to Anand on many occasions after her death, but she always fades away, suggesting that these hallucinations stem from the protagonist's overwrought condition.

The only departure from this is in the climactic moment when Madhavi traps Ugra Narain Singh by appearing in Madhumati's attire. It is a dark and stormy night when Anand paints Ugra Narain Singh's portrait, engaging him in a discussion on wandering spirits of the dead, a suggestion that makes Ugra Narain quake with fear. At the appointed time Madhavi appears, dressed as Madhumati. Terrified by her appearance, Ugra Narain backs into a corner while she recounts the events of the fateful night she was murdered. Ugra Narain corroborates her story, acknowledging his attempt to rape her and her death while escaping.

After Ugra Narain is arrested, Anand turns to ask Madhavi how she knows about the circumstances surrounding Madhumati's death. Madhavi remains silent, smiles knowingly, and recedes slowly toward the stairway. Suddenly a car pulls up and the "real" Madhavi dressed as Madhumati runs in through the doorway, apologizing for being late due to car trouble. Madhumati herself—*her* lingering vengeful spirit and not Madhavi dressed as Madhumati, that the viewer is set up to expect—

confronts Ugra Narain Singh. In part, such twists create the surprise that sustains the viewer's interest and pleasure. But this twist is also a deliberate effort to make divine retribution appear possible, where the oppressed even after their death might gratify themselves by revisiting their oppressors to torment and punish them.

Set in the mountains, the film is ambiguous about specific location, a hallmark of Hindi cinema. It is somewhere in the Himalayas, a place considered sacred as the source of India's rivers, spiritual as a retreat for meditating ascetics, splendid in its untainted glory. But that location is also perilous because of the oppressive aristocracy who dispossessed the indigenous population, leaving them a fraction of their former territory.[41] It is this political past that is the central organizing principle of *Madhumati*, framed as remembering a process of dismembering. Madhumati's fate is an allegory for India's indigent tribal population.

The film is premised on faith in an epistemology that lies beyond the reach and in defiance of rationalist positivist forms of truth and knowledge—a so called indigenous, native, tribal sensibility. Past and present lives come together through the mnemonic capacity of the central protagonist. The spirit of the dead Madhumati hovers around her lover, calling him, speaking to him, erasing the demarcation between life and death. As such, the film interrogates the modernist discourse, with its abiding faith in western material ontology, through a postmodernist discourse of noneurocentric sensibility.

While apparently a story of innocence and love that transcends one life and continues in life after death, the fantastic rupture of amnesia, meant to maintain an insurmountable distance between the two, serves as a simple mechanism to link individuals to classes and social forms across different periods, along a historical axis—to enable connections between the social ordering of the contemporary and the past. It is not too far-fetched to believe that Ghatak deliberately chose to mix history, politics, the occult, and melodrama in the genre of the popular film of which he truly was a master.

Framed as a flashback within the metanarrative, the protagonist's remembering his past through a chance encounter with the site which triggers his memory transports the narrative into the colonial period—somewhere between the last quarter of the nineteenth century and the first quarter of the twentieth century. Although the film does not specify the exact timeframe, it signals the period when feudal lords held sway and the modern bureaucratic managerial class emerged, supplanting princely power and influence, which continued in a diminished but demarcated space under British rule. The term *babu*—appended to a white-collar worker's name, usually by his social inferiors—was also used by the British to scornfully designate the bureaucratic class of Indian "mimic men" who occupied the colonial bureaucracy's lower levels. (It is also used deferentially by members of the underclass, the "subalterns," to address men with authority.) For a film with its primary narrative set in colonial times it is remarkably inward-looking, critically appraising indigenous institutions and the corruption within. This is in keeping with the tradition of most literary and cultural productions of the 1940s and '50s.[42]

Though the setting and historical time period are not specifically identifiable, the film tells a generalized tale of the brutal modernization process from the viewpoint of the middle managerial class: the professional literati, a figure instated as heroic across generations. The film rehearses an epochal narrative of modern Indian history and the dismembering of a local polity—the story of virtually all modernization narratives. But the middle-manager professional is clearly presented, in this case, as the heroic one in the modernization process.

Other institutions and social classes are also foregrounded. Ugra Narain Singh, the decadent owner of the lumber estate, represents the last remnants of the feudal state. Descendant of a once-benign aristocracy, he is the absentee landlord taken flight to the city, who visits the countryside occasionally to strike terror in the village folk. The film also depicts the dispossessed indigenous population, driven to the outposts of their own terrain after failing to resist encroachments by the estate. These estates were known to be cultivated by and loyal to British rulers.

Madhumati is the woman figure who, as always, symbolizes her community. She is the native—playful, childlike, and trusting. Anand *babu*, the manager of the feudal estate reborn as the engineer, Deven, in postcolonial times, are the sympathetic but fictional narrators who tell her tale, while the master narrator is the writer, Ritwik Ghatak. The continuing tragedy of Madhumati is that she does not figure to recount her own story. She is speechless beyond the sound of her choking sobs, recuperated by the male hero.

Madhumati's "double" is the urban Indian woman Madhavi, who, unlike Madhumati, shares the male protagonist's middle-class origins. In the film's final scene, Deven arrives at his destination, the train station, to meet his wife. Some passengers have been injured in the train accident caused by the previous night's weather. As Deven searches anxiously through the crowds his wife appears in the doorway of one of the carriages. Radha, to the surprise of the audience, is Madhumati— but in the form of Madhavi, not Madhumati. This is a significant telltale sign, exchanging Madhumati for Madhavi and Madhavi for Radha, the urban middle-class woman who quietly displaces the tribal woman to assume her place beside the male protagonist.

The film *Pratighaat* (1987), directed by N. Chandra, appeared forty years after independence and also instates a Madhavi figure as its central protagonist. Here she is Laxmi (Sujata Mehta), a college lecturer in provincial Dharma Pura. Laxmi grows steadily indignant as she discovers the level of violence the hoodlum Kali and his mob unleash. Kali's excesses are endless: kidnapping and murdering the lunatic Karam Vir's wife, Janaki; displacing five thousand weavers with a cloth mill employing only two hundred workers; killing Durga's husband, a weaver, for refusing to pay the illegal *hafta*; and murdering the upright cop, Ajay Srivastava, who was plucky enough to arrest him.[43] When Laxmi shows gumption by reporting the incident to the police, her lawyer husband, Satya Prakash, and her in-laws demand she withdraw the report for fear of reprisal. Kali arrives and teaches Laxmi a lesson by disrobing her in public. A crowd gathers to observe the spectacle in stunned silence. The screen turns white; the audience sees only her silhouette in film negative. The lunatic Karam Vir arrives with Durga to cover her naked body with the national flag; Durga and Laxmi forge an alliance.

When Kali attacks a senior freedom fighter, Gopal Dada, for opposing his candidacy for the Member of the Legislative Assembly (MLA) ticket, Laxmi rallies around Gopal Dada and stands for election against Kali. A band of supportive college students, the dislocated weavers, and marginalized workers add to the groundswell of her campaign. The prospect of losing the election sends Kali and his hoodlums on a

5. Laxmi's nakedness draped in the national flag. *Pratighaat* (Retribution), N. Chandra, 1987.

rampage, and they rig the polls to win. In the last scene Laxmi appears in a red saree, ostensibly to make her congratulatory speech at a large victory meeting. After the speech, she presents Kali with a garland from a large platter. Then, raising an ax from the same gift platter, she kills him. The police arrive and arrest her, despite protests from the crowd. As the police whisk her away, her husband arrives, tells her how proud he is of her, apologizes for his own cowardice, and promises to be a worthier husband.

The most dramatic aspect of the leap from *Madhumati* to *Pratighaat*, a period spanning thirty postindependence years, is the depth of cynicism, the transformation of public life, and its representation in Hindi films—"the nation's storytelling in an attempt to make symbolic sense of itself."[44] The film documents the extent and spread of the rot, the reign of mafia terror. It exposes the complicity of the state (the police and judiciary) that can no longer be relied upon to arbitrate matters of social justice. Karam Vir, the lunatic, once a dutiful police constable, reveals the pervasiveness of the malaise. Reminiscent of eminent mid-twentieth-century writer Saadat Hasan Manto's protagonist, Toba Tek

Singh—the lunatic who sees with perspicacious clarity—Karam Vir stands at the main *chowk* (crossroad) in the town, identifies the city's elite members, and exposes their crimes and misdemeanors.[45]

Kali, the local mafia don, attempts to gain legitimacy by entering electoral politics. He is abetted by politicians and appeased by weak-kneed police officials; worse, he is endorsed by citizen apathy: the fearful business community, Laxmi's students, her complacent middle-class neighbors, even her husband. Karam Vir's courageous remonstrance against Kali's last act of desperation, "capturing (voting) booths," ends with his death. Stabbed in the back by Kali, Karam Vir falls on the ground. His daughter runs toward him against the screen that turns white, her little figure rushing toward the viewers in slow motion, screaming heartrendingly, "*Bapu, Bapu . . .*" (Father, Father). She is equivocally invoking her father and Mahatma Gandhi, "the father of the nation," and the traumatic massacre of nationalist principles he stood for.

N. Chandra set a new benchmark for the level of violence in films. *Pratighaat*, an example par excellence, uses violence against women as an index of the suffusion of violence in public life. As if the molestation of Karam Vir's wife and the murder of a cop in full view of the public were not enough, the violence escalates until the shocking scene when Laxmi is publicly disrobed and humiliated.

When Laxmi returns to teach, to her dismay she finds nude female figure sketches on the blackboard while her male students mock her with their gaze. (Earlier, the same students hostile to her authority in the classroom had attempted to embarrass her by making her translate the word "breast" from the Sanskrit classic she teaches. On that occasion she deflected the fetishized sexualization of the female body, de-eroticizing breasts by invoking women as mother figures.) This time, she breaks into a song exhorting her male students (and all men in the audience) to look upon women not as sex objects, but as life-givers, nurturers who have sustained them. Her resistance takes the form of pitting *mamta* (nurturance) against *vasana* (lust/desire). Her students are eventually chastened by this plea.

This dichotomy in Indian culture between venerating and protecting women by appealing to their role as real or potential mothers on the one hand, and as sexual objects on the other, is striking, particularly since nurture and desire are irrevocably interconnected in the Freudian order of things.[46] *Pratighaat* suggests that violence against women is affected by commodifying women's bodies; it places the unwanted male gaze and the disrobing incident on a continuum. And yet, ironically, the film suggests also that women are subjects with their own desires. Laxmi inverts the traditional mode of sexual play by openly expressing desire for her husband.

Women here are not so much a trope for the nation, but active agents—saviors who will deliver the nation into the future. Initially Laxmi is a figure similar to Rajni, the protagonist of a television serial by the same name, extremely popular in the mid–1980s. Rajni is an urban middle-class woman with a civic conscience and in each episode she tackles corruption in the bureaucracy. Laxmi goes on to challenge not just constables who do not do their job and students who molest women, but Kali himself. She foils his agenda for legitimacy by entering electoral politics. For this she unites with Durga, and here the figures of Madhumati and Madhavi are, in a wishful move, brought together across class boundaries.

The film makes an obvious reference to Durga and Laxmi, goddesses in the Hindu pantheon. Using such icons might read as a strategy of containment that ascribes unique mythic qualities to gods and "heroes" who are distinct from ordinary folk.[47] However, it is also possible to read a very different form of social victimization the two women represent. Durga's means of livelihood—like Madhumati's community's land—is snatched away. For Laxmi, silence in the face of social injustice occasions a moral crisis. The principled stand she takes destabilizes her relationship with her husband and his family.[48] Middle and working-class women uniting—Madhavi and Madhumati, Laxmi and Durga—seem to dissolve class boundaries and offer up a sign of hope in women as bearers of a new liberatory potential.

The most troubling feature of the film, however, is the "masculinized" discourse that identifies society's ailment as a "lack" of potent male power. Even more disconcerting is the fact that female subjects articulate this prognosis. Masculinity is equated with strength and valor, and cowardice with sexual impotence. A minor subplot in the film focuses on a wrestler who spends hours exercising his body and yet is unable to challenge Kali, or inseminate his wife. Karam Vir declares (in English) at the end of Laxmi's charged disrobing incident that the inability of the people to respond is a sign of "the impotence of the intelligentsia."

Laxmi displaces the figure of Anand *babu*, who signified a generation of men now scorned as effete and mocked for their cowardice in failing to live up to the hopes and expectations they once represented. At the same time the voice of Madhumati, temporarily erased, returns to join the urban middle-class woman set forth as the new conscience and savior of a nation besieged by corruption and sustained by violence and terror. Villains are no longer the invisible aristocracy, feudal kings or landlords, but the politician king and his hoodlums who affect every aspect of urban life.

The film is unambiguous in its effort to replace one hero with another. Rather than place faith in collective action, the "new woman" is expected to become the nation's conscience. In the last shot, a low-angle shot of Karam Vir's daughter, a little girl holding the national flag fills the screen. She represents hope in a new generation that will replace Anand and Karam Vir, men without an alibi for the failures of the entire postindependence era.

Chapter 2

The Idealized Woman

Writings on the portrayal of women in popular Hindi cinema have long been split between the figures of the Madonna and the vamp—remaining truncated and not extending beyond a content-analysis methodology. As necessary first steps in examining Hindi films' representations, these studies provide a rich and abundant characterization of its idealized women figures: passive, victimized, sacrificial, submissive, glorified, static, one-dimensional, and resilient. What remains insufficiently explained, however, is why women have been fashioned so relentlessly in this manner in the period immediately following independence when in all other matters of development and national reconstruction, Hindi cinema was relatively forward-looking.

Rather than read popular screen characterizations of women as mythology's "timeless cultural resources," as some Indian critics do, searching history for continuities and shifts in the idealized representation of women offers clues to the way it structures our present culture and law. As Kumkum Sangari urges, we must comprehend "cultural processes which enable the symbolic empowerment or mythification of women."[1] Critics reconstructing an understanding of nineteenth-century Indian women are hard-pressed to find texts in which women represent themselves, speak in their own voice, and search for identity in the midst of cataclysmic changes that were underway. There is a notable absence of autonomous accounts by women in official archives, attesting to their invisibility in the nation's hegemonic discourses.

One option is to draw on a popular genre of memoirs (*smritika*), women's autobiographies and biographies that emerged in the nineteenth century and coincided with the beginning of women's education and the development of a new "individualism." These memoirs, inculcated by male guardians, were considered germane to women's needs: a technique used merely to record direct experiences of one's life. Women were not expected to express themselves or to develop their personalities so as to need more demanding writing abilities and stylistic embellishments. Yet what is striking about the autobiographies and their textual strategies "is the way . . . the very theme of disclosure of self remains suppressed under a narrative of changing times, changing manners and customs, and changing values." Women do not describe the self but the "times." Partha Chatterjee cautions us "to remember that sovereignty over language, a tricky business under the best of circumstances, is doubly vitiated for those subordinated to both colonialism and nationalist patriarchy."[2]

A century later, in today's texts of Hindi films, we are reminded of how women are still doubly vitiated and subordinated by a nationalist patriarchy and a sexist film industry. Women have no access to the means of film production and are still virtually unrepresented as directors, producers, or screenwriters. As actors they perform—directed by male fantasies and patriarchal values. Reading women's lives from the film texts alone would be flawed, particularly when the lives of actual women, especially in the film industry, are an apogee to their screen representation. Star texts—the lives of film stars occupying public space and knowledge—are useful counterpoints to constructions in film narratives. Changes in the film text and the extra-text are equally significant to note when mapping the trajectory of women's lives and the cultural space in which their lives change.

In another effort that attempts to hear women speak in their own voices, Susie Tharu and K. Lalitha edited two anthologies of writings by women in India. Their project ambitiously spans the period from 600 B.C. to the present. Undaunted by the absence of women writers from official archives—which at times offer only a glimmer, a fleeting reference to their works—the editors resorted to oral histories and word of mouth, searching personal libraries and private collections in distant places far from the established centers of the academy and its affiliated institutions.

In doing so, they clarify their objective: it is not to retrieve women's writing as texts to be reinstated within established and venerated cultural institutions from which these women were accidentally dropped and forgotten. Nor is the purpose to monumentalize women's writings as an institution unto itself. Rather, their effort focuses on using these writings to reveal the stakes involved in the battles for self and agency within patriarchy's margins, "reconstituted by the emerging bourgeoisie of empire and nation."[3] Translation, the editors acknowledge, involves a relation of power where two cultures collide. They therefore demand that readers "translate" past women's selves into specific sociocultural contexts, following the logic of these women's lives and the concerns of the world they inhabited. The writings they select reveal the response of women to history and the politics of everyday life.[4]

What purpose does this bear on a project that attempts to retrieve a history of filmic representation of women in Hindi cinema? Whether these popular texts are hauled onto the high ground of critical theory or whether theory is carried to a democratized, cosmopolitan world of cultural texts aided by free-flowing translation is a matter of judgment. As third-world cultural critics we are native informants, translating culture and texts—and also transposing the wherewithal of critical cultural armor upon them. These two worlds require traversing a slippery terrain.

In India there is a network of institutions that frame "womanhood" in law and the popular imagination. These institutions deploy discursive strategies that subordinate women and make them pawns in the rush for national identity. A useful focal point is the contest staged around the middle of the twentieth century, centering on reformulating women's legal rights within the private sphere. The sexist discourse in the Hindu Code Bill, and resistance to it in the form of the Uniform Civil Code, draws the State, religion, communities, and the nation into the fray.[5]

In the nineteenth century a model of "Indian womanhood" was created in the popular imagination in response to colonial rule, and jettisoning it has been difficult. Art, literature, drama, and poetry amalgamated to mold a popular vision of Indian womanhood, but the version of the "new" woman was actually the modernists' reinvention of the *traditional* Indian woman tempered by the mix of dominant Victorian and upper-caste Brahminical values. The Indian woman in popular Hindi cinema is very much the product of this Victorian-Brahminic axis, especially during the first two decades of independent India.

The exemplary film *Purab aur Paschim* (East and West, 1970) brings this historicized construction of womanhood into sharper focus. The film explicitly manifests the ideology mythifying the "essence" of Indian womanhood. By zeroing in on the colonial encounter, which led to the first modernist enunciation of the women's question, we can see how the film is directly connected with the symbolic world of women's images in Hindi films today. Written, directed and produced by the self-proclaimed patriot and actor Manoj Kumar, *Purab aur Paschim* is the saga of several families traced along two generations, presented with an elaborate prologue set during the peak of the independence movement in 1942. Om, a freedom fighter fleeing from the British police, visits his home. Harnam, a family friend, informs the police, and Om is tracked down and shot.

About twenty years later, where the main narrative begins, Om's grown son, Bharat (Manoj Kumar), leaves for higher education in England, which to him symbolizes the spiritual lack of western civilization. He lives with the Sharmas, an Indian family that has become caught up in the alienated, hedonistic world of 1960s excess. Mr. Sharma's daughter, the leather-miniskirt-wearing, cigarette-smoking, bar-frequenting Preeti (Saira Banu), pursues a relationship with Bharat, and they are soon engaged to be married. When Preeti refuses to relocate in India, Bharat promises to live with her in England on the condition that she visit India once. On the visit they tour temples and attend carnivals. Preeti slowly becomes enamored of the country and transformed by the "spirit" and "essence" of the land, kicks her smoking and drinking habits, and chooses to live like a "traditional Indian woman." The family never returns to England.

There are a few moments of the film worth elaborating on before launching a search for its imaginative genealogy. When Bharat, the protagonist—an avowed nationalist—leaves for England, his grandfather points to an ironical reversal: in ancient times people came to India for higher education. Bharat explains that the nation needs to learn science and technology, the very purpose of his sojourn. Science and technology are the ground on which the west's superiority is conceded.

6. Preeti, a decadent "westerner." *Purab aur Paschim* (East and West), Manoj Kumar, 1970.

But the west—specifically England, once the colonial master—is an emotional wasteland of derelicts without "family life": alienated individuals seeking refuge in sex, alcohol, and promiscuity. The most glaring feature of the west in the film is its free-floating libidinal excess, signified by overexposed women's bodies (such as the scantily clothed Preeti Sharma). Her journey to the east and its enthralling "essence" brings back her "lost origin."

Preeti's gradual transformation leads her to reflect on the East/West divide. She is struck by the devotion of the family servant's wife, who waits forty years in her home village before her husband brings her to the city, and by Bharat's female childhood friend who never confesses her love for him, constrained by an appropriate coyness. Preeti's brother, a Hare Rama Hare Krishna cult member, expounds on *lajja* and *sharam* (coyness and shame), the "rare jewels" the Indian woman possesses. When Preeti's mother, unable to cope with the lack of creature comforts on the tour, decides to curtail her visit and return to England, to her surprise she finds Preeti dressed in a bridal saree, worshipping at the temple. Gone are the leather skirts and boots. The errant girl finds her origin, embraces Indian womanhood—that defining essence of

Indianness—proving Bharat's thesis about India: "*apne yahaan ki mitti kuch aise hai ajnabi ko bhi sanskaar sikha deti hai*" (the soil of our land is such that even a stranger learns its culture). The power of nation, tradition, and culture are invoked with unusual vigor in this film—and their reverberations can be felt in the entire corpus of popular Hindi films.

Fixing the Figure of the Woman

Historians puzzle over the surge of interest in women's issues in the first part of the nineteenth century in India, and its disappearance by the end of the century when nationalist politics overtook the nation's concerns. Partha Chatterjee argues that in India the women's question receded from public discourse in the early twentieth century because the ideology of nationalism offered a resolution through the spiritual material divide.[6]

Transposing the spiritual/material onto an inner/outer—*ghar/bahir*, home and world—social space is divided, playing a significant role in the everyday practice of life. Gender differences fit into this division: men occupy the material world outside while women preserve the home, its essence unaffected by the material world. "Modern" ideas recasting the "new woman" became acceptable—so long as women's roles in the domestic sphere remained intact.

For example, nineteenth-century popular literature ridiculed Bengali women who mimicked the manners of European women; such literature expresses a common anxiety about Indian women. The message was that imitating the west was necessary in the material sphere, but, if it entered the home, it could threaten and destroy Indian identity. The new Indian woman was superior to her European counterpart precisely because she maintained her spiritual essence. The new woman also maintained her distinction from women of lower caste and class.[7]

Uma Chakravarti points to nineteenth-century discourse that was keen to emphasize the high-caste Hindu woman's decline in status compared to ancient times. High-caste women became recast in the superwoman mold, "the spiritual Maitreyi, the learned Gargi, the suffering Sita, the faithful Savitri and the heroic Lakshmibai."[8] Susie Tharu surmises that the emergent woman figure in the nationalist imagination was "in keeping with the now naturalized Victorian ideals of domestic virtue, patient and long suffering and autonomous, conscious of her power and of the strength she could find in tradition: a gentle but stern custodian of the nation's moral life. And this was the figure that was to dominate the literary imagination for several decades to come."[9] These two dominant strands are layered together: a tradition reinvented from the upper-caste Hindu notion of a "glorious past," and a Victorian legacy of purity and sexual restraint. Both traditions mutually accommodate and reinforce each other.

Woman's deification as mother was another dimension of womanhood occupying a powerful position in the national imaginary. By the end of the nineteenth century, in the early phase of nationalism, popular literature, song, drama, and painting—in fact the entire gamut of art and culture—was concerned with the problem of expressing "national identity," and used the mother icon to personify the nation. Images of the mother as a victim—a figure inspiring a strong sense of duty, an intense, almost filial, relationship to the nation—abound in the nineteenth century.[10]

Works that forcefully articulate the mother as a nation include Kiran Chandra Bandhopadhyay's play *Bharat Mata* (Mother India, 1873), with its figurations of the nation as a "dispossessed woman, often a widow or a woman deranged by suffering"; the first anthology of patriotic songs, *Bharat Gan* (India songs, 1879); and Bankim Chandra Chatterjee's 1882 novel *Anandamath*, where a mother is rescued by brave sons, the "agents of deliverance."[11] Bankim fused the concepts of *shakti* (power), the mother goddess, and motherland in *Anandamath*, forging a powerful emblem with far-reaching consequences.[12]

We can only speculate about this excessive investment in the mother image. It may derive from nineteenth-century popular religious practices and imagery servicing nationalism.[13] Or, the reiterated image may be linked to a general anxiety about the Bengali male's "diminished capacity of physical courage" and used to elicit compensatory images of valor.[14]

The suffering woman—or rather the suffering mother, a metonym for the nation—became a powerful and inspiring image evoking a sense of duty among the sons: they are required to protect the mother, the primordial nurturing force. Such a history of cultural imagery is central to understanding the construction of femininity and masculinity in Hindi cinema. In popular film the young male continues to be anointed the agent while the woman is powerless, an object to be acted upon.

The female figure as mother and nation also embodies sacrifice and forbearance. Fixing the figure of the woman in this context within the national unconscious occurred culturally along with the idea of reclaiming a reinvented "Indian" past. As nationalist politics unified around the struggle for political autonomy, independence from colonial rule took center stage. The fierce debates surrounding the "women's question" became contained as *race*—and this became the anticolonial movement's organizing principle. With brown set against white, nationalist ideology elided issues that could drive a wedge between diverse communities and classes or between men and women.

Woman, Community, Nation

If the above elaboration explains how women's idealized mythification crystallized in the nineteenth century, it does not explain the need to sustain this image after independence. Though tensions between several interest groups were contained in pre-independence India, the eruption of Hindu-Muslim strife (played up by the British) culminated in the worst holocaust on the subcontinent—India's Partition—that accompanied its independence in 1947. To stem the fissiparous tendencies and resolve contradictions between different communities the figure of the woman, already cast as a powerful trope for the nation, was once again deployed to shore up a sense of unity.

Yet such a formulation is problematic, especially if we turn to the debate on the passage of Personal Laws versus a Uniform Civil Code that raged for about fifteen years in the middle of the twentieth century. The furor surrounding rewriting the rule of law ends with the woman as a signifier of the home, the private, and the personal in the Sovereign Republic. It reinscribes iterations adapted under colonialism in laws dealing with marriage, family, and inheritance. Half a century after independence, the Uniform Civil Code remains a secular ideal to be achieved in the private sphere, which religious laws continue to regulate.[15]

In 1772, Lord Hastings designated Hindu texts as the source of Hindu law governing "personal" matters such as marriage, divorce, inheritance, and adoption, authorizing Brahmin pundits to interpret Hindu texts and impose an upper-caste Brahminic code on the lower castes, who were traditionally governed by customary practices. The Permanent Settlement of 1793 was the origin of the Anglo-Indian legal system. A judiciary was devised with laws facilitating market transactions and the accumulation of private property. Parallel to these public laws were the private laws—personal law functioning under the rubric of customary and religious norms and proscribing individual freedoms.[16]

Aspects of Muslim Personal Law (the *shariat*) were modified in 1935 by the Muslim elite (landowners and the middle class) and the *ulema* (the Muslim clergy). Enacting a central law applicable to the entire country's Muslim population, the *ulema* set themselves up as the *shariat's* authoritative interpreters on matters of adoption, wills, inheritance, personal property maintenance, dower, guardianship, gifts, and *wakfs* (endowments held in trust for Muslims). The *shariat* gained unifying and symbolic significance for minority Muslims in the postpartition period. By consolidating Muslim identity around religion and the practice of religious laws, and placing themselves at the helm of this group, these Muslim leaders, with political ambitions of their own, were a force to contend with in independent India.

For Hindus the *dharmashastras* (moral code) governed conduct; the code's source lay in religious Hindu texts, the *Vedas* and the *Smritis*. Rules governing Hindu life were meant to maintain "the cosmic and moral order": marriage was considered sacred and indissoluble, succession of property was through male heirs, women had limited property rights, and polygamy was permitted. There were significant regional variations. For example, some women in parts of south India exercised political power and could dispose of property as they wished. Lower castes had less restrictive customs. In the patrilineal joint Hindu family, sons shared common property rights; their wives had a right to maintenance, but not inheritance.[17]

Between 1921 and 1936 the women's movement campaign to codify Hindu law, grant Hindu women property rights, and the right to divorce (led by the All India Women's Conference, AIWC) was obstructed by the Hindu orthodoxy. In 1944 the B.N. Rau Committee's draft of the Hindu Code focused on marriage and inheritance: a widow's share was to be equal to her son's; a daughter was to get half a son's share; polygamy was prohibited; intercaste marriage was legalized; and grounds for the dissolution of marriage were established.

The Hindu Code left the elite deeply divided. Etched in this debate were notions about the ideal Hindu woman. Opponents drew the ideal woman's image from the *Manusmriti*, an orthodox Hindu guide: she needed protection, and "in this position of dependence she was worshipped as a goddess." The Hindu joint family was regarded as the appropriate property ownership unit, providing for women "in a manner superior to the individualistic basis of Western society." A member of the Constituent Assembly, Bajoria, argued that the notion of gender equality was British: "Hindus would be better protected by a nationalist government." With Pakistan awarded by the departing British to the Muslim League, a compensatory demand for a "'Hindu raj' (rule) in which Hindu values would be central" seemed legitimate.[18]

The putative pledge of Congress Party leaders to include social equality while drafting the Constitution failed to translate into support for the Hindu Code bill. Libertarian principles of gender equality, a fundamental right in the Constitution, precluded equal rights for women in marriage—in the private sphere. Implicit in a woman's right to divorce her husband or inherit property was the threat of her freedom from men's dominion.[19]

In 1945 a great deal of public interest was generated in the bill by the Rau Committee's tour around the country, the sale of translations of the Hindu Code into vernacular languages, and the appearance of 378 civilians at the Committee's hearings. Despite opposition, the Rau Committee's Hindu Code Bill was submitted to the Legislative Assembly in 1947 and debated in the Central Legislative Assembly and the Constituent Assembly between 1943 and 1944, and again between 1949 and 1951.

Publicity surrounding the bill grew because of the public hearings, while the controversy around it intensified because it was assigned to Dr. Ambedkar, the *dalit* Law Minister at the time. A *dalit* leader's support, combined with the bill's association with educated "westernized" women, provoked unmitigated hostility from the patriarchal Brahmin orthodoxy.[20] Notwithstanding the bill's publicity, the debate reached only the educated urban community, barely 5 percent of the population, leading detractors to question women Assembly members' ability to represent women at large.[21]

The highest ranks of the Congress leadership were divided on the Hindu Code Bill. Ambedkar's announcement to secure the Bill's passage, his open criticism of Hinduism, and his resignation protesting Nehru's short-circuiting the legislative process by abandoning the Bill deeply offended orthodox Hindu politicians.[22] Mahatma Gandhi opposed a legalistic approach while Nehru, in spite of his vacillation, favored legal reform and the Hindu Code Bill. All other senior leaders opposed Nehru—including the then-President, Rajendra Prasad, and the Deputy Prime Minister, Vallabhbhai Patel. The President went so far as to threaten a constitutional crisis by refusing his assent to the bill even if the Parliament passed it.

Nehru treated his overwhelming victory in the 1951 general election as a mandate of support for the Hindu Code Bill, securing its passage in 1955. After a controversy that had raged for fifteen years, the Hindu Code Bill was divided into five separate acts and passed. These were: 1) the Special Marriage Act (1954); 2) the Hindu Marriage Act (1955); 3) the Hindu Succession Act (1955); 4) the Hindu Minority and Guardianship Act (1956); and 5) the Hindu Adoption and Maintenance Act (1956).[23] The Indian Republic inaugurated secular principles in criminal and commercial laws and all aspects of property— except inheritance. Inviolate personal laws would govern the private sphere, varying according to each community's dictates. However, these laws, requiring contemporary interpretations of medieval and ancient scriptures, failed the test of delivering gender justice.

Though the AIWC demanded reform in Hindu law, they proposed the idea of a uniform civil code as early as 1940 to displace religious personal laws and bring the entire domain of the private/religious into the public/secular sphere. Minoo Masani, Hansa Mehta, and Rajkumari Amrit Kaur, leaders of the AIWC and members of Advisory Committees to the Constituent Assembly, voted in favor of establishing the Uniform Civil Code as a fundamental right, arguing that it would break down barriers between different communities.[24] Muslim leaders, however, made the community's identity contingent upon preserving the *shariat*, demanding Muslim personal laws be kept beyond the purview of the Uniform Civil Code.[25] The Constituent Assembly debate posited preserving religious identity through personal laws versus consolidating national unity—equating the Uniform Civil Code with assimilating minority identity. This highly reductive nature of such religious/community identity was constructed in response to an Orientalist colonial and bureaucratic regime.[26] The discourse elides what lay at the heart of this debate—the control of women.

Protesting the failure to make the Uniform Civil Code enforceable, Hansa Mehta, in her speech in the Constituent Assembly, insisted that such a code was far more important to national unity than creating a national language.[27] Her words turned out to be prophetic in the light of what happened thirty years later, in the mid–1980s, when a tenuous national unity was severely strained by a sixty-five-year-old Muslim woman, Shah Bano. In 1985 Shah Bano's litigation, demanding a paltry alimony maintenance of 125 rupees (now $3) a month, rocked the nation and threatened its fragile unity. When the Muslim orthodoxy threatened insurgency, the government capitulated.

The debacle began when Mohammad Ahmad Khan appealed to the Supreme Court, challenging the High Court's decree directing him to pay a small maintenance to Shah Bano, his divorced wife. Invoking Muslim Personal Law, he claimed he was not obliged to pay his divorced wife beyond the period of *iddat* (court proceeding). Section 125 of the Criminal Procedure Code of India enjoins the maintenance of divorced wives; under this clause Khan was obligated to pay. However, the Muslim Personal Law Board disputed the Supreme Court's right to interfere with Muslim personal law.

The Muslim fundamentalist leadership mobilized mass protest against the Supreme Court's ruling, demanding exemption for Muslims from section 125 of the Criminal Procedure Code on the grounds that it contravened the *shariat*, offended Muslim sentiment, and even endangered their minority status. Initially the government stood behind the Supreme Court, but later it relented, reversed its position, and succumbed to conservative Muslim leaders, effectively buying electoral support at the cost of women's rights. The 1986 Muslim Women (Protection of Rights on Divorce) Bill was passed, ostensibly to preserve cultural diversity, the rights of minorities, and to protect their religious identity.[28] To maintain the ideal of multicultural, multilingual identities the prospect of a uniform civil code, it was argued, had become anathema.[29] Here the figure of the woman, once deployed to consolidate national identity, is used analogously in the name of the Muslim community's identity in a way that diminishes Muslim women's rights and fragments Indian women's unity.

On another register, Hindi cinema also uses a specific construction of traditional Indian womanhood to connote a unified nation. Mastery over women plays a central role in such a signifiying practice. Men equate women's legal equality with losing community identity. Postpartition tensions around Hindu-Muslim integration center around each community's right to retain control over "their" women. The *shariat* and the Hindu Marriage Act ossified patriarchal law. At stake for feminists now is disrupting a patriarchal discursive and social regime in which the woman remains a signifier of the religio-ethnic community.

Thus, the symbol of woman as home and nation turns out to be an unstable signifier. Varying political contingencies animate the woman as a sign: she is a stand-in for the nation at one historical moment, and for the religious community in another. Consequently, launching the woman as a symbol of the nation is at once progressive and regressive. It works as a symbol of unity, a Pan-Indian consciousness that Hindi cinema strives to project at a moment when political fragmentation is imminent. Yet such signification frequently fails, and women become sites of contest each time a community asserts its identity, threatening the fragile amity among religio-ethnic communities. Shah Bano's case, taken up by Muslims, and Roop Kanwar's immolation, a rallying point for some Hindus, are instances testifying to such lapses.[30]

The symbolic image of the traditional Indian woman in Hindi film could well project a wishful desire to unite the nation around the figure of the woman, while repressing debates on identity and community which have propagated patriarchal laws signifying "difference" in the name of cultural diversity. To use woman to represent the entire nation blurs the boundaries contested by different communities. The double-bind, however, is that using woman as a stand-in for nation may work in favor of secular consciousness, but at the same time it continues to promote egregious gender injustice. Yet all communities and castes dally with this venerated image of womanhood, claiming it as their badge of honor. It is clear, however, that women's interests have been sacrificed at the altar of national unity.

The "Social Butterfly"

Popular Hindi cinema in the postindependence years exercised monumental repression, denial, and disavowal of communal politics, presenting an idyllic oneness, unity among undifferentiated "Indians." Difference is acknowledged only in stereotypical representations of communities, through communal fraternizing typified by the Hindu protagonist's Muslim / Sikh "best friend," or the historical genre celebrating Hindu-Muslim amity.[31] Yet boundaries between them remain firmly in place. For instance, film narratives assiduously avoid suggestions of intercommunity marriage that might effect genuine integration.

Yet Hindi films also use heterosexual romance and love as the "transcendent" power flouting strict endogamous codes that ensure social distance across class and caste boundaries. The divides between rich and poor, urban and rural, upper- and lower-caste are constantly surmounted by romantic love. This victory of romantic love is particularly intriguing in a society where a large number of ethnic religious groups (and multiple subsects within each) are all deeply conscious of their identity, and anxious to maintain their purity through the endogamous codes of an arranged marriage system. Love and romance culminating in marriage has enormous symbolic power and appealing triumph in its ability to bend social norms and push social boundaries. Yet in the history of Hindi cinema it has been impossible to enunciate or even suggest a Hindu-Muslim romantic union—at least not until Mani Ratnam's *Bombay* (1995), made in Tamil and dubbed in Telegu and Hindi, a trend as unusual as the film's aesthetics, a cross-pollination of popular and art film.[32]

The protagonist, a Hindu journalist Shekhar (Arvind Swami) visits his home village and falls in love with a Muslim woman, Shaila (Monisha Koirala). Defying their families, Shaila runs away to marry and live with Shekhar in Bombay. Anonymity in the metropolitan city works well for them and their twin sons, until riots erupt in Bombay's streets disrupting their private tranquil.[33]

With the passage of time their families relent and finally accept the grandsons as legitimate offspring of an "anomalous" union. However, the ire of that once-benign metropolis, Bombay, gives way to unimaginable ferocity in the form of Hindu and Muslim mobs, who identify and kill members of the other community. The twin boys, about age five, are lost in a riot. Disclosure of their hybrid origin intensifies their vulnerability, even threatens their survival. The irony is, of course, that they are both Hindu and Muslim yet neither purely Hindu nor Muslim, and hence unsafe from fanatics on both sides.

The Shah Bano controversy had barely subsided when the right-wing Hindu Bharatiya Janata Party began claiming that the fifteenth-century mosque in Ayodhya, the Babri Masjid, was the Hindu god Rama's birthplace. The party sought to expand its base by calling to replace the mosque with a temple. The mosque's desecration on December 6, 1992 set off month-long riots in several major Indian cities and towns—a conflagration on a scale the nation had not witnessed since the 1947 Partition. Ratnam, in keeping with his penchant for combining contemporary politics and film, strategically set the film in Bombay, a city that burned in December and January of 1992–1993, bewildering secularists who thought that its long industrial history and unique cosmopolitan culture had inoculated it from sectarian prejudice.[34]

Critiques of the film insisting that a narrative constructing a romance between a Hindu man and a Muslim woman asserts Hindu cul-

7. Riots disrupt the private tranquil. *Bombay* (Mani Ratnam, 1995).

tural dominance liaise dangerously, and even buy into, a discourse in which the woman is a sign of her community.[35] Other critiques concede that demands to ban *Bombay* condone Muslim patriarchal sentiments, but still faults the film's ploy of using romantic love. Yet romance in *Bombay* is almost reduced to a subplot, resolved in the first half of the film. A Muslim father and Hindu mother would not change the identity of the syncretically named hybrid twins (Kabeer Narayan and Kamal Basheer), whose fate becomes the focus in the film's latter half. Furthermore, the charge that the film suggests that integration is accomplished in the private sphere is belied by the manner in which the eruption in the public sphere intrudes upon the supposedly safe haven of the family—here metonymic for a composite nation turning on itself.

Notwithstanding *Bombay*, a dominant trend for almost fifty years of Hindi cinema has been the omission of conflicts driven by community identity and a deliberate representation of communal fraternizing—*Amar, Akbar, Anthony*–style. Promoting a generic Pan-Indian identity, this tactic erases "difference," especially between religious communities. What remains vital in this erasure, however, is maintaining "difference" of another kind—gender difference. Hindi cinema's casting of "the traditional Indian woman" during the postindependence period is symbolic of a wishful desire to unite the nation around the figure of the woman and to repress the searing debates on identity and community.

If Hindi films routinely use romantic love to transcend all kinds of social schisms, in Guru Dutt's film *Mr. and Mrs. 55* (1955), heterosexual love—or, more specifically, the modality regulating it—is thrown into crisis. The film raises the question of how female agency is expected to negotiate the private (love/marriage/family) and the public (legal/national/political) spheres. *Mr. and Mrs. 55* is unusual because Guru Dutt, canonized as a leading 1950s auteur for combining sharp social commentaries in his noir-like films, uses romantic comedy to depict a picaresque world of female anarchy and trouble.

The plot in *Mr. and Mrs. 55* deals with the infamous Hindu Code Bill, notoriously controversial in the public's view because of a divorce clause granting women the right to annul a Hindu marriage, thereby transforming marriage from a sacrosanct, lifelong act to a legal, terminable contract. As the film interrogates this bill it subjects it to merciless derision, employing romantic comedy as an effective cinematic genre to probe India's troubled gender politics. The film's narrative line manifests familiar symptoms of male anxiety about women repositioning themselves in society—symptoms that include publicly mocking women or trivializing and caricaturing their demands. Most insidious and effective of all, the film pits the misguided, "westernized," "individualist" woman against the model, self-effacing, traditional woman, making the modernized woman finally learn the virtues of an "Indian" sensibility. An unlikely storyline is plotted in Mr. and Mrs. 55 to indict women demanding legislative changes in the institution of marriage. Instead, the film affirms a deeply conservative version of marriage and man-woman relationships. In the process of this reaffirmation, the film mobilizes sentiments about both gender and class.

The women under siege in the film are at once upper-class, westernized, man-hating and money-minded. The film turns the Hindu Code Bill on its head, here referring to it as the "divorce bill"—a term assigned to it in popular parlance. Most interestingly, we get a glimpse of women never before seen in popular Hindi cinema: women getting organized, entering the public space, and bringing to it matters deemed personal and private. In the film Anita (Madhubala), the young heroine, is a rich young woman raised under the guardianship of her father's sister, Sita Devi (Lalita Pawaar). Sita Devi, an activist campaigning for the Hindu Code Bill, has become singularly devoted to the cause of women and their liberation. Her home provides a place for women's meetings; she is a public figure, organizes deputations to petition the government on behalf of women, and is recognized by members of the press. Anita finds herself impatient with her aunt and views the aunt as the demonized male-hating women's liberationist.

On her twentieth birthday Anita learns the terms of her father's will: She will inherit a sizable amount of property if she marries within a month. As the will explains, the father was aware of his sister's aversion to men, and he feared his daughter would be forced to remain single. Sita Devi decides to deal with the will's technicality through a legal counterstrategy. She finds a man, Pritam (played by the actor-director Guru Dutt himself), who is unemployed at the time, and arranges a registered marriage—that is, one that is to remain on paper alone. On the condition that the marriage remain a secret—that is, that Pritam does not seek to have intercourse with Anita—and that he be willing to divorce Anita on request, the aunt offers Pritam a monthly salary.

Pritam, already in love with Anita (although she is unaware of this), agrees to the marriage. To Anita, it appears he is in it for the money; initially she despises him for this. But Pritam refuses to cash his monthly check, attempting instead to win Anita's love. When he fails, he responds with the malevolence of one spurned in love, letting Anita go by conjuring false evidence against himself so that Sita Devi can procure the divorce she desires in the court of law. The case proceeds under a floodlight of publicity, with the best lawyers and all the false evidence money can buy. Sita Devi expects to win the divorce case for her niece. Anita in turn wavers in her affection for Pritam, but when she finally learns the truth about her aunt's machinations to win the divorce case at all costs, she grows uncharacteristically defiant, challenges her aunt, and in the end successfully unites with Pritam, still rightfully her husband. The confrontation between the aunt and niece toward the film's end is unabashed in its misogynist raving, the dialogue rendering the film's conservative ideological underpinning transparent.

In a broad sense the film can be read as a clever, clairvoyant parable (recall the Shah Bano debacle) anticipating men's worst fears— that the new legislation permitting divorce and its incumbent system of alimony ("maintenance") might open the floodgates to women's independence. Although the male protagonist receives "alimony," he remains innocent; his complicity in a marriage of convenience remains uninterrogated because he refuses to accept financial support from his rich wife. In the first half of the film, Pritam also refuses to annul the marriage. For him, marriage means a lifelong contract. By refusing to cash the checks, the hero has the moral high ground. A significant aspect of this subtext is patriarchal culture's dreadful fear of alimony— having to pay up for institutions men could enter and exit with complete immunity. Herein lies the culture's lesson to all women, which the film states openly and unabashedly: a woman's place is to find happiness and love in marriage, circumstances notwithstanding.

The film skirts the chasm between Pritam's and real women's

circumstances in corresponding situations. While women's access to opportunities for employment and economic independence are acutely limited within Indian society, the film's narrative reshuffles these elements by making the male protagonist unemployed and therefore financially dependent. Pritam eventually finds employment as a newspaper subeditor. However, although his initial monetary lack gives way to financial power, there is a substantial class distance between him and Anita that continues even as financial developments avert his acute dependence on her.

By inverting traditional gender positions—setting up the woman as the one with means and the man in a state of penury, the converse of social reality—the film shifts attention onto a playful, imaginative scenario that although improbable is not altogether impossible. Such gender inversions in romantic comedy disrupt the "social hierarchy of male over female," placing "'the woman on top.'"[36] The film's superb cast, entertaining gags, and comic interludes add to the general mood of irreverence generated against women of leisure. In a masterful oscillation between solemn conviction and lighthearted, disarming humor, we are asked to stretch our imagination, to envision alarming scenarios that any readjustment in the time-honored arrangement of Hindu marriage might provoke. And the film counterbalances this comedy with numerous moments when the air of frivolity is abandoned—moments when "serious" interventions are made to bring order into heterosexual relations supposedly thrown into turmoil by the anticipated effect of the new legislation and its reconfiguration of the man-woman relationship.

Now for a closer look at how the film depicts women getting organized. *Mr. and Mrs. 55* opens with a young newspaper boy's full-throated sales pitch: "*Assembly mein zordaar behas—'talaq'* . . . " (heated debate in the Assembly—divorce), which refers to the passing of the contentious 1955 Hindu Marriage Act. A crowd gathers, clamoring for the paper, and the camera follows a young bespectacled woman buying a copy. Soon after this opening scene, the camera pans to a meeting of a women's organization. In a few deft cuts, it singles out Sita Devi as she addresses a group of women, telling them of recent developments: in the past month the Women's Union sent a deputation to the government to lobby on behalf of the "divorce bill." "You all know," she declaims, "how important this bill is for women to gain self-respect in our patriarchal society where a woman's place is at her man's feet and she is expected to be happy as his slave."

As she rails against women's oppression at the hands of men, the camera cuts to two women who sit inattentively and discuss various beauty treatments for the skin: orange peels versus milk cream. A third woman joins in after initially hushing them: "Try a mudpack," she suggests. This satirical introduction to political issues is a quick summation and promise of what will follow in the film: the heavy-handed caricature of upper-class Indian women, their obsession with women's rights, and the specter of the "divorce bill."

The film creates a scenario that mocks marriage as a contract— good today, void tomorrow; it valorizes eternal commitment and women's pleasure in subservience to men and marriage. Such issues were also phrased in this way in the political discourse of the time. In the widely publicized debates that occurred in the Legislative Assembly around the bill, Pandit L. K. Maitra from West Bengal contrasted his "humble wife married according to *shastric* rites . . . nurtured in the ideals

8. Women organizing in *Mr. and Mrs. 55* (Guru Dutt, 1955).

of our Hindu homes" with the women who supported the Hindu Code Bill. The latter he characterized as "the lavender lipstick and vanity bag variety."[37] Bajoria, another Assembly member, dismissed educated Hindu women as "butterflies with social affectations."[38] Even the then-President, Dr. Rajendra Prasad, turned away a women's delegation lobbying for the bill on the grounds that he could not imagine his own wife supporting the divorce clause in the Hindu Code Bill.

The local media reacted against AIWC's "Indian Women's Charter of Rights," declaring it "represented the demands of a few overeducated women."[39] *Roshni*, the AIWC newsletter "complained bitterly" in June 1949 of being characterized as a "few educated women passing the same Hindu Code Bill resolution for thirteen years."[40] The strong hostility provoked by the "educated Indian woman" throughout this period is striking, suggesting a deeper sense of threat and fear. While the AIWC was faulted for being elitist and for failing to reach a wider base of lower-class women, the fact is that the men opposing the bill occupied the same elite strata; their locus standi—questionable on grounds of class and gender—strategically is never mentioned.

In *Mr. and Mrs. 55*, the young woman who buys a newspaper in the opening scene, Mona (the comic sidekick of the megalomaniac Sita Devi), informs the rustic, middle-aged house cleaner, "Nanny," that the "divorce bill" is going to pass. The house cleaner responds with sarcasm: "Well, go light up some oil lamps [and celebrate]. Night and day it's 'women's-liberation-and-the-crimes-of-men.' Is there anything beyond this that you women know?" Mona hushes her, reminding her of the imminent women's meeting. The maid responds in her brusque and nonchalant way: "The hell with your meetings! I am not afraid of anyone. God knows what's happened. Wherever one looks there's a meeting or a lecture. *Sab ke sab angrez ban gaye hain!* (Everyone's turned British!)." Nanny reiterates this every time she makes her brief appearance, leaving no doubt about her disdain for westernized, upper-class Indian women and their mimicry of the ex-colonizer. In doing so, she invokes a common insult, which oddly finds common usage among the already westernized.[41] And such statements are often used to bludgeon the very idea of women autonomously organizing to fight politically for equal rights.

The press was divided on the issue of the Hindu Code Bill. The opposition staged demonstrations against the government each time it was debated during a parliamentary session.[42] A smear campaign against the bill maintained that it promoted incest. Although female inheritance was the issue dealt with in the central clause, public attention and propaganda focused mainly on the issue of permitting divorce. This public furor does not appear in *Mr. and Mrs. 55*, but the film joins the bill's opponents in mocking any contractual or legalistic approach to marriage. In the plot, the series of events that build toward the initial climax clearly enunciate the film's perspective on the institutions of love, marriage, money, and class.

After the marriage is registered in court, Pritam defies the terms agreed to with Sita Devi. Disguised as the aunt's chauffeur, Pritam waylays Anita and takes her to his brother's house. Here they are greeted by his *bhabhi* (sister-in-law), a rustic village woman presented as the model woman and wife. She inquires if Anita is married yet. Pritam responds on Anita's behalf: "Not yet, and not for another twenty years. These are very wealthy people. They have a lot of money tucked away in their homes. . . . What do you know about these city girls? Unless there's a fat benefit involved, these women don't get caught in the hassles of marriage." Unwittingly the film script acknowledges the connection between marriage, money, and gender. Wealthy women don't really need to marry—not for financial security. The implicit threat that women with money pose is their lack of dependence on men; in a conservative way, the film subjects that threat to an open challenge. The film naturalizes the normative by postulating that the greatest pleasure for women lies in conjugal bliss. And in romantic comedy's inimitable style, heterosexual love in this film ultimately negotiates the difficult terrain of obstacles that are barriers to the couple's union. The woman's desire is the "principal object of comic transformation."[43]

Anita's initial antagonism dissipates temporarily in the romantic interlude that follows when she responds to Pritam's overtures. In a convention that has become Hindi cinema's signature, the couple break into song. Anita's uncertainty, wavering affection, and dilemmas of the heart get settled, at least temporarily, when Sita Devi arrives. Infuriated by Pritam's impertinence, Sita Devi offers him ten thousand rupees to release Anita. Pritam, still defiant, tears up the check and, assuming the role of Anita's protector, declares she will not leave against her wishes. But when Sita Devi pulls out a telegram Anita sent to summon her, a belittled and infuriated Pritam lashes out at her. He accuses Anita of conducting a charade. Then, filled with regret and sorrow, he berates himself for not knowing women like her better: "The likes of you butterflies cannot be trusted." Anita protests and storms out with her aunt. Thus begin the series of complications which the remaining narrative has to resolve.

The "butterfly" as a recurrent metaphor for "women of leisure" in popular discourse (recalling Assembly member Bajoria's dismissal of educated women as butterflies) distinguishes between normative and wanton womanhood. The butterfly metaphor evokes images of restless, flighty, colorful creatures who are difficult to pin down or control. Most important, the similitude admits compelling charm and captivating lure for the beholder. And herein lies the troubled relation Hindi cinema has with women, particularly the archetype of the westernized heroine. She entices with her alluring appearance but is hard to get. The challenge lies in conquering her, despite the hero's and the culture's disdain for her "inconstancy" and "capriciousness."

In *Mr. and Mrs. 55* this conquest occurs when the uptight woman is "brought to her senses." It happens in a last-minute reversal when multiple narrative complications and misunderstandings that separate Anita from Pritam dissolve. Anita realizes that her malevolent aunt's machinations have impeded her "true love" for Pritam. The initial oppositional desire of men and women in romantic comedy marks the woman as the narrative problem and tracks her progress toward "correct values . . . articulated and represented by the hero," and culminates in their union at the price of the woman's conversion.[44] This conservative aspect of the genre challenges assumptions about screwball comedy violating norms in the forwardness of its women and its non-sentimental, even combative courtships. If anything, the resolution in romantic comedy is remarkably conventional in that the ideology of love structures the woman's correct path. Heterosexual love, staunchly asserted as the "natural" channeling of female desire, is romantic comedy's *deus ex machina*, a "magic force" that defines rationality, like fate in 1940s' noir.[45] Woman's rebellion in romantic comedy remains tolerated because it is short-lived and ultimately serves the hero's interests; the "unruly bride" is ultimately disciplined.[46] The "woman on top" in *Mr. and Mrs. 55* loses her grip and falls uncontrollably in love with the hero, who then, of course, takes firm charge of her.

No longer the irresolute young girl, Anita comes into her own and challenges her authoritarian aunt's ideology, politics, and personal style with uncharacteristic courage. The narrative pits these two women against each other and imposes its own well-defined ideology of class and gender. When Anita defiantly informs her aunt of her intention to meet Pritam on the eve of their divorce settlement, Sita Devi responds with alarm about its impact on the litigation.

SITA DEVI: The matter has reached the court, it has received publicity in the press. If you turn back now, it'll be very humiliating.

ANITA: Do preserve your sense of honor—even when someone's life is on the line! Whatever you do, you do for your own selfish interests. This leadership business is just about your ego. These illogical ideas you impose upon others are also for your own sense of honor.

SITA DEVI: My ideas are aimed at improving the lot of women. Everything I've learnt is based on experience.

ANITA: Then expand your experience! Instead of standing at the podium and turning your nose up at lower class women, go into their homes and see the pleasure an Indian woman derives from marital bliss.

SITA DEVI: Those illiterate women think of slavery as pleasure. What do they know about liberation? I will teach them about liberation and all I've learnt from women in America and Europe.

ANITA: A lot more can be learnt from them: to change one's husband four times like the change of seasons!

SITA DEVI: If an illiterate woman were saying this, I would understand. But an educated girl like you praising (women's) slavery is astounding.

ANITA: If finding pleasure in one's household chores, if keeping

one's family happy is called slavery, I'll praise such slavery a
thousand times! The slavery in which a husband and wife love
each other, respect one another, are concerned about each
other's happiness, is better than your liberation, which has
nothing more than hatred for men. . . . You always wanted my
happiness. I have found my happiness. Why should it make you
unhappy?

SITA DEVI: I warn you, one day, you'll return in misery.

ANITA: I'll never return to you!

The confrontation ends with Sita Devi locking Anita in her room to
physically debar her from leaving.

Constructed as a dialogic encounter between the voice of the elite
vanguard of the women's movement and the subaltern, "true" Indian
woman, the exchange in fact takes place between two equally privileged women for whom the subaltern is a mere chip in the argument
and on whose behalf both claim the right to speak. The most damning
evidence, however, comes when Sita Devi admits to the Indian women's
movement's relation to western imperial powers.

This is the weapon which indigenous patriarchy wields against
women's assertion for rights and liberty—their complicity with the west.
That argument against women's rights and autonomy conveniently represses the fact that the two preceding centuries of Indian history,
struggle for national liberation, and assertion of a modern nation were
predicated on ideas that were equally "western." Such an argument
against women's rights brings us back full circle to the ideas of the nation, the Indian, and womanhood cast across the woman's body. In the
years after national liberation, this argument prevailed legally not only
because it positively defined the virtues of womanhood but also because
it could clearly demarcate, distinguish, and mark the westernized Indian woman as horrific, malevolent, and capable of fomenting a fascist
reign of terror—as in the caricatured representation of Sita Devi and
her women's organization.

Kathleen Rowe invokes descriptions of comedy in terms of Northop
Frye's "liberating a wilting world," Bakhtin's "carnivalesque," Victor
Turner's "liminal" world, and C. L. Barber's "'green world' of festivity

and natural regeneration." But she also concedes that comedy expresses fears about what might happen if oppressed groups become liberated. Women in comedy can appear as "fearsome or silly, symbols of repression and obstacles to social transformation."[47] Sita Devi is the "eccentric woman" whose eccentricities relate to her high-class status.[48] In this she joins the ranks of a long list of spinsters, dowagers, prohibitionists, mothers-in-law, suffragettes, "battle-axes," career women, "women's libbers," and lesbians. In a way that is similar to Hollywood romantic comedy, Hindi films combine the figure of the rich woman with the educated westernized Indian woman, the "social butterfly," as the target of the misogynist hero's comedic aggression. Class and gender conflicts are rolled together as the struggle for women's rights itself becomes a fanciful pursuit for the leisured rich, a sign of female anarchy that the hero effectively contains.

Women's class status, visibility, and power that stem from material resources come under attack. The fact that they organize independently, free from male tutelage, becomes questionable, and with it comes the confounding question of "authenticity"—the impossibility for these women to represent or speak for all women. Such an interrogation of the Indian women's movement and its class domination points to a significant problem. Those who raise the question (in this case the celebrated filmmaker Guru Dutt), remain hidden in the margins, obscured within the text of their critique. The effectiveness of the film's narration lies precisely in the fact that the narrators using the filmic apparatus in *Mr. and Mrs. 55* can remain invisible, suppress their own class origins and their own stake in the viewpoint naturalized within a fictional narrative.

I have traced here the historical forces shaping archetypal Indian womanhood and reproduced endlessly in Hindi films. For more than a century now, the invention of the "new woman" has captured the Indian imagination, constantly reinvented according to the exigencies of the times. Although layers of meaning have accreted around the Indian woman figure over time, its foundation rests on establishing her difference from everything western. A sign for Indian tradition and culture, she is of course an interplay of Victorian and Brahminical ideas. The figure of the woman was first used as a symbol by nationalist ideology to mobilize against imperialism, and later by majority and minority communities as a sign of community identity; ultimately it impinged on legal reform discourse, which sacrificed women's rights as equal subjects. Post-independence Hindi cinema denies communal differences by using the woman as a sign—a wishful desire for a utopian unified nation.

Chapter 3 — *Heroes and Villains*

Narrating the Nation

I T IS ABUNDANTLY clear that Hindi cinema constantly narrows the gap between the public and the private by forcing connections between the nation and the family, bringing the former the same kind of affective relations of love that sustain the family. While Euro-American eruptions of melodrama during the interwar and postwar years are viewed as "dramatizing the retreat into the private sphere in the face of crisis within the public sphere," in Hindi films these two spheres—family and "nation"—coalesce in the film hero's personal narrative.[1] The hero fights the nation's "enemies"—threats to the nation at the moment of the film's making. These enemies took the form of unprincipled profiteers in the 1950s, foreign aggressors in the 1960s, "smugglers" in the 1970s, separatist "terrorists" and politicians in the 1980s, and authoritarian patriarchs in the 1990s. While vanquishing enemies signifies the hero's passage to manhood, another battle, against the enemy within the family, marks his rite of passage.

Masculinity

Hindi cinema's narratives are unfailingly centered on a hero and heroine, who together constitute its fundamental templates in which masculinity is the flip side of femininity. Changes in masculinity in response to the nation's history are discussed in popular Hindi cinema film criticism.[2] An aspect of constructing masculinity is the hero's role as a primary agent shaping the nation's history. Like all heroes, the Hindi film hero upholds the law; or, on occasion, he is the heroic outlaw. He undertakes dangerous journeys, takes risks, and battles evil forces to return victorious, having won not only glory, but romantic love. Another extraordinary feature in many popular Hindi films is the purposeful deployment of masculine agency to rescue the mother figure, by performing valorous acts through which he declares his intense love for her. The Hindi film hero may even die for his mother. The mother-son relationship in Hindi cinema is striking because of the particularly charged intensity with which it is staged.[3]

The actions undertaken by the hero in the name of the nation bear a paradigmatic relation with the "family romance" (mother, father, and son). The methodological tools employed for this analysis are both sociological in appraising the importance of social institutions, and psychoanalytic, which is the only theoretical resource developed by film theory to explain the construction of subjectivity within patriarchal culture. Psychoanalytic film theory has been highly contentious for several well-known reasons, not least because we lack verification of its theories about the unconscious. The response to this charge is that the unconscious would no longer be the unconscious if it were verifiable, thus making its theories a self-fulfilling prophecy. The psychoanalytic method becomes more problematic when applied beyond the context of filial patterns in late-nineteenth- and early-twentieth-century western Europe. For the last several decades the universalizing imperative of grand master-narratives have justifiably been under siege. The critique of psychoanalysis notwithstanding, a Lacanian poststructural revision of Freudian analysis points to the importance of symbolic processes involved in constructing subjectivity.[4] Furthermore, conditions of coloniality (and now postcoloniality) have effected far-reaching changes, overhauling patterns of familial organization—particularly within urban culture in nonwestern societies. Steady transformation from the extended to the nuclear family suggests that individual and family histories in urban nonwestern culture are now more susceptible to psychoanalytic exegesis.

It is worth remembering how Frantz Fanon creatively uses psychoanalysis to analyze the collective social unconscious in the colonial encounter, rather than focusing exclusively on the individual.[5] Invoking Pierre Naville, Fanon makes a case for locating a society's dreams and a collective unconscious that acknowledges the economic, social, and cultural conditions, "because the content of a human being's dreams depends . . . in the last analysis, on the general conditions of the culture in which he lives."[6]

We are reminded by Homi Bhabha that Fanon understood that the individual and collective psyche were constituted within the history of colonialism, and that in the transition from Nature to Culture the "Psyche and Society mirror each other."[7] Fanon points to important connections between the European family and the nation where the child very easily learns "the centralization of authority in a country . . . [entails] a resurgence of the authority of the father. . . . There is no disproportion between the life of the family and the life of the nation." Accepting state authority is a reproduction of family authority that shapes the individual.[8]

When I invoke psychoanalysis, I also evaluate its relevance for the Indian family and Hindi films. Psychoanalytical film theory applied to Hollywood films explains the voyeuristic and fetishistic visual pleasure the female body offers by resolving the oedipal castration threat. Hindi cinema deploys the female form in much the same manner as Hollywood, but theories about the castration threat and its resolution are belied by the indomitable presence of the mother-son relationship, the son's stagnation in the pre-oedipal stage, and his apparent inability to arrive at the oedipal stage.

Sudhir Kakar argues that India's "hegemonic narrative" does not resemble that of Oedipus or Adam and Eve, but the *devi*, the mother-goddess. Although the mother is a powerful figure in western psycho-analysis, a certain form of the maternal-feminine, a central feature of the Indian psyche, is distinct from its western counterpart.[9] Kakar attributes this centrality to the desire for oneness with the mother. The mother's and the child's sexual desire are obstacles to this oneness, a fusion threatened by phallic desire. Desexualizing the mother by disavowing her as a sexual being, idealizing her, and making her a divine object of worship and adoration are ways of denying female eroticism in Indian culture.[10]

The mythical story of Ganesha and Skanda, sons of Shiva and Parvati, demonstrates how the Indian male experiences a pull from two opposite directions. Parvati, the mother, promises a mango to reward the son who travels around the universe and returns first. While Skanda, the image of the virile male, embarks on the journey, Ganesha, the infant-god, goes to his mother, circles around her, tells her she is his universe—and receives the mango. For Kakar the myth articulates the two powerful oppositional tugs the male experiences in the pre-oedipal stage. One, to individuate, separate, and go out into the world; and two, a desire to re-immerse with the mother, to seek fusion with her at the cost of independence.[11] Culling further evidence from mythological figures, Kakar attributes Shiva's *ardhanareshwara* (half-man, half-woman) form to male desire—to become a man without completely separating from the mother.

In this lack of complete separation from the mother the Indian male experiences a different oedipal trajectory from the western male subject. Corroborating the evidence of Dr. Girindrasekhar Bose, founder of the Indian Psychoanalytic Association, Kakar argues that the Indian male does not experience the castration threat.[12] Rather, he experiences "a desire to be female," and since the Oedipus figure represents a combined parental image, "much of the motivation of the maternal deity is traceable to this source."[13] Indian patients reveal identification with both parents and an amazing degree of cross-sexual identification. Kakar offers rather cursory information about the father-son relationship. Father-son rivalry, he says, occurs later in the Indian context. It takes the form of "the son's guilt over a fantasized and eventually unconscious patricide."[14] The father's envy of the mother-son relationship and the son's persecution anxiety create father-son rivalry.

It is interesting, then, to examine the father's position in Hindi films. Initially present, the father becomes absent, displaced, or avenged by the son, who ultimately instates himself close to his mother, successfully excluding the father. How does one reconcile the mother figure's centrality and the father's exclusion in a stringently patriarchal society? How do we come to terms with the strong mother fixation within patriarchy, and what can we elicit about patriarchy from the obsessive repetition with which the son wins his mother by going against his father? What is at stake in a masculine delineation that draws battle lines within the family triangle, thus making winning the mother grounds for the boy's successful passage to manhood?

In the North American context, the discursive impact of medical and psychiatric practices on notions of masculinity offers a concept of manhood first measured against the norm of "responsibility," which gives way to an open, reactionary individualism.[15] In India the logic for large extended families lies in a predominantly labor-intensive, land-centered agrarian economy. The pressures of the large, extended family traditionally created a diffuse sense of responsibility among its male members. That sense became more acute as industrialization, urbanization, and migration caused the family to disintegrate into nuclear units. The young male thus became weighed down by the responsibility of becoming the caretaker of a new generation of children as well as his parents.[16] But with this shift in responsibility young males were also increasingly able to wrest paternal authority. The son thus became the new figure of patriarchal authority, the male with the physical and financial power—guaranteeing the perpetuation of patriarchy while the process of the generational power transfer created its own ripples within the family.

The intense mother-son bond not only appears repeatedly in popular film narratives, but their passion is often central to the plot along with other acts that define the hero coming into his own—becoming a man, as it were. Traditional genre divisions associated with gender—women's "weepies," the maternal melodrama, and men's gangster/action films—collapse in Hindi films. Here, maternal melodrama and gangster action coalesce. These films project masculinity in a unique way. The moment that culminates in heroic success and proves an idealized masculinity is one in which the hero, as in most action films, achieves success by upholding the nation's law. But in Hindi cinema the hero is typically also motivated by a consuming desire to avenge the sins against his mother, which drives the narrative forward. *Mother India* (1957), *Aradhana* (Prayer, 1969), *Deewar* (Wall, 1975), and *Trishul* (Trident, 1978), resonate with the son's desire to redeem his mother's suffering and to fuse with the maternal figure. In some exceptions the hero's search for his mother is attenuated by a narrative that includes the father, such as in films like *Zanjeer* (Chain, 1973) or *Yaadon ki Baraat*

(Procession of Memories, 1973), in which the child grows up to avenge the death of both parents. But more often than not, the son rescues the mother from suffering or humiliation caused by the father. Representations of the mother-son relationship appear to resonate as powerfully with women in the audience as they do with men, erasing gender divisions in spectator genre preferences.

How these films define masculinity involves investigating the ways in which a heroic ideal is determined by contemporary events and the nation's anxieties. Filmic relationships that specifically and repeatedly affirm the mother-son dyad are also indicative of broader social changes taking place in the nation. Films in which the nation is collectively imagined through narratives in which the hero fights off enemies and delivers the nation are closely tied to those in which the hero's role is that of his mother's savior. In examining how Hindi films deal with "masculinity and its discontents," the nexus between both types of films will become evident.[17]

Heroes and Villains

In the 1950s the hero in Hindi films was a crusader for the nation and optimistic about its future, notwithstanding his critical appraisal of problems besetting the nation. The enemy, of course, is the villain, a constant in Hindi cinema, standing in for the nation's "problems." These problems change over time, coinciding with shifts in the nation's anxieties.

The hero represents an idealized longing for a nationalist spirit: his patriotic characterization sharpens when he pits himself against—and defeats—the antinational villain. These hero and villain characters articulate national discourses that are essential to and determined by contemporary ideas about what troubles the nation. In identifying the enemy the films define the nation's difficulties, its exigencies. While the 1950s' films are self-conscious in their commentary about the formative years of the nation and the responsibility to build it, later films, particularly those of the 1980s and 1990s, simply assume the nation is a natural political entity. The malaise the hero struggles against and overcomes in these later films contains a "message" about the state of the nation and its problems.

A range of influences are discernable in the past fifty years of Hindi cinema, from the politically didactic Indian Peoples' Theater Association (IPTA) to the globally influential Hollywood James Bond films. Films by Guru Dutt, Bimal Roy, and Raj Kapoor in the 1950s, known as "socials" in the industry, were influenced by IPTA in the way they addressed the nation's problems. Raj Kapoor's *Shri 420* (Mr. 420, 1955), Guru Dutt's *Pyaasa* (The Thirsty One, 1957), Bimal Roy's *Sujata* (1959) and even Vijay Anand's *Guide* (1965) envision a utopian future where casteism, corruption in high places, and the chasm between the avaricious rich and the noble poor disappear.[18] Yet the future imagined is uncertain; in numerous film endings the protagonist walks away with his lady love into an ill-defined misty space, an unknown place. Neither do action-oriented films of the 1970s, 1980s, and 1990s have an optimistic vision; the task of uncovering the underworld, and of apprehending and punishing antinational traitors, is a pressing concern in film after film.

Kapoor's *Shri 420*, scripted by the prolific K. A. Abbas, is the quintessential 1950s' film about the hero's journey and his quest for truth, accompanied by his sobering "inward-looking" reflection that slowly turns into a critique of the daunting pressures on the young nation.[19] The narrative, in Kapoor's characteristic maudlin style, orbits around Raj, the protagonist, whose innocence is lost but finally regained. He journeys from small-town Allahabad to the big, bad city of Bombay, where he succumbs to its trappings of wealth, glitter, and latent treachery. Toward the end he recovers his lost *imaan* (integrity/honor), and in the last frame leaves the city with his paramour, Vidya (Nargis), to travel to a nowhere land. The moment of revelation, the truth about the "enemy of the nation," occurs when he discovers that corruption (referred to as *chaar sau bees*, four hundred and twenty) is the root of the postcolonial nation's enervation; it brings home the importance of the integrity he steels himself to uphold.

The film is embedded in populist commentary embraced by Hindi cinema under Nehruvian influence. Nehru's vision, robust and vital at the time, held promise among the literati. The screenplay for *Shri 420* became the master narrative for many films to come and is therefore worth attending to in some detail. Abbas was an active member of the Indian People's Theater Association (IPTA), which promoted

Nehruvian socialism. Sumita Chakravarty points to a typical idealism
vested in the figures of the "happy peasant, . . . honest laborer, the ide-
alistic schoolteacher, [and] the philanthropic doctor" in IPTA productions. Film narratives typically locate these protagonists in the city—a
"microcosm of the nation,"—place them in conflicting situations, and
end with resolutions that idealize the "traditional" against the "modern" even as the protagonists retreat to "a nonexistent space, to nowhere, a space that the films do not indicate visually at any point in
the narrative."[20]

Hindi cinema positions itself as a national cinema not only by privileging the traditional over the modern, but by naturalizing and idealizing the nation's imagined community as one that commands fierce love
and loyalty. It also narrates the nation's problems, which the hero single-
handedly solves by displaying physical and moral courage. In *Shri 420*,
Raj (Raj Kapoor), an unemployed youth, arrives in Bombay in search
of a job but fails in his efforts to make an honest living. However, as a
casino trickster and a right-hand man for a shady businessman, he becomes wealthy. He floats several fraudulent schemes to make money.
In the end, his conscience prevents him from defrauding his former
homeless friends. He recants and gives his business associates up to the
police.

Shri 420 presents the world in black-and-white terms, with no ambiguous gray areas. The characters are stand-ins for principles and causes
from which they remain unshaken. Vidya (meaning "knowledge"), the
woman Raj loves, is a school teacher with a social conscience; Seth
Sonachand Dharamanand (literally "merchant of gold, silver, and religion"), is the villain posing as a respectable member of society because
of his wealth—ill-gotten gains made at the expense of the poor. Maya
(a name referring to the world's illusory nature in Hindu philosophy)
is the wily westernized woman, the vamp, Vidya's opposite who lures
Raj to an opulent, decadent, and deceitful world. And finally there are
the loving, generous, simple-minded working-class folk, among them
Ganga *maa* (mother), Raj's surrogate mother, and the nameless street-
beggar, a wise old man, who offers critical exposés of the modern world.

The only character afforded any complexity, if one may call it that,
is Raj. His poverty drives him to crime despite his innate goodness and
because his attempts to live with integrity fail. Once Raj discovers how

to make a fast buck, he sinks deeper into white-collar crime, and the deceit and guile transform him. But the transformation is not as thorough as it appears. In a dramatic moment Raj stands before a mirror, confronted by his alter ego—modeled on Charlie Chaplin. He sees his "real" self in the mirror, wearing a tattered suit, a studied contrast from his present self.

Scenes where the protagonist looks into and speaks to his or her image in the mirror are well-worn devices weighted with connotations of duality, the split between the "real" self and the "image" of the self, or between the different selves inhabiting the same body. In this instance, what appears in the mirror, the "image," is purported to be the "real" self, while the "real" self standing before the mirror is the ephemeral chimera. In a brief exchange between the two, shot in medium close-up to extreme close-up of Raj's face, the viewer is made to empathize with Raj's feelings of emptiness and loss even as he is immersed in wealth. When Raj sees not a reflection of himself as he appears to us, but his earlier disheveled self, he is surprised.

RAJ: You?!

IMAGE: Hmmm me!

RAJ: What are you looking at?

IMAGE: You! What can I say, you're looking very natty! This collar, this bow tie, this suit! Wow! What can I say?!(snickers) Why Raja, did becoming rich give you all you wanted? Are you happy now?

REVERSE SHOT: EXTREME CLOSE UP OF RAJ'S FACE, HIS EYES, HIS SILENCE

IMAGE: Why? Aren't you happy?

RAJ: No Raja, I'm very unhappy. (Lowering his eyes) I don't know what's happened. You know I'm not a rich man! I don't know what to do! Where did you go. . .(Looks up)

IMAGE DISSOLVES

(Raj, stepping forward, leans on the mirror, in desperation and anguish) . . . Raju! Raju! Raju!

Viewers are assured that Raj has only changed superficially, that he still retains his earlier probity, the childlike innocence with which he first arrived in Bombay, eager to succeed with a combination of resources—a graduate degree and integrity (*imaandari*). The latter, an abstract quality, is signified with literal devices such as the gold medal awarded to him in college for his *imaandari*. In Kapoor's films, these narrow the gap between the symbolic and the real. He flags the hero's journey, his descent into and escape from the underworld: the pawned gold medal, his innocent swaggering to buy it back after he "buys Bombay out," the pawn shop owner's sardonic comments about how every immigrant's fantasy is to buy Bombay but how they sell themselves instead, Raj's subsequent loss of integrity in a hedonistic world, his loneliness, and finally his change of heart, which recovers his integrity.

When Raj arrives in the city he is buffeted by its machinations, learns the devious ways in which it operates, and plays with its dangers, but finally recants and single-handedly defeats the mafia. When Seth Sonachand Dharmanand initiates a scheme to defraud the poor—Raj's homeless friends—by faking a plan to provide them all with *janta ghar* (people's housing) in return for their life's savings, Raj refuses to continue working for him. His elaborate plan to escape turns into mayhem when the mafia go after him to grab the bag of money in the climactic chase scene, only to discover Raj has duped them by stuffing the briefcase with newspapers instead. "What you people are fighting like wolves for, is paper, useless paper," he says equivocally. "But what don't you do for that? Money laundering, floating 'bogus companies,' burning down your stores in order to claim the insurance money. I am leaving with evidence of your misdeeds. People will soon know all about Samaritans and philanthropists like Dharmanand!"

After recovering from the reversals heroes experience in the build up to the final climactic sequence, Raj discloses the mafia's fraudulent scheme. In an unusually long speech delivered to the crowd of homeless folks thronging to Dharmanand's premises he recounts the nation's ills:

> Take a good look at the faces of these 'great' people. They
> appear to be very nice, honorable, respectable, wealthy. These
> people are not one, ten or fifty. They are a good four-twenty.
> 'Shri 420.'
>　　And take a good look at yourself too. Who says you are

poor, unemployed and homeless? Today you all own one million seven hundred thousand rupees. This money was accumulated for the *janta ghar*. I did not want to betray you. I want to bring you together. If you like, you can take your money back. But if you ask me, don't squander your money like this. Don't lessen your strength. No home can be made with a hundred rupees. But with a hundred thousand rupees several homes can be made. You could go to your government and tell them, 'Here's a hundred and fifty thousand rupees. Give us land and we'll build our own homes.'

And now take a good look at me too. I am one of you. When I came to Bombay I had everything: integrity, education, the aspiration to be a rich man, to have a home, a family, raise children who would grow up to study in a school and college. But because of my greed for money, I lost everything. And today I have nothing but regrets. But blessed be the person who saved me from continuing in the world of deceit and trickery, who told me that the solution to poverty and unemployment is not greed and deceit but courage and hard work. The solution is the nation's development and people's unity. . . . I just wanted to say, the mistake I made, you must never make.

This nonsensical declaration at the end of the film indicates the confusion that permeates the film's message: a trenchant albeit populist critique, the hallmark of Hindi films. It ends with a last-ditch effort to reinstate the official rhetoric, smooth the ruffled feathers of hegemonic ideology, and plead—against the grain of the entire film—for a truce with status quo. Vidya too consistently defends this status quo. It remains unclear how Raj and Vidya are going to realize the "dreams" they share.

Speaking on behalf of a generation that faced the onerous task of nation-building after inheriting a disfigured postcolonial legacy, *Shri 420* addresses the contradictions between commitment to the nation and the Herculean challenge posed by meeting the needs for food, shelter, clothing, and education. Raj and Vidya dream about a home and the means to raise and educate children, but they are worn down by it. In the song that became a classic of Hindi cinema of the time, the couple sing tremulously of their love, their elation sobered by apprehension about the future. In a memorable scene of glossy streets wet from the rain, they walk together on a misty night under a large black umbrella singing,

> pyaar hua, ikraar hua, pyaar se phir kyon darta hai dil
> kehta hai dil rasta mushkil,
> maaloom nahin hai kahaan manzil . . .
> (we have loved, we have cared, then why is my heart so afraid,
> my heart says, the journey is difficult,
> we don't know what lies ahead)

Later, the sea change in Raj estranges him from Vidya. They meet again after he becomes part of the mob. Raj reminds Vidya of the dream they shared.

> RAJ: . . . Vidya, whatever I've done, it's to make those dreams come true. . . If I'm treacherous, it's only directed against those who are themselves liars, crooks. Do you have any sympathy for those people?
>
> VIDYA: . . . You wanted to make me your wife. (Leans against the iron bars of the fence behind her). Tomorrow when you're in jail, whose wife would I be? A convict's? . . .
>
> RAJ: (Walking toward her) But think Vidya, what can we folks do without money. In this world you need money even to breathe!
>
> VIDYA: (exasperated) Money! money! money! O Raj! (Crying on his shoulder) What have you done! . . . Why have you done this? . . .

With anger, sorrow, and exasperation, Vidya castigates him again as on previous occasions. This time Raj is unable to resort to the ironic defense he put up earlier: "The advice to be honest and upright is given only to the poor—to work hard and have integrity."

And though Raj embraces this advice in the end, the film strains to assert confidence in the future. In the last scene, Raj comes on the screen walking his Chaplinesque walk on the highway that brought him to Bombay at the beginning of the film. He sings the opening song once again,

Mera joota hai japani, ye patloon englishstani,
Sar pe lal topi rusi, phir bhi dil hai hindustani . . .
(My shoes are Japanese, these pants are British,
A red Russian cap on the head, but still, my heart is Indian)

The camera swings to the left corner of the screen. Vidya emerges from the other side to join him, and together they walk up a hill receding farther from the audience. When they get to the top of the hill they pause and complete the last line of the song, drawn out slowly and purposefully: *mera dil hai hindusthani* (my heart is Indian)! Far in the background, a faint image of the housing sprawl appears (the "nowhere land"). In a symbolic closing shot, they walk toward it.

In Sumita Chakravarty's view this song privileges "the core (heart, sentiment)" over peripheral "(limbs, outward appearance)," where the body signals "randomized global accumulation of accessories . . . a map on which nations can appear to coexist in harmonious yet distinctly separate spheres. . . . By transforming the social marginality of the filmic hero into the centrality of the Indian citizen, material needs are displaced onto a more intangible (emotional) level of experience." It is, she argues, an internationally conscious figuration of the nation in the

9. Raj, the Chaplinesque figure. *Shri 420* (Mr. 420), Raj Kapoor, 1955.

Nehru era, in which the vagabond laughs at his impoverishment, "a reflection of the society of which he is a part."[21]

I am struck more by the irony in this scene: the hero, an internationally recognized Chaplinesque look-alike framed in a long shot, sublimates his chosen material lack with sentimental pride in his "Indian" heart. Such pride in the spiritual, sentimental, and emotional connotation of a special Indian identity is meant to compensate for that material lack (or in this instance, meaningless materialism identified with other nations). These are common and enduring strategies of rhetorical inversion used by popular Hindi cinema to define the nation—the elevated spiritual Indian versus the crass Western materialist.

If *Shri 420's* Raj voluntarily enters a world ruled by the mob, in *C.I.D.* (1956), the protagonist, the incorruptible Central Investigation Department police officer Shekhar (Dev Anand), is framed by the mafia. Fashioned after noir thrillers both in form and content, with chiaroscuro lighting that its director Guru Dutt reveled in, it powerfully communicates the danger lurking beneath the surface of everyday life. The film fits neatly into the master narrative set in place by *Shri 420*. It begins with a murder. Editor Shrivastava of the *Bombay Times* newspaper refuses to be bought or intimidated by an anonymous phone caller. The editor calls Shekhar to report the threat, but is killed by a hit man midconversation. Shekhar's investigation leads to "Master," the tailor (Johnny Walker), the comic sidekick, who is accidentally present at the crime scene.

Master identifies the killer, Sher Singh, in a line-up. Sher Singh, however, dies in police custody after Shekhar allegedly tortures him in the interrogation chamber. In the following court proceedings, the so-called facts are pieced together and read as proof of Shekhar's guilt, while the real killers, hirelings of the gangsters, are exonerated. Shekhar is sentenced to jail, and the case makes headline news. Shekhar alone sees the connection between being falsely framed, the death in police custody, editor Shrivastava's death, and the need to get to the mastermind behind all these events.

In a desperate last-minute move Shekhar, determined to prove his hunch, escapes from the police. Now sought by both the police and the gangsters, Shekhar negotiates the dangers of the underworld as a fugitive suspected by his colleagues and his boss. Miraculously, he lands in the gangsters' den and encounters Kamini (Waheeda Rehman), the mafia boss's girl. The ruthless treatment of gang members like Sher Singh prompts Kamini to defect and help Shekhar. However, as Kamini enters the police station to testify she is injured in a drive-by shooting, seriously threatening Shekhar's efforts to prove his innocence. Granted one last opportunity by his boss, Shekhar tricks Dharam Das, the gang leader, into visiting Kamini. Sabotaging Dharam Das's plan to kill Kamini, Shekhar redeems himself. In the last scene, Kamini recovers and announces that she is ready to testify. Once again, a hero undertakes a perilous journey alone, against the whole world, and brings down the "enemy."

Like several successful films of the time, *C.I.D.* expresses a fascination with big-city Bombay, where everything is not what it appears and where the deceitful and treacherous wealthy pose as philanthropists. The motifs of crime in high places and the capricious nature of the city are woven together to "expose" the machinations of the rich and respectable. Like Seth Sonachand Dharmanand, Seth Dharam Das in *C.I.D.* is a well-known philanthropist and businessman who leads a notorious underworld ring. The primary problem motivating the narrative is finding the means to expose him. Unlike *Shri 420*, *C.I.D.* focuses exclusively on the gangsters' style of functioning without ever describing the precise nature of their operation.

Despite obvious commonalities in theme and content, *Shri 420* and *C.I.D.* are strikingly different in genre and style. In *Shri 420* the subaltern and elite world of Bombay is represented with crowded images of chaos in the streets, bazaar, and nightclub, while Guru Dutt, visibly influenced by noir films, images the same city in *C.I.D.* with an eerie sense of order: uncrowded streets, orderly traffic, and tidy queues of people waiting for buses. Perhaps this has to do with the more powerful sense of irony that Guru Dutt tends to rely on, as opposed to Kapoor, for whom symbols are denotative rather than connotative in the Barthesian sense, and metaphors are made literal. Compare for instance the opening scenes, the introduction in each to "the big city."

In *Shri 420*, a slow dissolve after the opening sequence becomes a montage of images reflecting Bombay's chaotic city life. The noise and bustle of crowds, traffic, pedestrians, street hawkers, and fruit and vegetable sellers fill the screen, while passersby show scant regard for one

10. Dutt's ironic depiction of Bombay's orderly surface. *C.I.D.* (Guru Dutt, 1956).

another or for the protagonist, who stands at the center, awestruck. Even more telling is the exchange Raj has with the old man begging at the street corner; it serves as a narrative exposition at the beginning of the film. In Abbas's structurally ordered narrative style this exposition anticipates the ensuing action, complication, and resolution.

The old man at the street corner begs for alms: "*Baba, baba*" (sir, sir), he implores, extending his hand. People pass him by with complete indifference.

> RAJ: Why brother, are the people who dwell in your Bombay all deaf?
>
> OLD MAN: (Reluctant to engage) Deaf and blind too! Their ears hear nothing but the jingling of money. This is Bombay my brother, this is Bombay. Buildings here are built of cement, and human hearts of stone. Here only one thing is worshipped—money. But step aside please, this is time for business.
> (To a passerby) Sir . . .
>
> RAJ: Business? You mean work? That's what I've come here for from Allahabad. Why brother, what does one do to feed oneself in your city?

OLD MAN: What I do. Beg!

RAJ: No. Tell me about work.

OLD MAN: I'll have to think about it. Are you educated?

RAJ: A graduate. Take a look, here's my degree. I carry it around
with me.

OLD MAN: Are you honest?

RAJ: I received a medal for honesty and integrity.

OLD MAN: Are you young? Can you work hard?

RAJ: I could work twenty-four hours. Try me.

OLD MAN: Then you can't get any work.

RAJ: Can't get any work?! An educated hard-working youth can't
get any work!

OLD MAN: That's because this is Bombay my brother, Bombay!
Honesty and integrity can't find you any work. And yet you
could be dishonest and make money in four hundred and
twenty ways.

RAJ: Thank you boss, thank you. (Doffing his hat) Today I've learnt
a lot from you, a lot.

A similar refrain about the commercial nature of life in the big city
and the impossibility of honesty and decency is repeated in *C.I.D.*,
where nothing is what it appears. After establishing the murder that
takes place, the comic figure, "tailor master," breaks into a popular film
song. The lyrics are replete with irony and sarcasm:

ae dil hai mushkil jeena yahan
jara hat ke, jara bach ke
yeh hai Bombay mere jaan . . .
beghar ko aawara, yahan kehte hans hans
khud kaate gale sabke kehte ise 'business'. . .
(dear heart it's difficult to live out here,
just step aside, be careful
this is Bombay my dear . . .
those scoffed at—are the homeless, called vagabonds here
yet slitting peoples' throats—that's called 'business')

In both films Bombay is reified, and big business reviled. This parallels
the connections Cornell Woolrich makes between noir film in the

United States and the nineteenth-century "fictional genre of 'mysteries of the city' with its discourse of anti-urbanism."[22] Money, specifically big business, is tainted by being implicated in crime. In both films the wealthy mafia, masquerading as philanthropists, gain social respectability, which shields them from public scrutiny. The heroes enter that world, unveil them, and hand them over to law enforcement authorities.

In Vijay Anand's *Johnny Mera Naam* (My Name Is Johnny, 1970), the hero Sohan, played again by Dev Anand, is a police inspector with a hazardous charge: to round up a ring of smugglers. To do so, he masquerades as a gangster. This film is the prototype of the popular gangster-action genre, in which siblings separated at birth or during childhood traverse opposite paths and after a series of circuitous chance events reunite. Sohan and his brother Mohan (Pran) are a conscientious police officer's sons who, as boys, are never able to outdo each other in middle-school boxing matches. Ranjit, the mob leader, retaliating against police action, assassinates their father, disrupting a happy family. Mohan follows his father's killer and stabs him, but accidentally falls into the hands of gangsters, who end up raising him as Moti. He eventually becomes the second-in-command to Rai Saheb Bhupender Singh, the leader of an international smuggling ring.

Sohan, groomed under his father's boss, Mehta, grows up to be a police officer. Posing as a gangster under the pseudonym Johnny, Sohan infiltrates the mob when he is hired by Rekha (Hema Malini), the heroine. His mission is to uncover the smugglers' mode of operation. Johnny and Rekha travel to Kathmandu, in neighboring Nepal, where the gangsters transact their business. The plot thickens, and the intrigue and danger heighten when Johnny discovers that Rekha is in the game to reach her father, Rai Saheb Bhupender Singh, who operates behind the scenes unseen by the gang members. Rekha and Johnny join forces to win Moti over.

Johnny wins the gangsters' confidence by accomplishing several missions: transporting bullion, stealing jewels from a temple, concealing diamonds in Indian musical instruments exported overseas, and so on. Moti trusts Johnny until an old partner of the gang, Heera (Jeevan), tips off Moti that Johnny is an undercover cop. Moti and Johnny have a showdown. In this protracted fight scene the brothers recognize each other through their boxing styles. They embrace, come together and round up the rest of the ring with ingenious and entertaining gags. In the denouement it becomes clear that Rekha's father, Rai Saheb Bhupender Singh, is indeed innocent, a captive of the villainous Ranjit (Premnath). Ranjit is Bhupender Singh's evil brother, the real leader of the ring—the man who once killed Mohan and Sohan's father. Ranjit simply uses Bhupender Singh's name to destroy his brother's reputation and work out his sibling rivalry.

The boxing match between Sohan and Mohan as young boys at school, their playful matches at home, and later, when they are grown men playing cops and robbers in the "real" world, is a telling ode to brotherly love, masculinity, and male bonding. Virility, physical strength, and power are important features of the masculine self, split between the figures of the hero and the villain. The contest is between two evenly matched combatants dedicated to opposing ends—national and antinational, good and evil. The villain is the darker half—the ideal masculine subject gone awry.

Johnny Meraa Naam is testimony to the relatively high quality of screenplay writing and production in 1970s' Hindi cinema. Elaborate and carefully worked out narrative details (notably lacking in these genre films of the 1980s), compelling motivation, kinetic energy in narrative developments, complete narrative closure in all the subplots, and an excellent cast all helped to set a high standard that has unfortunately slipped away. Films in the 1980s became belabored, discontinuous, and poorly executed. (*Karma*, a film I discuss later, is an example of such a decline.) Powerful themes in contemporary politics are diffused by vague allusions to the enemy, the "terrorist" or politician located in a nonspecific time and place.

If *Johnny Meraa Naam* is specific in details, it is dogged by another kind of obfuscation. Double-speak regarding wealth pervades the film, and others of its kind: there is a persistent fascination and vilification of wealth and the wealthy. There is more at stake than the audience vicariously enjoying the pleasures of wealth; it is also impeached for its relation to crime and corruption. "Smuggling," a trope for antinationalism, was a particularly effective aspect of the nationalist discourse from the 1970s onward. Nationalist protectionist state policies conflicted with the growing taste for "foreign" goods in cosmopolitan centers.

But the smugglers shown in films invert this dynamic to fit a colonial and Orientalist imagination: they drain Indian wealth, conceived as gold, diamonds, and precious jewels. The films at once flaunt international cosmopolitanism (with its dazzling high-tech show of Bond-style spectacle) and a commitment to state policy that favors the indigenous bourgeoisie over the comprador. It is a discourse that cleverly consolidates and privileges the national, in antipathy to the "foreign." The hero defends the nation from the antinationalists' squandering, but a sanctioned support for the indigenous bourgeoisie is repressed within the double-speak.

The hero and villain, signifying the nation and its enemy, are polar categories imbued with an emotional charge that derives from their status as siblings. Once the Hindi film established the convention of big business as criminal, it became unnecessary to explain the nature of its operation in later films. The villain associated with it is simply a sign, a register of the nation's troubles. If the family is metonymic for the nation, the rivalry between the good and bad sons or brothers, standing in for nationalist and antinationalist, reiterates this.

11. Bond-style setups in *Johnny Meraa Naam* (My Name Is Johnny), Dev Anand, 1970.

From the mid–1970s to the end of the decade Hindi cinema experienced unparalleled vitality, attributed to the rise of the "angry young man" films with the working-class protagonist that became the insignia of and vehicle for Amitabh Bachchan's superstardom. Shortly after his debut film *Saat Hindustani* (Seven Indians, K. A. Abbas, 1969), Bachchan's career in popular cinema took off with successes like *Zanjeer* (Chain, Prakash Mehra, 1973) and *Deewar* (Wall, Yash Chopra, 1975). His working-class hero roles recur in the 1970s in *Namak Haraam* (Traitor, Hrishikesh Mukherjee, 1973), *Trishul* (Trident, Yash Chopra, 1978), and *Kaala Pathar* (Black Stone, Yash Chopra, 1979), but decline after *Coolie* (Porter, Manmohan Desai, 1983), with a last hurrah in *Hum* (We, Mukul Anand, 1990).

In the body politic of the nation, these films showcase working-class disenchantment. Always a subaltern figure—coal miner, dock worker, factory worker, porter, or slum dweller—the Bachchan figure challenged employers, factory owners, mafia men, and capitalist bosses either from his underdog position, or by rising to the top to vindicate past (inevitably familial) humiliation. In the process he exposed the machinations of "the system."[23] Structurally these films are not different from Abbas's master narratives in *Awaara* (Vagabond, 1951) or *Shri 420*, but unlike Raj Kapoor's portrayal of earnest unemployed youth, Bachchan played an urban ghetto product who barely concealed the rage simmering beneath a self-assured but melancholic persona.

While this gave Bachchan's wildly popular films an edge and him unsurpassed star iconicity, their success was obviously propelled by more than his star power. The extraordinary screenplays, terse scripts, and sharp dialogue written for Bachchan by Salim-Javed were inscribed with a trenchant critique that resonated powerfully with a disillusioned post-Emergency nation. If films like *Upkaar* in the 1960s exhorted the nation's citizen-soldier-peasant to the national cause, Indira Gandhi's Machiavellian strategies to stay in power in 1975 by declaring an Emergency unleashed a cynical mood that encompasses the films projected on the nation's screen.

The effects of the 1965 war, chronic food shortages and student-peasant rebellion in east India, were temporarily cast aside with the 1971 Bangladesh liberation war's success, which returned Indira Gandhi to power in 1972. However, the nation was teetering after the 1973 oil shock, a sharp rise in commodity prices, and the protracted all-India railway workers strike. Jaya Prakash Narayan's anticorruption movement, among others, was building popular opposition against the state. This was effectively snuffed out by the Emergency declared by Indira Gandhi, giving her powers to arrest political leaders and suspend citizen rights for nineteen months. It was during this period that Bachchan became an indomitable screen presence in violent gangster-action films considered to have a new air of "realism" at the time.

Subhash Ghai's *Vidhaata* (The Protector, 1982) continues in this genre, tracing the making of a mafia chief. An honest working-class locomotive driver, Sher Singh, is transformed into Sobhraj, the don of a notorious underground mafia operation, the Mizia group. Centering on working-class rebellion and containment, it is a carry-over of themes popular in the 1970s. The master theme "poverty begets crime" (as in *Shri 420*) is modified; in *Vidhaata* the state's loss of legitimacy leads to crime. The antihero Sher Singh/Sobhraj is played by Dilip Kumar, who returns to the screen as a mature actor two decades after his heyday in the 1950s.

When Sher Singh's son, a police officer, is killed by the notorious gangster Jaggavar, he becomes the sole protector and grandparent of his infant grandson. Sher Singh kills his son's assassins (because the police have proved ineffective), and becomes a fugitive from the law. A chance meeting with a tycoon provides him with employment, propels him into the underworld, and finally to the inheritence of the tycoon's estate. In another chance meeting he befriends Abu (Sanjeev Kumar), a lower-class Muslim widower. Together they parent the child Kunaal. They agree to let Abu raise and discipline Kunaal, away from his grandfather's overindulgence.

Kunaal (Sanjay Dutt) returns to his grandfather's home when he turns eighteen. From Abu, whom he considers his mother, he learns to value honesty and hard work. Kunaal's desire to marry Durga (Padmini Kolhapure), a working-class girl, creates a conflict with Sobhraj, in the course of which Abu is accidentally killed by Sobhraj's men. These events lead Kunaal to discover that Jaggavar and his grandfather are mafia men. In the torturous events that follow, the confrontation between Sobhraj and Jaggavar comes to a head; both are killed.

The film uses an old paradigm—the reign of criminalized big busi-

12. Police apathy toward a gunned-down cop and the loss of the state's legitimacy. *Vidhaata* (The Creator), Subhash Ghai, 1982.

ness in public life—that Hindi cinema's *Shri 420* set in place in the mid 1950s. It is only now, however, fifty years later, that concern about criminality in business is being publicly aired in the news media. Surfacing as a hotly debated aspect of political discourse, for the first time the imbrication of crime, big business, and politics has appeared in fora considered more "enlightened" than popular Hindi cinema—the parliament, journalism, and television.[24] Revealingly, the discussions are no different from the guarded allusions made in Hindi films: they are singularly nonspecific, refusing to name individuals, political parties, or the bureaucrats linked with crime.

Recurring elements in Hindi gangster action films make them interesting treatises on masculinity. The law enforcement authority is always portrayed as a well-meaning but bumbling force. The police's late arrival at the end of *Vidhaata* (after the hero defeats the villain) is an admission of this.[25] But the film also explicitly singles out police ineptitude and the breakdown of civil life. By the 1980s there was widespread cynicism about police corruption and the state's loss of legitimacy. *Vidhaata*, a sympathetic portrait of the antihero, the "godfather," tracks the desperation driving a law-abiding man to become an outlaw. The police force's apathy toward his son, a gunned-down police officer, is the last straw.

By the 1980s, filmic representations of the dangerous and exciting inner workings of big business had shifted from fraudulent housing schemes meant to hoodwink the masses (such as in *Shri 420*) to the machinations of the shipping, textile, and chemical industries. Along with this change came an escalation in crime only hinted at in *C.I.D.* These latter-day films emphasize the imbrication of big business in crime and corruption. That the filmic presentation is far more graphic and less "spoofed" is only partially a sign of the technological advances in Bombay cinema.

Another recurring feature of the gangster-action films is the plot of the hero escaping poverty only through corruption and crime, and being ruined by his temporary gains. The hero-turned-antihero then must either die or revert to his original persona.[26] At every stage passionate family relationships motivate the plot. The hero takes to crime to support his family; but he eventually disavows crime to win his family's approval.

Karma (Action, 1986) once again configures parent-child, father-son relationships in the context of the overriding nationalist-patriot theme. This time a patriotic father, lovingly but stern, trains his recalcitrant sons to love, fight, and die for the nation. Set against a decade of terrorist violence unleashed by Punjab's separatist politics during the 1980s, the film reiterates sentiments articulated by other frontier states such as Assam and Tripura during the 1970s, and Kashmir in the 1990s. *Karma* unequivocally targets the new enemy: the mindless separatist terrorist, who strikes at the roots of a unified nation.

Rana Vishwa Pratap Singh (again played by the veteran Dilip Kumar) is the police chief of a major penitentiary. He arrests Dr. Dang (Anupam Kher), the leader of Black Star (BSOA), a terrorist organization operating a military camp across the border.[27] Dang, an egomaniac, retaliates in a hysterical fashion. He stages a spectacular get-away on a helicopter, murdering every prisoner, reducing the penitentiary to smoldering rubble, and killing Rana's two young sons. Only Rana's grandson and his wife survive, and she suffers a loss of speech from the shock.

Rana resigns from his position, but is supported by the state in an experiment to apprehend Dang and his organization. Rana selects three convicts from penitentiaries across the country and establishes a training camp near the border. The three men, Johnny (Anil Kapoor), Khaeru (Naseer-ud-din Shah), and Baiju (Jackie Shroff)—notably a diverse band made up of a Christian, a Muslim, and a Hindu—are at first scornful of Rana Vishwa Pratap's patriotism and suspicious of the state's intentions. But the men's original goal to use the mission as an opportunity to escape evaporates when they begin appreciating Rana Vishwa Pratap's deep conviction.

Toward the end of the film Rana Vishwa Pratap is injured and taken captive by the BSOA. The three men attack the dreaded BSOA camp. As the battle becomes full-blown, Rana Vishwa Pratap and some Indian POWs held by BSOA escape; they join Johnny, Khaeru, and Baiju and together they release Rana Vishwa Pratap's wife, grandson, and others taken hostage by Black Star. Khaeru sacrifices his life willingly for the national cause. Rana Vishwa Pratap, the "son of the soil," kills the megalomaniac Dr. Dang, decimates his terrorist encampment, and liberates the Indian POWs. But once the mission is complete, Baiju and Johnny refuse to leave, insisting on a place within Rana's family—the place his own two sons once filled. An altered but reunited happy family is once again metonymic for the recuperation of the nation after a bloody holocaust.

In *Karma*, director Subhash Ghai seized upon contemporary divisive politics that threatened the problematic concept of the Indian nation. Ethnic nationalism generally wins popular support in the face of issues such as job scarcity and uneven development. Throughout the 1980s, a violent secessionist movement in Punjab received widespread support. Terrorist acts in service of this movement were at first directed against high-placed public officials. When security around these officials became impenetrable, the target shifted to common people and mass killing in public places. By the end of the 1980s, popular support for the movement had petered out.

The politics of the separatist movement, however, is still grist for Hindi cinema's mill, which identifies it as the new enemy threatening the core idea of nation. The separatist "terrorist" was depicted in another blockbuster success directed by Ghai, *Khalnayak* (Anti-Hero, 1993). Here the terrorist, a direct affront to national unity, is isolated and attacked. Ironically, the film highlights the tenuousness of the nation, the very thing it defends. The film presents a plethora of symbols to invoke nationalism—and it does this with a desperation that underscores not only the precarious nature of such a strategy, but also the confusion it unleashes when ethnic nationalism evokes the same level of passion.

In *Karma* the issue of secessionist politics is entirely side-stepped by presenting terrorism as a sign of mental derangement in the form of Dr. Dang. The political motivation for Dang's antinational feelings is merely a personal and psychological matter: his father was killed in the 1947 independence movement. To be fair, the band of men Rana Vishwa Pratap mobilizes to defend the nation are also nothing more than sociopaths. When Baiju is requisitioned for the mission, he is neither interested in the nation's friends nor its enemies. He is not even interested in himself. Yet the three men learn from Rana Vishwa Pratap, their aging paternalistic teacher. Their collective dementia is redeemed when they center their energies on the nation.

Peculiar to this centering is the rhetoric of nationalism that mobilizes a particularly morbid set of symbols common to both sides, with their militia encampments divided by an imaginary national border.[28] Ghai is scrupulously silent about particularizing the place: the references are restricted to "here" and "there." No names, not even fictional ones, denote the place to which they travel, the site of their mission. Physical location until the late 1990s has remained an ambiguous sign in Hindi cinema (unless reference is to the cosmopolitan big city, such as Bombay).[29] It is a strategy that works to preempt localized identification in lieu of a generalized one. Yet references to nation, soil, and "this land" abound, along with other symbols: the flag, patriotic songs, phalanxes of uniformed police and military forces, and the map of India, as well as invocations of death, sacrifice, martyrdom and blood.

These are invoked passionately on both sides (nationalist and separatist) as emblems of a new secular religion. But it is only the nationalists' patriotism that is depicted as honorable. The pathology and dementia of the ex-convicts is erased by their allegiance to the nation. The antinationalists (and, by implication, ethnic nationalists) remain deranged. This despite the fact that the actions on each side are the same—war, violence, blood, death, and martyrdom. Unknowingly (and perhaps even contrary to its intention), *Karma* lays bare the similarity between the state-owned nationalist force and the terrorists, each side goading its soldiers with an ideological preparation for war. Ethnic and secular nationalism elaborated in the film are eminently exchangeable, their origins relying on a similar well of emotions for which the soldier is expected to do or die. Perhaps the soldier Khaeru's words are worth re-iterating here. In one scene he confronts Rana Vishwa Pratap, who de-mands that a soldier know only about his weapons and nothing about romantic love. Khaeru's response as a soldier is a telling one, if for a moment we forget the fact that he is really referring to being a con-vict: "*hum hamesha kaidi rahenge. humen kabhi azaadi nahin milegi* (We [soldiers] will always be prisoners. We will never be free)."

In *Vidhaata*, *Karma*, and *Johnny Mera Naam* the concourse between gender, nation, and family—as well as villains, heroes, and antiheroes—is inscribed within an infinitely malleable master-narrative. By stretch-ing the narrative's archetypal representations of masculine, parent-child, and hero-villain relationships, it makes the nation's troubles transpar-ent. Just as Abu Baba is cast as Kunaal's mother without being either the biological mother (or even a woman), Rana Vishwa Pratap, an official in the coercive and punitive state machinery, is the loving father even when he sends his "sons" to die in war. And in *Johnny Meraa Naam* a benign, father-like police chief sends off Sohan to Nepal without any reassurance. "So far the police has supported you," he says. "Now you are playing with your life and entering another country. You are exposed to unknown danger and should prepare to make sacrifices."

All missions are brought to fruition in the end. The ultimate ex-ample of rescuing the nation from its enemy is conveyed by Rana Vishwa Pratap's grandiloquent speech in the climactic confrontation with Dr. Dang. Pushed against a wall, Rana fires a barrage of bullets at Dang. When he is finished, the bullet marks reveal a map of India drawn around him. Rana's electrifying speech goes on: "You handful of wretches think you can break this nation into pieces . . . you will never be able to . . . Impossible! (screaming) . . . Impossible! When a monster like you comes into the nation, you will be erased by this country's tri-color (camera pans up, the reframing reveals the Indian flag)." Rana Vishwa Pratap's fiery patriotism reifies the flag and nationalist fervor—

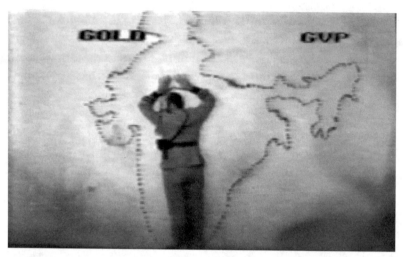

13. Rana's bullets reveal the national map. *Karma* (Action), Subhash Ghai, 1986.

the power that inspires heroes, consolidates the nation, and deals with its enemies.

Sons and Mothers

In maternal melodrama the mother's devotion to her son is profound. *Mother India* (1957) and *Aradhana* (Prayer, 1969) exemplify this. Salman Rushdie wickedly satirizes Mehboob Khan's grand production *Mother India*: "Motherness—excuse me if I underline the point—is a big idea in India . . . Ladies-O, Gents-O: I'm talking *major* mother country."[30] Conversely, films tracing the quintessence of masculinity are told from the son's point of view, narrativizing, among other things, the hero compensating his mother for suffering at the hands of the father. This is prominently featured in Raj Kapoor's *Awaara* (Vagabond, 1951), and Yash Chopra's *Deewar* (Wall, 1975) and *Trishul* (Trident, 1978). These films were amazingly successful with both men and women. As such it is a telling story about the uneasy and intensified restructuring of the Indian family during the second half of the twentieth century.

These films collectively articulate a metanarrative: changing family politics within India's feudal-patriarchal culture giving way to capitalist patriarchy. Commenting on the repetition in the mother's representation in North American popular culture, Ann Kaplan suggests that it "touches something basic in white middle-class cultural uncon-scious."[31] She justifies using psychoanalysis as a way of understanding fiction because it bears up where other methods do not.[32]

Male identity is acquired by successfully overcoming the pre-oedipal stage, the phase when the son experiences his mother's body as one with his own in a perfect loving dyad. Getting past the pre-oedipal phase guarantees gaining an adult sexuality—but it is one that is potentially regressive at any point in time.[33] The ". . . phallic regime of masculine identity is by no means a secure option that can be taken for granted. . . . It has to be consolidated and perpetually protected against various forms of deviance and disruption."[34]

Peter Matthews argues that the constant symbolic replay of mater-nal loss tells of a "suppressed desire" that must be "mastered." On both sides the mother-son relationship rests on a desire for pre-oedipal one-ness with the mother, as experienced by the woman with her own mother and now by her son. The mother's yearning for her son is a "safe" investment of women's passion.[35] For the son, the mother is a pre-oedipal figure of primal love; displaced by the process of oedipal sepa-ration, she becomes a lost object who recurs in the mother-son fantasies replayed in popular films. This pre-oedipal desire is scripted in films in narratives that are retold with varied emphasis on the subjects' point of view—the mother's or the son's—and tapping into a reservoir of un-resolved conflicting desire. Wider social and institutional shifts, how-ever, are also significant in accounting for the unique fixation on the mother-son relationship, the absence of the father, and the constancy of family drama in Hindi cinema.

In Yash Chopra's *Deewar* two sons are raised by their mother after their father abandons them. Growing up in hardship and poverty, Vijay (Amitabh Bachchan), the older brother, raises himself from the posi-tion of a dockyard worker to an underworld mafia man. Ravi (Shashi Kapoor), moving through relatively advantageous channels and hav-ing the opportunity for education, becomes a police officer. As a pow-erful mafia man Vijay buys his mother the very high rise building where she was once hired as a poor construction worker. But once Vijay's live-lihood is disclosed, his mother and brother turn on him and Vijay be-comes a pariah in the family. Ravi therefore "wins" the mother. Being a dutiful police officer, he hunts Vijay down for his criminal offenses.

While on the run, Vijay learns that his mother is terminally ill. Unable to bear the separation, Vijay visits her despite his injury during an encounter with the police.

In the end, Vijay dies with his head on his mother's lap. The intensity of their relationship, referred to obliquely throughout the film, is now made explicit. The rift between the two brothers is exacerbated by the fact that the mother chooses Ravi over Vijay. But in this emotionally charged denouement, the mother shares a tender moment with Vijay. As he dies she reminisces about the very special pleasure she enjoyed when he slept with her as a boy. This is about the most candid reference in all of Hindi cinema to the passionate mother-son relationship.

In part, the mother's passion is a way of directing female desire to the "safe" confines of her children and is as much a manifestation of the woman's own impossible desire for merging with her mother.[36] Mehboob's film *Mother India*, on the other hand, is a paean to the sufferings of womanhood and motherhood. The protagonist Radha (Nargis) is married to a peasant, Shamu (Raj Kumar). The film plots the tribulations of peasants dependent on the vagaries of nature. A series of misfortunes ruin Radha's life. First her husband is crippled; then, unable to cope with burdening the family, he deserts Radha. Radha tills the land herself and raises her children in terrible poverty: when a famine strikes the village she mortgages the land to the local moneylender and then has to ward off his sexual advances.

Ramu, her older son, grows up to be responsible, but Birju, the younger son, turns into a rebellious daredevil. He attacks the moneylender's house and retrieves his mother's bracelets (*kangan*), once pawned in his shop. Then he fights to get their land back. But he is unable to read the ledgers that show the mortgage as still unpaid. Birju's violent confrontations in the village with the powers that be make it difficult for Radha to cope. The final straw comes when Birju makes a sexual advance on a girl in the village. Radha responds to this excess by killing Birju in cold blood. In the last scene (also shown as the opening scene of the film), as "Mother India," Radha is asked to inaugurate a new dam in the village. The dam, a symbol for modernization and progress, promises to displace the old feudal order.

Rosie Thomas has brilliantly argued that *Mother India* is, unambiguously, a "complicit" text.[37] The complicit text is a maternal melodrama consonant with the dominant master-mother-discourse within patriarchy, while the resistant text questions this discourse.[38] Thomas is right when she points out that Birju's subversive potential is first mobilized and then carefully contained. His inability to read the ledgers is indeed the most poignant moment in the film. It powerfully underscores the pathos of their disempowerment, the bane of illiteracy. Radha, although assigned agency, only subverts Birju's protest and the possibility of change it could bring. She defends the status quo.

Though this reading is valid, it is difficult to relegate the entire film to this complicit category. Within the tradition of mother-son narratives in Hindi cinema it is more ambiguously positioned. Birju's intense attachment to his mother motivates much of his behavior, including his rage against the moneylender. The fetishized bracelets are cultural tell-tale signs marking Birju's passion.[39] On the other side of this fusional relationship is the mother, whose passion is considered safe when her yearning is invested in her sons. Popular culture often reveals a strong attraction to the maternal sacrifice myth, taking either the form of the overinvested mother or the powerful "phallic mother."[40]

Mother India offers a spectacular twist on the traditional mother-son narrative, offering up a figure who is at once a sacrificing mother *and* a phallic annihilator. This duality has never been replayed on the Hindi film screen. Maternal love legitimately channels the woman's passion and her search for oneness experienced with her own mother, and sons become "substitute erotic subjects" on whom she lavishes her love.[41] (Garbo, for example, often died for her sons in films.) But the son's pre-oedipal attachment cannot be condoned or forgiven. Almost admitting a guilty secret, Radha kills her son. No less telling are the circumstances in which he is killed. Birju makes a sexual advance on a girl from his own village, violating the incest taboo. (In north Indian village culture men and women of the same village are conventionally considered siblings.) Here the subtext depicts the violation of the incest taboo as a stand-in for the transgression of the son's relationship with his mother; Birju's act is therefore punished with death. This act of the life-giver as capable of smothering and annihilating makes the film ambiguous, and difficult to judge as either entirely complicit or resistant. And the mother as annihilator is a stunning spectacle. As Rosie

Thomas herself admits, "The most powerfully horrifying image is of Radha leveling a shotgun at her son."[42]

In conventional mother-son narratives the protagonist's unfettered pre-oedipal love for his mother and his anger for being separated from her are projected onto the mother as her pain. They sanction the son's hostility toward the father, the enemy within the family. Unlike father-daughter depictions in films where the mother is absent, the mother-son filmic portrayal takes full cognizance of the father. Narratives account for first his presence and later his disappearance, displacement, or his punishment.

In Raj Kapoor's *Awaara*, a muted father-son rivalry is played out in a courtroom drama. Raj (Raj Kapoor), the protagonist, is tried for murder. Raghunath, the judge who presides over the trial, is, unknown to all at the time, Raj's father. Rita (Nargis), Raj's lawyer and his lover, defends him; the father-son story unravels in court. Raj grew up in an urban slum and becomes a criminal, it turns out, because his father abandoned his mother and her unborn child on the unfounded suspicion that the child was not his. In the denouement of the film the judge discovers that Raj is his own son.

In Yash Chopra's *Trishul*, Vijay (Amitabh Bachchan) works his way

14. Radha levels a gun at her son. *Mother India* (Mehboob, 1957).

up the corporate ladder to undercut and undo his business rival, none other than his own (illegitimate) father, Raj Kumar Gupta (Sanjeev Kumar). Vijay punishes his father for the ordeal his unwed mother suffered by not only stealing Gupta's business contracts, but also destroying Gupta's family by turning both his legitimate children against him. In a narrative reiteration of his desire to vanquish Raj Kumar Gupta, Vijay speaks to his deceased mother's photograph after his first victory against Gupta. "This," he says, "is just the first battle, there's a whole war ahead." Later, his business partner and lover, Geeta (Rakhee), discerns and objects to his personal vendetta in professional business. He responds enigmatically, referring to his mother's victimization: "I am not earning money. I am accounting for my mother's tears."

In film after film, the father is configured along with the mother-son dyad; he becomes an absentee parent, as is often the case in the opposite dyad, father-daughter, that also recurs frequently in Hindi films. Yet each film accounts for the father: in *Mother India*, he first loses his arms, a disfigurement signifying his sexual impotence, and later he leaves home forever.[43] In *Deewar*, too, the father runs away from home; in *Aradhana*, the lover dies, causing the mother to suffer social censure for bearing his child out of wedlock; in *Trishul* and *Awaara*, the fathers are arrogant, self-centered and weak-kneed. In every film the mother and son pay the price for the father's cowardice—the father who either shuffles away, dies, or is later confronted by the son for his misdeeds against his mother. Psychologically, the mother's torment warrants an unfettered playing out of pre-oedipal scenarios with the hero's mother. The resolution of the oedipal conflict is a fantasy to displace the father.

Hindi films such as these deal explicitly with the masculinized hero's rage and melancholy, conflicts and resolutions, and the power the hero asserts, described in terms of the relationship he shares with his mother. Why does the son compete so desperately with the father to "get" the mother? Why do the narratives always end with a real or allegorical assurance of a permanent and inseparable bond between the mother and son? What do we make of the constant portrayal of the father's compliant, deferential, quiet surrender to the son and the privileged mother-son relationship?

The young male's coming-of-age and his rites of passage are produced by cultural notions of masculinity. Changes within the family economy and shifts in balance of power within it have been underway for the better part of the twentieth century in India and elsewhere. Film narratives have responded to that transformation. No longer under the umbrella of the aging patriarch, the new and smaller nuclear family unit finds itself under the power of sons who have asserted themselves as the new patriarchs, wresting control and power from their fathers.

It is this momentous transfer of power that replays itself over and over in the "family romance" projected in Hindi popular films. The narratives settle the issue unequivocally through the son's victory over his father. As the competing and ultimately succeeding patriarch, the son asserts himself again and again by reclaiming his mother against the father, who either makes himself absent, disappears, or is dislodged by the son. The mother is the ground of contest and the site of resolution, with an outcome always already determined in favor of the son, the hero. She is the trophy, symbolizing masculine achievement. Popular representations—in film and elsewhere—repeatedly celebrate the moment of passage to manhood; the mother-son bond is germane to and anticipates this power shift. The narratives in Hindi cinema reinforce this shift, depicting patriarchy's regeneration: the baton passed from father to son and the transfer of phallic power, staged through the contest over the same woman.

Chapter 4

Heroines, Romance, and Social History

As ONE OF MANY discursive practices, Hindi cinema is exceptionally powerful in constructing gender with its knowledge/power dynamic.[1] Women, the prominently visible "heavenly bodies" with little material or directorial control in the industry, are the putative ventriloquists' dummies reassuring men of their dominance.[2] The emphasis on women as objects to be seen, and the lack of film narratives where women's subjectivity is central, screens the inside, hidden, private female subject.

Instances of women's resistance are diluted to collude with the dominant discourse. Thus, filmic representations of women resisting through self-punishing acts of valor and honor turn them into victims, martyred to aggrandize patriarchal values. Yet there are lapses in the solidity of such representations. In this chapter I pry open popular Hindi film's reigning ideology to find moments of resistance and unintended leaks which subvert the text. Such critical reading against the grain destabilizes Hindi cinema's hegemonic values.[3]

Women's roles, assigned in relation to the hero—his lover, mother, or the "other" woman—maintain the male protagonist's centrality. In film plots the heroine repeatedly appears as the girl the boy meets, the romantic lover, a figure in the margins—a dim outline with little or no substance. The range of women characters are limited to archetypal Madonna/whore, lover/"other" figures, while tales about male subjects abound in details about their struggles against society, quests for justice and freedom, anxieties of loss and separation, or the satisfaction of avenging personal and societal losses. If a woman character in Hindi cinema is privileged with complex characterization, she is typically a pitiable victim in an elaborate saga of despair and tribulation. *Mother India's* suffering mother, Radha, is this quintessential figure. When women are afforded centrality, they suffer: their sacrifice, restraint, forbearance, chastity, and stoicism strengthen and ennoble them in the face of hardship.

Hindi films do not openly account for the sea change in women's lives since independence. A growing section of the female urban population—and, for a much longer time, low-income rural women—have been in the work force, impacting the public and private sphere. Disavowing these changes, the films at best refer obliquely to their struggles and the tenuous balance between public and private life. When films center-stage emancipated women, they are turned into objects of derision.

Reinvented traditions affected by the modernization process afflict women in specific ways: dowry deaths, acts of *sati*, and new technologically sophisticated forms of female infanticide all add to traditional forms of violence against women. These rarely appear in the virtual world of women in popular cinema. Repressing that reality is a sign of general male anxiety about social change and the desire to cathect this anxiety onto images of unchanging women—forever feminine, innocent, childlike, sexual, desirable, and devoted. As Teresa de Lauretis points out, the tension between "woman as representation" on the one hand and "women as historical beings, subjects of 'real relations'" on the other, is sustained by a contradiction in culture: women are "at once within and without representation."[4]

Reading Resistance

A film historian plotting women's social history in postcolonial India through popular Hindi films confronts endless scenarios that sexualize, victimize, or marginalize women. Women characters may be ubiquitous in popular cinema, but they are inevitably denied depth or dimension. How then does one write a social history of women, based on their hypervisibility and metaphorical silence in the films? Feminist journals and journalistic film reviews in India interminably lament the severely delimited "image of women" on the screen. A rather bleak scenario emerges in critical discourse that takes a dim view of Hindi cinema's gender politics. Steering through this pessimism, how do we write a history—how do we map a narrative of women through Hindi films that might still serve "affirmative" politics?

Given the lack of narratives *about* women and films made *by* women, the remaining choice is to examine women's roles in the margin: to recenter their position, look more closely at their silhouettes and find traces, however faint, from which to read more about what these women might actually represent. In other words, I view women's filmic presentations as inscriptions of and by dominant cultural discourse which clouds their concerns, sensibilities, and aspirations.

How does one extricate women's resistance from cultural representations?[5] Since resistance is always a response to domination, it is important to understand its extent, the nature of control, the points through which it is exerted, and the possibilities of intervention or protest. No power structure, however totalitarian, is monolithic. Even popular Hindi cinema condemned by feminists is not so successfully hegemonic in its patriarchal discourse. Portraying subordinates in a system as passive is a "woefully lopsided account of social reality."[6] Power, constantly threatened by resistance, needs to be continually secured.

Commercial Hindi cinema, with its objective of gaining popularity and a narrative logic requiring situations exacerbating conflict in social relations, cannot but pit the voice of the subaltern against the elite, or present the woman figure straining against male control. True, this is an aspect of a carefully controlled representation that always reinstates hegemonic ideology. Yet leaks in the dominant discourse, especially in narratives that are dialogical, present women and men, both subaltern and elite, in encounters that force cognizance of the "real" situation. These moments of fracture open opportunities to read the text against the status quo ideology that the narrative imposes. The fault lines in the patriarchal order enable reading against the grain and reading resistance—a process Teresa de Lauretis calls "self-representation" in the "space-off" of the hegemonic discourse.[7]

Since women appear predominantly in the role of the girl who meets the boy, there are limits imposed in examining heterosexual romance and tales of love, sexuality, and mismatched expectations. Of course, such limited analysis replicates the films. In applying this analysis the intent is not to rehearse the hierarchy set up by Hindi films between robust masculinity engaged in the public sphere and feminine susceptibility to sentimentality, obsession with the "private"—the concerns of love, home, and the hearth. Rather, the idea is to disclose the public and political nature and ramifications of the "private" that women are identified with in cultural representations such as Hindi cinema.

Close readings of films produced across several decades are examined here individually and intertextually. I read the film texts against the grain of normative culture, as well as against each other, to demonstrate that the films do not present a monolithic discourse. The film texts are also read in conjunction with "star texts," a salient aspect of film culture in India and a site where public and private narratives coalesce in revealing ways. Through this layered reading it is possible to piece together a history of the social text.

In the hermeneutic of women's representations popularized in Hindi films, reading against the grain would mean scrutinizing texts not explicitly about resistance—with, as Sunder Rajan says, an implicit "political agenda of feminist criticism . . . [to] *read* resistance."[8] Given the excessive use of the term "resistance" in literary criticism, it is necessary to add caveats so as to retain its critical edge. Through a series of negative assessments, I explore the political purpose and process of reading resistance. I assess a few different contexts in which resistance is read to clarify the diffuse meaning it assumes. While resistance is a matter of a particular reading, I eschew the methodology of feminists whose "political" acts of reading resistance in dubious actions (of death/suicide/*sati*) are rather strained. This deflects the discourse onto a metaphysical plane and reduces resistance to textual and semantic terms.[9] Such readings, far from being strategic interventions, can potentially offer alibis for a sinister right-wing agenda, which devalues human lives in general, and women's lives in particular.

Likewise, Sunder Rajan, reviewing *Women Writing in India*, makes important cautionary remarks. She points to (a) the conflation between the subversion inherent in women's writing and the act of writing, and (b) the critical reading of it. She notes problems inherent in both: in the first case it is important to historicize conformism in women's writing where it exists, and, in the second, she points to the problem of generally inflating the critic's role to the point of speaking "for" the subaltern. To be sure, resistance in Hindi films can be read as a sign of "intention" and "agency" of the characters.[10] It is generally produced by a situational or institutional crisis within the diegesis, although this might only be temporary and the demands of narrative closure restore the status quo.

Another caveat is that just as dominance is not monolithic, resistance cannot be construed as entirely autonomous. In reconstructing a history of women's writing some critics have experienced the dilemma of finding it a process at once "violent" and "hegemonic." Violent, because it has to break with existing traditions, and hegemonic in terms of the hazard of setting future agendas.[11] Undoubtedly, this is the nature of disciplinary practices that are constantly charting new frontiers.

To the paradigm of the dominant discourse and situating acts of resistance in its context, I wish to add another important constituent force: the subject, the "woman as subject" to be precise.[12] Addressing the problem of constituting women as subjects in the face of the contemporary onslaught of "Eurocentric postmodernism" and its declaration of the death of the subject, Nita Kumar points out that to announce the death of a subject one should first have had the right to speak as one, thus suggesting that subjecthood is a luxury not granted to all.[13] In defiance of current poststructuralist trends, Kumar insists on the construction of women as subjects as a way of speaking of autonomy, resistance, and protest. Although critical of poststructuralism, Kumar feels free to borrow from it, and suggests a modified Foucauldian approach to reconceptualize the subject as one who is constituted by discourse— a plurality of discourses, a recognition of subjection by these discourses as well as the possibility of resistance against it. We have to recognize that women are neither liberated nor repressed. What we have are discourses about "purity" and "honor" that have exerted power at different periods.[14]

The different forms of discourse through which women are constructed—language, speech, proverbs, songs, written texts, and even writings by women in autobiographies, letters or diaries—can be instrumental in revealing their confusions, aspirations, doubts and desires.[15] The dominant discourse that women appear to accept passively is easy to read and deconstruct. But what is not easily accessible is that which is on the "inside, private, hidden and silenced, . . . mysterious and indistinguishable. Not only can we not interpret it right away, we cannot even locate it easily."[16] Yet women constantly create new spaces from which they speak or act, based on their own notion of "autonomy" and "power," very dissimilar from the masculine subject with his "operative will."

Contesting the Laxman Rekha *(Laxman's Line)*

B. R. Chopra's film *Gumrah* (Deception, 1963) is unusual for its time not only because the protagonist is a woman, but also because the film deals with the even now tabooed subject of a married woman's continuing relationship with her former lover. In the film's prologue Chopra is careful to insert an episode from the classic epic *Ramayana*: While in exile in the forest Sita asks Rama's brother, Laxman, how far she may stray from the home. Laxman responds by drawing the famous *laxman-rekha* (Laxman's line), encircling her. This is literally a line drawn around Sita—around all women, marking quite plainly the boundary every woman must stay within, placing limits on her moral and sexual "wandering." This mythic line embedded in the patriarchal imaginary prescribes limits on the behavior expected of women and is carefully upheld by Hindi cinema.

Over the last four decades there are moments in Hindi film when this encirclement of women—their incarceration in the prison house of exacting Brahminical-Victorian morality—is challenged, when the mythic line is contested, or its boundary stretched even minimally. These contestations can be linked with the social and historical moment to which they belong. Points of rupture, break, and destabilization can be traced within the dominant paradigm, and they sometimes—speaking optimistically—point to the possibility of change. Love and romance in Hindi cinema is a compelling locus to examine womanhood: how does romantic love constitute women? Does this reveal change over time? Discourses on love, romance, sexuality, and the family are sites where women's subjectivity is located, shaping how they are imagined.

Filmic representations of women in these scenarios are shot through with a common patriarchal ideology.

It is therefore no surprise that the time-honored love story formula, the benighted love triangle, always shows a woman torn between two men. Narratives of love foreground women caught in dramatic moments of conflict with their conscience: they wrestle with love, desire, and duty. Men do not face conflicts in love: their universe expands beyond love into lofty struggles against society, for social justice, and against evil forces. The male hero wins the woman he wants, while she struggles within her narrow moral universe to make the "right" choice—choosing the hero. Perhaps the only popular film that dealt with the idea of a man "falling in love" with a woman other than the heroine/wife was *Pati, Patni aur Woh* (Husband, Wife and the Other, B. R. Chopra, 1978). The film created a sensation because its audacious title named the unmentionable—the other woman. Significantly it chose comedy as the genre to present a not-so-serious extramarital affair parodying the seven-year itch—a temporary diversion from the boredom of marriage. The film explores a middle-aged man's roving eye that settles on the young office secretary. He eventually gets over her—without the fling posing a deep conflict.

As for women facing the dilemma of love there is an abundance of films addressing this; here I focus on few highly successful ones. *Gumrah* boasts the most unusual narrative, and I discuss it in relation to other films depicting similar dilemmas posed by the love triangle which traps the woman: *Sangam* (Confluence, Raj Kapoor, 1964), *Pyaasa* (The Thirsty One, 1957), and *Guide* (1965)—all extremely popular in their time and now considered Hindi cinema classics.

In *Gumrah*, Meena (Mala Sinha) is a happily married young woman whose life is thrown into turmoil when her ex-lover, Rajinder (Sunil Dutt), re-enters. We learn that years ago Meena had abruptly terminated their relationship without any explanation. Rajinder now demands to know why she left, and Meena recounts events that interrupted their affair. After her sister's unexpected death, she married her brother-in-law, Ashok (Ashok Kumar), to take her sister's place and to mother his children. Although she is happy in her relationship with her husband, Rajinder's return re-ignites their unfinished affair, which

15. Meena meets her lover in his city apartment. *Gumrah* (Deception), B. R. Chopra, 1963.

becomes more impassioned under the circumstances of secrecy. She moves from a small town to a big city; despite this change their lives remain interconnected, and soon Meena finds herself drifting uncontrollably into a sexual relationship with her ex-lover. An elaborate but benign ruse set up by her husband forces Meena to struggle with her feelings of deceit, guilt, loyalty, desire, and duty. In the end, she confesses everything to her husband and chooses to stay with him, the man she is pledged to by the sanctity of their marriage vows. The *laxman-rekha* drawn in the prologue is successfully defended by her choice in the end.

Unlike the *Ramayana*, with its prototypes of good and bad men, the narrative in *Gumrah* has no villains. Each character has effective motivation. The first-person narrative in Meena's voiceover gives us not only her version of events but also access to her thoughts, conflicts, and struggles. It also lends credibility to the narrative. Ashok is kind, trusting, and gentlemanly in a paternal sort of way, removing any hint of tragic loss from Meena's choice in the end—an agreeable decision for the audience. The film is undoubtedly more candid than others about the extent to which Meena is drawn into the extramarital relationship, despite the dangers it signals to her (*badnami nahin seh sakungi*, I cannot bear a bad reputation). Within the narrative economy, Meena's indiscretion is compensated for by the fact that she selflessly chooses to marry Ashok and mother her sister's children.

Sangam deals with a similar love triangle between Radha, Gopal, and Sunder. This time, however, the scenario shifts to Gopal "sacrificing" Radha, his childhood sweetheart, to allow his friend Sunder to court her. Sunder's narcissistic self-absorption prevents him from recognizing Radha and Gopal's relationship.[17] Neither can Radha tell Sunder about her commitment to Gopal, and under complicated circumstances she ends up marrying him. Sunder's adoration for Radha, his childlike ebullience, and their relocation in Europe, make it easier for Radha to reconcile with her situation. Gopal, however, keeps returning in their lives. Radha is clearly not over Gopal, and when Sunder discovers an old love letter to Radha his jealousy and suspicion turn into self-destructive rage. During the film's climax, the three face each other and Gopal, after confessing his longstanding love for Radha, kills himself.

The constant refrain is that heterosexual love demands "sacrifice"—conveying the need to obfuscate desire, to belie the intrinsically

16. The final confrontation in *Sangam* (Confluence), Raj Kapoor, 1964.

narcissistic logic of monogamy which lays claim to the desire to be exclusively desired. *Sangam* attempts to reclaim heterosexual love by mobilizing it in favor of a spirit of selflessness. Such a spirit calls for repressing the individual, obliterating the self in favor of some higher goal—nurturing motherless children as in *Gumrah*, or relinquishing one's self in the name of *dosti* (friendship), an exclusively male phenomenon in Hindi films.

Both *Gumrah* and *Sangam* have a highly charged denouement when the women speak out. In *Sangam* Radha interrupts Sunder and Gopal, who speak of her as a trophy they are both willing to forfeit for the other in the name of friendship. "Have either of you thought of what I go through," she interjects angrily. Then, rationalizing her experience, she says, "*Pyaar ho jata hai, par shaadi, shaadi dharam hai* (one falls in love, but marriage, marriage is a matter of duty)." Likewise Meena defends her loveless marriage in an impassioned speech: "*Shaadi farz hai*" (marriage is a duty). These moments of reconciliation indeed bare alarming implications: women (and the audience) accept marriage as an institution, a duty, a *dharma* (one of the four stages in the life cycle Hinduism traditionally enjoins) which can exist *without* love.[18] The films' narratives show us that love is possible outside marriage.

Obviously, the weight of duty serves as insufficient ballast to keep the marriage afloat. The reappearance of ex-lovers in both Radha's and Meena's lives seriously destabilizes marital equilibrium. However, the imaginary line of patriarchal authority—the *laxman rekha*—keeps it in place. Interestingly, in *Gumrah*, it is not the woman's conscience that functions as the mechanism of control; it is fear of chastisement and social disgrace in the event of discovery. Meena's desire is quite clearly kept in check by the social/patriarchal authority that places a premium on a woman's reputation. Not only does she represent the family name and honor, but the country and community as well. Ashok roundly declares this toward the end of the film. But if the woman is claimed a signifier of family honor, the film also suggests something else that contravenes, interrupts, and challenges marriage: the woman's own desire. The *laxman rekha*, although intact, is under severe strain.

This "overvaluation" of women's desire (rather than, say, dealing with their material condition, where much more is at stake) is dictated by the discursive cinematic practice which sexualizes women while simultaneously circumscribing their conduct within a strict code. In the films I have taken up here the women characters' "uncontainable desire" is a reactive move against that dominant tendency. An oppositional reading of film must seize upon transgressive moments that challenge the strict sexual/moral code imposed on women. Women internalize the code, simultaneously resisting and subverting its excessive demands—and this is what the film narratives inadvertently tell us. Or perhaps not so inadvertently, since the narratives point to social contradictions that elicit rebellion (only to have the rebellious women quickly returned to subordination and patriarchal control). Constant eruptions within the institution of monogamy betray its troubled, unstable nature. Yet as psychoanalysis would have us believe, within the schema of family pathology, we are always already inscribed within monogamy.

In *Pyaasa* the female figure locked in a loveless marriage—coincidentally another Meena (Mala Sinha)—again has an ex-lover, Vijay, who re-enters her life. Vijay is a recreation of the legendary, self-destructive Devdas figure introduced in Saratchandra Chatterjee's 1917 novel *Devdas*, and reformulated in the film as an iconoclast.[19] This male figure is powerfully imprinted in the popular imaginary through numerous filmic iterations, especially through the performances of certain leading stars of their time: K. L. Saigal in the 1935 film *Devdas*, directed by P. C. Barua, Dilip Kumar in the 1955 version by Bimal Roy, and Sharukh Khan in the extravagant 2002 remake by Sanjay Leela Bhansali. Devdas suffers separation from and then loss of his childhood love, Parvati, and rejects the world because of it. In *Pyaasa*, Vijay spurns Meena along with the world. By choosing to marry a wealthy publisher instead of the poet-dreamer Vijay, with whom she once had a college romance, Meena comes to represent the shallowness and hypocrisy of the bourgeois world Vijay abjures. She has neither Parvati's austerity nor firmness in love, nor is her decision driven by sacrifice or circumstance.[20] Financial security drives her pragmatism. She lacks remorse and fears only that her domineering husband will discover her past. This justifies Vijay's misogynist aggression. Such male vindictiveness, presented as justifiable, is characteristic of so many films by Guru Dutt.

Meena stands in contrast to Gulabo, the prostitute in *Pyaasa*. A liminal figure, an outcast, she becomes the marginalized hero's partner.

In the last shot they walk away in a dim gray fog, entering a nowhere
land, an unspecified space—an ending common to so many 1950s' Hindi
films.[21] The film reclaims Gulabo as the hero's legitimate partner, a
hooker with the proverbial golden heart. The first to recognize the
worth of Vijay's iconoclastic poetry, she selflessly works on publishing
it, and is unfailingly by his side throughout his travails.

In Hindi cinema the alluring courtesan figure and courtesan culture elicits an obsessive fascination.[22] These are women whose work
depends on their being women, yet they are released from the cycle of
monogamous love and romance. They are, as Sumita Chakravarty says,
"at once economically dependent on and yet distinct from the world
of men"; their autonomy depends on their sexual/moral conduct.[23] One
would expect that the existence of this group of women would be explained by a nontraditional understanding of heterosexuality, love, sex,
romance, and womanhood within patriarchy. But as Chakravarty argues,
in the historical/legendary courtesan film genre, the woman, a victim
of social conditions (or the victim who is also the apotheosis of maternal love) is transformed and refitted into the site of romantic love,
where she longs for the "protection" of one man.

In an excellent discussion of the figure of the courtesan, Fareed
Kazmi uses Julia Lesage's analytic framework to examine how the female subject becomes emotionally involved in narratives that victimize women. Kazmi examines eight films of the "Muslim social" genre
and shows how in each case the protagonist, a subaltern Muslim woman
living autonomously, ekes out an existence under extenuating circumstances and demonstrates outstanding courage by confronting or defying the dominant power. Yet in each case the dilemma of love—the
longing for one man, romance, and glamour is an amazing elision of
real-life circumstances, deflecting women's problems and concerns.[24]

While the genre of the "courtesan film" strains to domesticate the
whore and fit her into a wifely role—to the point of projecting her as a
trope for virginal purity—in one significant film it reverses this process
and traces the movement from the opposite direction. In Abrar Alvi's
Hindi film classic *Sahib Bibi aur Ghulam* (The Lord, His Wife, and Slave,
1962), based on Bimal Mitra's novel, the domesticated upper-class wife
adopts a courtesan's ways. An extraordinary film in several respects, this
period piece, set in turn-of-the-twentieth-century Calcutta, provides an

outsider's view of the goings-on in the Chaudhari clan, a fast-declining, decadent feudal family that is overtaken by an enlightened bourgeoisie and outwitted by a modernized, managerial-technocratic class. It is a complex period film: the decaying feudal order is juxtaposed with the Subinay household. The latter is affiliated with the *Brahmo Samaj* movement, which works actively toward social regeneration in keeping with a late-nineteenth-century agenda of political action.

The story is told from the point of view of the household servant, Bhutnath, who oversees the work of demolishing the old *haveli* (mansion) that lies at the center of the narrative. The dismantling scene can be read as a literal dismantling of the old order, replacing it with the new. The entire film is a flashback, focusing on Bhutnath's memories of several decades earlier when he first arrived in the city as a servant in this *haveli*. Although there are several important characters and subplots, the main narrative deals with the youngest daughter-in-law, Chhoti Bahu (Meena Kumari), and her claustrophobic life within the *haveli's* walls.

Through Bhutnath's admiring eyes we first encounter Chhoti Bahu, who is astonishingly beautiful and hopelessly bored. Bhutnath is her only conduit to the world outside. Her husband, an alcoholic, spends his time entertained by courtesans patronized by the feudal households. His two older brothers are profligates who waste themselves in equally frivolous pastimes. Among the women the oldest sister-in-law, Badi Bahu, has lost her mind and wanders aimlessly through the *haveli*, a victim of the acutely lonely and oppressive *bhadramahila's* (upper-class Bengali woman) life. The middle sister-in-law, Manjali Bahu, keeps herself entertained by ordering fineries and jewelry.

Chhoti Bahu's ennui, her disenchantment, constitutes the central narrative. Determined to draw her husband into her life, she tries several strategies to win his attention. One evening she refuses to let him leave. Their not-very-subtle exchange is replete with references to sexual desire and sexual needs. The husband declares he is the "hot-blooded" scion of the Chaudhari lineage, and no *bahu* (daughter-in-law) of the family can fulfill his (sexual) needs. Chhoti Bahu insists on being given a chance. She attempts to seduce him. The young Chaudhari asks her if she can drink, dance, and sing licentious songs. Chhoti Bahu, horrified at first, takes up the challenge and initiates herself into what ends up being a life of alcoholism. In one of Meena Kumari's most exquisite performances, we see her grapple with the angst of loneliness, loveless-ness, a craving to be desired, and an unabashed desire for her inatten-tive husband.

Chhoti Bahu's actions reflect her refusal to conform to the norms of an upper-class wife. Not only does she make sexual demands on her husband, she also learns lovemaking as an art: the terrain of the pro-fessional courtesan. The film couches all this in the rhetoric of love and service to her husband, but the film's frame, in a moment of ex-cess, betrays an altogether different meaning. The viewer cannot miss the sexual charge in the eroticized moments when Meena Kumari tosses her head back to strike a "kiss me" pose or when, on another occasion, she performs a dance number. A little high on alcohol, she dances and expresses her passion, her desire to be loved, to seduce and be seduced. This scene—in fact the entire plot involving Chhoti Bahu—is about the need to desire and be desired, a theme traditionally absent from filmic and cultural representations of women.

Meena Kumari's portrayal of Chhoti Bahu is a classic example of a

17. Chhoti Bahu strikes a kiss-me pose. *Sahib, Bibi aur Ghulam* (The Lord, His Wife and Slave), Abrar Alvi, 1962.

film star encouraging identification with a key protagonist. Pam Cook, referring to Richard Dyer's work on film stars, notes that "their charisma produced an excess of meaning which, by captivating the spectator's gaze, disrupted involvement with narrative progression. Even if the story made sure that a strong female character got her comeuppance, her dazzling image lingered in the spectator's mind, overriding the knowledge of her punitive destiny."[25] Get her comeuppance she does, for at the end of Chhoti Bahu's song (pleading with her lover not to leave) she tries physically to stop him. When she asks if she hasn't kept him "happy," Chaudhari evasively and wryly suggests that she spend her time like the other daughter-in-law of the household, collecting jewelry and counting gold coins. Incensed by his condescension, Chhoti Bahu flies into a rage. In a scene memorable for its dramatic tension, Chhoti Bahu remonstrates against the idea of being compared to other women of her class after she has undergone such a thorough sense of physical and spiritual violation. "No other *bahu* has ever consumed alcohol to please her husband . . . Call me a mother," she taunts him insolently, obviously rebuking him for his impotence. Chaudhari Babu, infuriated, slaps her, knocks her down, and castigates her for drinking and behaving like a madwoman.

The rest of the story traces Chhoti Bahu's life going downhill as she becomes an alcoholic. Bhutnath watches the years pass her by. She alternates between moments of delirium and lucidity, but is always weighed down by an overwhelming melancholy. Her husband contracts a terminal illness; in her last effort to do something for him, she prepares to see a shaman whom she hopes will cure her husband. She dies in the carriage on her way to meet the shaman, a death instigated by the family patriarch. In the film's terms, this is punishment for her transgressive behavior.[26]

If Hindi film offers mainly moments of "punitive destiny" meted out to the women characters, where do we look for transgressive behavior, for narratives that plot the changes that have overtaken real women's lives and histories? *Sahib Bibi aur Ghulam*, in fact, shares certain biographical similarities with Meena Kumari's real life that became public after her death. She had a difficult relationship with her husband, and she was, in fact, melancholic, as were the characters she portrayed.

According to Dyer, the star persona, "across and between individual texts, can . . . work against the grain of negative stereotype," and star performance can militate "against the smooth passage of ideology."[27] Thus in *Sahib Bibi aur Ghulam*, Meena Kumari's drinking *with* her husband is projected as drinking *for* her husband. But the film reveals one of those moments of excess, as Pam Cook puts it, when the star's personal life story intervenes to further charge the dramatic filmic moment. Meena Kumari, estranged from her husband for fifteen years, was known to be an alcoholic, living a lonely life similar to the one she enacts in *Sahib Bibi aur Ghulam*. Her private life was devoted to writing, poetry, and the search for a primal kind of love that she stumbles around to find in *Sahib Bibi aur Ghulam*.

What do we make of the star's life?[28] Among the constituting elements of the Hindi film industry, the single most dominant group, the films stars, have a powerful grip on peoples' imagination, and narratives about film stars' lives occupy film magazines and film journalism—virtually an ancillary industry. These "star texts," supposedly based on rumor and scurrilous reporting, are marked by fascination with and admiration for the lives of the rich and famous. Female stars' lives are embedded in public discourses on love, romance, marriage, and sexuality—the traditional technologies of gender construction in Hindi cinema. But in this case the narratives' origins are different, arising from a social text rather than a masculinized imagination; they deal with "real" women's lives. The star text discourse and its narrativization style are strongly inflected by the historical moment of its publication.

Furthermore, other texts—the extra-text about the stars' lives—are sometimes parallel to or at an angle from the film narratives. Film texts can reflect or refract star biographies. The play between the film and extra-text heightens tension and dramatic potential, expanding the possibilities of reading multiple meanings in the interchange between the two that the audience reads simultaneously. In this context Hindi film culture is a continuous film text, which includes not just the film's narrative but also adjoining discourses by film critics, journalists, academics, and, most important, popular film and gossip magazines. Following the lives of the stars' offscreen lives provides another opportunity for politically reading the interstice between the film and the social.

Film/Star Text: Reading Social Change

We rely today on films to speak social history. But when the film texts are more or less formulaic, the sources and archival records must expand to include the social text beyond the film. Read against and parallel to films, star texts offer a wealth of information about cultural politics, particularly about a particular period—in this case, India's postindependence years. This methodological innovation responds to the exigency of the situation—the emptiness of official archives—and draws upon the domain of the popular to read the popular.

The construction of female stars in popular discourse intersects many issues the films raise: femininity, romance, marriage, sexuality, love—and women as subjects. Rachel Dwyer's description of Indian film magazines and close textual analysis of *Stardust*, the most popular one, points to their use by readers not as escapism or emulation, but as "ways of dealing with one's everyday life," a means to understanding the role of the individual, the family, the significance of the body, and the nature of consumer society.[29]

Print media purports to reveal the truth about the lives of the stars, and it is shaped by its own conventions and suffers particular constraints. By comparing the codes that operate in different discourses—in the films themselves and the genre of film reporting, which explores the topography of star lives—differences are revealed in their generic conventions. The parameters of the discursive practices in films and film magazines, what is included or excluded, and how the same themes are treated or inflected across discourses, change over time in response to other social and political influences. Thus, in the case of cinema, the women's movement of the late 1970s indubitably affected the discourse of both film and film journalism, although it penetrated extant discourses in different ways.

Two immensely popular female stars of Hindi cinema are Meena Kumari (fl. 1947–1972) and Dimple Kapadia (fl. 1973–). Taken together, their careers span the fifty years since independence. In reconstructing the offscreen lives and careers of these two women who have excelled in performances portraying "women's issues," I analyze their films and their lives as depicted in newspapers and film magazines. Both women have struggled against a patriarchal system within and outside the film industry—that is, in their public and personal lives—and public perception of them varies sharply. The point is not so much to compare their offscreen lives, but rather the narrative discourse shaping the life stories of two women working during the early and late periods following independence. By scrutinizing the language—what is and is not articulated—it is possible to discern the manner in which the discourse on "women" is ordered, framed, and focused for us. A notable change in this discourse enables plotting the history of social change in women's lives.[30]

The euphonious obituaries for Meena Kumari compared the melancholic "tragedienne queen" she enacted in films to her own life. That life was characterized by extended bouts with depression, a sense of disenchantment that reverberated in the Urdu poetry (nazm) that she wrote, and her early death due to alcoholism and cirrhosis of the liver. It is worth noting how the public narrative about Meena Kumari's life obfuscated these basic facts. Like many other actresses of her time, Meena Kumari's origins were shrouded in secrecy with insinuations about her links with an old, disreputable courtesan culture—considered by some to be the repository of a tradition of song, dance, theater, poetry, and the arts and letters. Her mother, Iqbal Begum, a stage actress and dancer, had a fledgling career in the film industry and Meena Kumari (originally Mahazabeen) began her film career as the child-artist Baby Meena. Her husband Kamal Amrohi, the writer-director who directed and produced *Pakeezah* (Pure Heart, 1971), her last and enormously successful film, was only one of the men with whom she shared a very troubled relationship. Publicized as a film made over a period of twenty years (its production was interrupted by their estrangement), *Pakeezah* was released after Meena Kumari's death. As many have speculated, that perhaps was part of the reason for its success.

The narratives about the last few years of Meena Kumari's life and the circumstances under which the "tragedy queen" died are mixed with an unmistakable tinge of melodrama: she was alone and impecunious at the time of her death and her poems reflect her loss of will to live. She lacked worldly wisdom and was inept, even indifferent, to money matters. In her will she bequeathed her property to her siblings and to charitable institutions without certifying it through proper court procedures. As a result, her estranged husband inherited a sizable amount of her property, her manager seems to have siphoned much of it off for himself, and the state took almost half of her assets for tax arrears. For her labor in Kamal Amrohi's *Pakeezah*, her grand finale, she had asked as payment one guinea—a token of her husband's good will—which suggests the hopeless romantic that she was until the end. She bequeathed her diaries and poems to the writer-director Gulzaar, a trusted friend and perhaps once a lover.

Meena Kumari's irrepressible charisma endeared her to audiences. As one journalist wrote, it was "her own personality that carried the impress of the culture and sophistication of Lucknow, the seat of the post-Mughal Muslim culture. Her studied reserve, cultivated smile, dignified mannerism, chaste diction, taste for poetry, polished and impeccable conversation and, finally, a golden voice that was a perfect combination of throatiness and nasalness."[31] Her literary pursuits "and claims to intellectualism," which the same journalist discounts, created an association between her and films based on literary works. Expectations that these films would benefit from her presence were never disappointed: Meena Kumari appeared to closely identify with the characters she played. This lent her portrayals an intensity that led the press to tirelessly draw parallels between her life and the roles she performed.

Meena Kumari became the site where fact and fiction ironically coalesced. The extra-textual accounts, as though observing an unwritten code, limit themselves carefully to elliptical allusion to her life, which seems to get more focused upon in her films. We never really read *about* her life—only about the impenetrable grief, turbulence, and pain she suffered. References to real events in her life appear unspeakable, unmentionable. What newspapers repeatedly discuss are the characters she played in her landmark films: *Daaera* (The Circle, 1953), *Sahib Bibi aur Ghulam* (The Lord, His Wife and the Slave 1962), and *Pakeezah* (Pure Heart, 1971), in which she enacted women "belonging to three different settings at three different times. Yet, they are united in their ultimate response to life—the voluntary option to self-mortification, self-punishment and self-destruction, *a characteristic of the masochism of the Indian female* [emphasis mine]."[32] The tacit understanding between readers, journalists, the film industry, and film viewers is that Meena

Kumari was not "acting out" a role, but "living her life" on the silver screen. This suffused her films with an extra edge of "realism." Viewers had the pleasure of seeing her on screen, knowing how the film text spilled over into the extra-text, the star text.

A documentary film made ten years after her death, Meena Kumari ki Amar Kahani (The Unforgettable Story of Meena Kumari, 1979) by Sohrab Modi, was meant to chronicle, commemorate and celebrate her work: seventy-seven films over a period of twenty-five years, not including her performances as a child artist.[33] Yet the documentary had to grapple with an effort to keep her "scandalous" life out of her work. In a move that is reminiscent of the print media's simultaneous obsession with and obfuscation of her life, the documentary pastes together a collage of her films to ignore scandals and to sanitize that life, in an effort to monumentalize her contribution to the annals of Hindi cinema.

In fact the public narrative of "the tragedienne" was necessary to make the unmentionable, unspeakable "scandals" in Meena Kumari's life invisible to audiences and fans. That narrative provided a convenient spin of self-inflicted torment and sadness on the life story of a woman who was extraordinarily intelligent, independent, and unconventional for her times. This melodramatic narrative also refused to commend her for her own quiet assaults on a patriarchal order. It insisted on reading her life in terms of a suffering, tragic victim, full of the "self-destruction characteristic of the masochism of the Indian female," as the journalist quoted above wrote in her obituary. This may have been part of Meena Kumari's self-perception as well. Such a conflation of self with the tragic role indicates the power of discourse—the technology of gender—that shapes consciousness and knowledge about experience.

Dimple Kapadia arrived on the film scene in 1973, a year after Meena Kumari unexpectedly died at age forty. The timing creates an interesting divide between two film stars whose lives and careers in significant ways took very different turns. In these two time spans within the fifty years following independence, the technologies of gender were gradually bent, reshaped, and reconfigured in the domain of star text discourse. The two women—in a sense like mother and daughter—belong to different generations. The discourses surrounding their lives operate as a measure of the social change separating their life histories.

Dimple Kapadia's trajectory is not only different from Meena Kumari's; it is in fact different from that of any female Hindi film star. Introduced to the film world at age fifteen as a protégé of Raj Kapoor, the grand master of the industry, Kapadia's debut film *Bobby* (1973) was a runaway success at the box office. The young starlet's appearance in a teenage love story launched it as a cult-film classic. It spawned an entire line of products, from motorcycles to accessories like sunglasses, handbags, and hair clips, all bearing the film's name. At the time, this was an extraordinary phenomenon.

But Kapadia's success as a star was truncated by an early marriage to superstar Rajesh Khanna, a man twice her age who forbade her from working in the industry. Without understanding what her heady success really meant, the idea of being proposed to by the nation's foremost superstar, she later recalled, was an even headier experience. After a courtship that lasted a week, she married, quit working in films, and by the end of three years had two daughters. Rajesh Khanna's career declined rapidly and reports of trouble in this "dream marriage," and subsequent cover-ups, appeared in the press. Nine years later, in 1982, Dimple Khanna, as she was now known, walked out of the marriage and returned to her parents' home with her two daughters. Eleven years after her debut, she returned to make a comeback film as Dimple Kapadia, remembered now as the "Bobby girl."

The return was not easy, and as the print media reports it, Kapadia fought a hard struggle. She desired to be thought of not as a "glamour girl," but a serious actress. Here the contours of Kapadia's life narrative—in sharp contrast to Meena Kumari's heyday—reflect the social changes that made a new kind of public discourse possible. Kapadia spoke out against her years of "incarceration" within marriage, her complete lack of self-esteem, and her sense of the terrible loss of the best years of her life. She was frank about how she had children thoughtlessly when she was a child herself, how her traumatic marriage placed an emotional strain on her parents, and how hard it was to walk out with two children and no money of her own.

She, too, told a complete victim narrative, but with a difference: She was a victim with tremendous grit and staying power, the ability to fight and win. She went back to an industry she had left when she was too young to understand its ways. It was a place where her ex-husband still had considerable clout, making prospective employers hesitant to hire her. She was emotionally vulnerable and faced constant comparison to her days as a starlet. She also contended with the "bad publicity" of being a mother of two trying to regain her stardom in an industry where such women are considered over the hill.

But Kapadia turned every disadvantage to her advantage. Speaking candidly to the press, she and the reporters plotted her life's narrative from the innocent teenager snared into an impossible marriage to the emergence of a mature "woman with experience." After the initial failure of a few films—*Zakhmee Sher* (The Wounded Lion, 1984) and *Jaanbaaz* (Gambling with Life, 1986)—Kapadia was back, fighting her way to the top, preferring to perform roles she described as serious and exacting rather than flippant and unchallenging. Film scripts began to be written around her, paralleling her life story. She and her directors openly publicized her roles as ones where she drew from the well of her own experience. *Aitbaar* (Faith, 1985), *Kaash* (If Only, 1987), and *Dhrishti* (Sight, 1990) brought her acclaim. Within five years, at age thirty, she received the Best Actress award for several of these performances.

In comparing the account of Meena Kumari to that of Dimple Kapadia, there is a discernable reversal in the style of journalistic reporting on women film stars. Kapadia's life was made the master text, the master narrative against which the films were read. In the earlier period, the press had merely alluded to Meena Kumari's life in relation to her film performances. In Kapadia's life, gone are the references to female masochism—even if the films Kapadia acted in repeat the narrative of the victim over and over again. In the clamor that arose from the press (although it should be noted that the regional, vernacular, and English press were not unanimous on this), Kapadia was hailed as the brave new, strong, seasoned, and "experienced" woman.

If there is a woman-as-victim aspect to Kapadia's narrative, she significantly undercut it by her own candid and consistent accounts of her life story that made it more than just a publicity gimmick or marketing strategy. The stories about her have no tragic undertones. Rather, they depict a woman with agency, making active choices and admitting faults and failings. She shows a readiness to learn, move on, and get ahead. She has no guilty secrets about the men in her life, past or present. She openly confesses having a relationship with a married man and working through the trauma it causes her children. She discusses a model of motherhood based on openness and "friendship" rather than hierarchy and authority. In the early 1990s, Kapadia even made public appearances as the ex-star Rajesh Khanna's wife during his election campaigns for Parliament. In short, in public discourse the victim searching for pity slipped away, replaced by a figure eliciting admiration. What intervened in the years between Meena Kumari and Dimple Kapadia was a new wave of the women's movement, a feminist consciousness with its own ideas about romantic love and agency. Though the reach of this new discourse was uneven, it entered crucial places in the public domain, especially the media—a site and agent for its dissemination. The "women's question" was reframed to interrogate patriarchal privilege and tyranny. Women's oppression was no longer a "characteristic of the masochism of the Indian female." Like Kapadia, women could choose to appropriate the discourse of feminism to represent themselves—a choice unavailable to Meena Kumari. She had to enclose her life in a shroud of secrecy and maintain the moral high ground, at the cost of terrible self-repression, turbulence, and grief.

Newspapers by no means construct entirely truthful accounts about stars. But it is not that veracity in question here; rather, it is how newspapers promote a discourse with sharp ideological underpinnings. Both film stars were highly successful in the industry, and singled out for screen performances portraying women's "reality." Screenplays and newspapers actively drew on their personal stories of an embattled life in patriarchal culture. The interpolation of a new star discourse, arising from the groundswell of the women's movement, indicates a slow but sure-footed change that is challenging, bending, and repositioning the old *laxman rekha*.

In her analysis of film magazines Dwyer rather pessimistically concludes that the discourse rejects feminism—despite the array of tabooed issues they air (divorce, the singles' sexual market, female star careers after marriage, homosexuality, and so forth).[34] I argue instead that the women's movement has a presence in the lives of "real" women, shaping "real" histories. When feminism creeps into the discursive texts narrating film stars' lives—apparent when we take a longer view—it reanimates the contested sexual/moral economy discourse in the public sphere.

What will happen to feminist cultural representation in popular discourse such as film and journalism is still uncertain, tentative, and very contentious. As screenwriter Javed Akhtar said, "Everyone in the film industry knows the image of the Indian woman is to change, but as to what the new image is going to be there is complete confusion."[35]

Chapter 5   The Sexed Body

DURING THE 1970s, Hindi films featuring women as central protagonists began to show evidence of change. These changes, initially im-
perceptible and trivial, gradually become perceptible in following
decades. Yet specific commercial films incorporating radical change nevertheless do so within an elaborate conservative scheme that clouds and
contains that radical moment.

Filmic Love

The introduction of Eastman Color in the early 1960s led to abandoning studios in favor of the open vistas of outdoor locations, especially
for romantic sequences and their critical incumbent, "song pic-
turization," as it is known in the film industry.[1] Films made under these
circumstances typically track the movement of a young cosmopolitan
man and woman traveling to an idyllic holiday resort where they meet
by chance, fall in love, and, after a few complications and reversals, become a couple. These films flaunt signs of modernity overtaking the
nation at the time: mobility, travel, and tourism worked to erase regional
and ethnic boundaries by allowing young people to break away from
traditional parochial bonds. Geographically bound regional communities began to dissolve into an expanded social space, the nation.[2] This

reified concept extends to picturesque far-flung places, included as part of one's own—albeit imagined—community.

Admittedly, the new cosmopolitanism in these films is limited: the protagonists are always Hindu, often upper-class (and, by implication, upper-caste), and radical action is at best conceived of in terms of violating class boundaries within heterosexual romance. Caste and religious community boundaries are never transgressed.[3] If signs of caste and religious difference are invoked at all, it is by casting a minority community member as the protagonist's faithful friend or loyal servant. Away from the protagonist's immediate community, family, and the reality of urban everyday living, the films enable the heterosexual romance by using an "emptied" social space against scenic sites in anonymous locations.

Visually, the exotic landscapes provide the untraveled spectator with the pleasures of unseen places.[4] Screen romance is germane to this fantasy world, where the everyday humdrum life vanishes. Against snow-capped mountains, panoramic shots of colorful valleys and expanses of blue skies, viewers follow the young couple's romance, their temporary separation due to a complication, and final union in the denouement. This is the formulaic strategy of innumerable films, memorable for the pleasures they provide through the accompanying music and lyrics. But what of the act of love? There has been a long and puzzling silence about this. Its absence in Hindi films calls for understanding the elaborate conventions Hindi cinema uses to represent sexual love.

The song and dance sequences stand in for sex scenes.[5] The focus is particularly on the heroine, the fetishized female sexualized through close attention to her costumes, graceful body movements, and carefully angled shots that heighten scopic pleasure. Whether the heroines lie languorously across the screen, roll down hilly slopes, or frolic playfully with the hero, they feign an unawareness of their sexualized bodies and the camera's voyeuristic gaze.

This holds for the generation of actresses successful between the 1950s and the 1970s, from Nargis, Madhubala, Waheeda Rehman, and Vyjayanthimala to Asha Parekh. In the song and dance numbers the camerawork and editing emphasize facial expressions in close-ups and eyeline matches, which convey the ecstasy of being in love. Perhaps this feature of Hindi cinema led one fan to comment nostalgically about

18. Vandana stretches languorously across the screen. *Aradhana* (Prayer), Shakti Samanta, 1969.

her fondness for romance in these films: "*Aankhon-aankhon mein he pyaar ho jaata tha* (Love—it was all said [in looks exchanged] through the eyes)." She regretted this loss in contemporary films which, according to her, displace romance with half-clad heroines.[6] The combination of music, poetic lyrics, and elegant sexual undertones evoke sensuality in the song and dance sequences. The love songs express intense emotions and promise eternal unwavering passion, always straining against overt sexual desire.

Victims to Vigilantes

Strongly influenced by Victorian principles, sex as an aspect of heterosexual love was broached gingerly in the popular cinema of the 1970s. Shakti Samanta's *Aradhana* (Prayer, 1969), faithful to the maternal melodrama tradition, is a narrative of excess: a woman's acute suffering, sacrifice, and a favored theme in Hindi cinema: her intense love for her son. An enormously successful film, *Aradhana* depicts a woman's youthful passion turning into lifelong trial and tribulation. The film begins with trenchant arguments in court where the female protagonist,

Vandana (Sharmila Tagore), is on trial. As the credits end, we hear the prosecutor's concluding statements. "Your honor," he says, "in the eyes of the law, there is nothing more grave than the murder of a human being. And when the one who gives birth to human beings, a woman, murders a man, the crime becomes even more heinous. I therefore plead with the court that the defendant not be spared because she is a woman. She should be punished severely so that people learn from this precedent and justice is served." As Vandana, dressed widow-like in austere white clothes, is incarcerated, the camera tilts up to the barred window, and in a protracted flashback, the story unfolds.

A young Vandana returns from college to live with her widowed father and falls in love with airforce pilot Arun (Rajesh Khanna), who dies just before they are to marry. Vandana discovers she is pregnant, suffers rejection from Arun's family, endures her father's death, and after further misadventures gives up her son to a childless couple, Ram Prasad and Anita. She gains employment as the boy's governess, but her happy years as a surrogate mother end abruptly when Anita's brother visits. He propositions Vandana but is killed accidentally in a scuffle with her and her son, Suraj, who intervenes to help her. To protect Suraj, Vandana assumes full responsibility for the death, and after twelve years of incarceration she is released from prison. Several coincidences later she meets the adult Suraj (also played by Rajesh Khanna) now an air force pilot. The film is unusually suggestive about how a son displaces a husband in a woman's life by having the same actor play both the lover and the son.[7] A war breaks out and Suraj is wounded in action, but during his convalescence, in the final denouement, he discovers Vandana's identity. To everyone's surprise, in the last scene he introduces Vandana as his mother and declares her the corecipient of his gallantry award.

In keeping with the demands of evolving genres, there is something new in the film despite its repetition of familiar themes. Its portrait of a suffering woman derives from the Indo-Anglian literary tradition developed in the shadow of Orientalist canons and Victorian norms.[8] Sexual restraint is intrinsic to this representation. While popular films absorbed principles of female chastity, *Aradhana* was the first to explicitly associate romantic love with sexual desire. Yet harking back to chastity principles, it also shows the ruinous consequences of extramarital sex for women.

Aradhana breaks with the taboo on explicit sex scenes in Hindi cinema, where song and dance sequences function as elaborate substitutes.[9] In keeping with the location shooting trend where heroines stretch languorously across the landscape as if innocent of the camera's gaze and their own sexualized bodies, *Aradhana's* opening depicts the "wonders of falling in love." Yet it somewhat daringly disrupts the sexual sublimation during the couple's courtship. Caught one day in an unexpected downpour, Vandana and Arun take shelter in a motel. Vandana changes out of her drenched clothes and swathes herself in a blanket.

As the camera cuts between Arun's gaze, fixed on Vandana, and the object of his gaze, the two circle the fire in the middle of the room, which within the mise-en-scène excessively signifies their passion (and perhaps a mock Hindu wedding). Shot against the silhouette of a couple in the neighboring room (divided from theirs by an opaque glass door) where the man is serenading his lover, Vandana and Arun, in an unusual moment for Hindi cinema, grapple with the intensity of their sexual desire. At the end of the famous *roop tera mastana* (you are irresistible) number Vandana steps forward, unbuttons Arun's shirt, and the camera averts its gaze, cutting to the glowing fire. The next shot is of a sunrise. The sequence is memorable for its elegance, skillfully skirting the censor board and Hindi cinema's own curious prudery on matters of sexual intimacy—incessantly spoken of (or sung about) but never "shown."

Yet the entire film exhibits the cunning of the maternal melodrama which operates on two levels—both condemning woman's victimization and punishing her for a reckless moment of sexual passion for which men get off scot-free.[10] Bereft of a man's protection when her lover dies, Vandana distances herself from her son to avoid the ignominy of unwed motherhood, hands over her rights and recognition as a biological mother, and, worst of all, becomes easy prey to strange men.[11] Though she wards off an imminent rape, its upshot—the death of her rapist—drives the narrative forward. Through this, and her voluntary incarceration to protect her son, her severance from him is complete. Typical of the genre of melodrama there is "a constant struggle for gratification and equally constant blockages to its attainment. [The] narratives are driven by one crisis after another, crises involving severed family ties, separation and loss. . . . Seduction, betrayal, abandonment, extortion, murder, suicide, revenge, jealousy. . . . are . . . the familiar terrain of melodrama. The victims are most often females threatened in their sexuality, their property, their very identity."[12]

Despite the film's powerful rendition, it betrays a disconcertingly conservative strain. At the end of the film, instead of the cathartic trial scene that rehabilitates the mother, we get this exaltation by the state as the son shares his success with his mother, or at least deflects his glory onto her. This resonates with several other films—from *Mother India* in 1957 to *Deewar* in 1975—which privilege an intense mother-son relationship. These films underscore the theme of a suffering mother finally apotheosized by the state.[13] This veneration reinforces suffering as a value in itself, monumentalizing it rather than resisting its patriarchal underpinnings. The suffering woman is held up as a model of womanhood—idealized, honored, and decorated. In a fantastic and wholly fabricated gesture, the films have the son/state recognize the mother's martyrdom, making her sacrifices "worth it."

This move, particular to Hindi cinema, is distinct from the 1930s Hollywood version of such narratives, which show the miraculous rise of women to power, fame, and success and returning on equal footing to the society that once rejected them. In turn, the 1930s Hollywood films reverse the European maternal melodrama in which the outcast mother sinks into anonymity and oblivion.[14] Further studies in melodrama will profit from historically specific analyses of cross-cultural deployments of this genre. So far, for example, cross-cultural comparisons between Euro-American and Chinese melodrama—defined in terms of its bourgeois origins—interrogate its relation to subjectivity and place in a putative "classless" China.[15] Certain cross-national trends in melodrama within Asian cultures are also worth noting; these trends reveal the efficacy of melodrama in enacting fundamental social conflicts by employing common tropes.

Family conflicts, central in Asian cinema, figuratively explore the nation's specific politico-historical experiences that are cast in common cultural antinomies of east versus west and tradition versus modern—

all undergirding one central conflict between the community and the individual.[16] Within the family, narratives privilege women in wife-lover and mother-figure roles, paying particular attention to mother-son relationships. In Asian cinema mother figures bear positive and negative valences: Japan's sacrificial mothers (*haha mono* films) appear in the 1940s and 1950s, the heyday of Japanese melodrama; during the 1960s the mother became the efficient home manager, and she morphed into the tyrannical mother-in-law figure by the 1970s.[17] In popular family drama produced in the 1980s by "fifth-generation" Chinese directors, mothers (and mothers-in-law) are pitted against daughters and daughters-in-law in contests over the son or husband.[18] To avoid conflating these figures across all Asian cultures, narrative exegesis must scrupulously attend to their specific historical, political, and cultural inscriptions—which in the case of China, Japan, and India range from varying degrees of Chinese Communism, Japanese capitalism, and Indian bourgeois democracy.

Whatever the attributes of the mother, in Asian melodrama individual desire is inevitably in conflict with the social (state institutions in China, and moral/cultural codes in India and Japan)—as opposed to "existential conditions" beyond human control in Euro-American melodrama. In Asian melodrama desire is dealt with safely when put in terms of female romantic love.[19] Thus in *Aradhana*, Vandana's sexual affair frames her as a desiring subject who is punished, but her sacrifice and atonement as a mother are honored by the state. Here melodrama, with its "poetics of hyperbole," emotional intensity, excesses and extremes, illuminates "priorities of valuation" and articulates what cannot be said—"demands inadmissible in the codes of social, psychological, or political discourse."[20] Thus in this moment of Indian social history, victim-woman melodrama is the patriarchal national-popular's acknowledgment of sexual difference, women's subjectivity, and compensatory validation for her subjugation.

Aradhana spawned a virtual woman-victim subgenre in the early 1970s. *Kati Patang* (Falling Kite, 1970), *Amar Prem* (Eternal Love, 1971), and *Julie* (1975) are among the most popular. The narratives recuperate all kinds of "fallen women," deifying them and their suffering, and setting them up as objects of reverence. While representing women as abject but idolized victims *Aradhana*-style became the dominant mode of such women's films, a decade later another subgenre replaced them, that of the avenging heroine.

During the 1970s, however, another female protagonist prototype was discovered: the garrulous "tomboy," lacking in "feminine" grace until she falls in love with a man and becomes a woman. Despite her latter-day conversion, this figure offered viewers a welcome respite from the pitiful woman-victim sagas. The tomboy image—albeit in a limited way—was tremendously promising in terms of subverting traditional gendered identities. In several films women appear as autonomous, independent-minded, and spirited characters—but somehow they never develop beyond fledgling roles. Moreover, discovery by the male protagonist completes her rights of passage to womanhood, with its accompanying feminine grace and charm. Examples of this subgenre include Jaya Bahaduri as a prankster in *Guddi* (Doll, 1971), as the self-employed street vendor in *Zanjeer* (Chain, 1973), and Hema Malini as a horse carriage driver in *Sholay* (Embers, 1975).

The *Aradhana*-style abject woman victim was contested by alternative representations, which were popular in the early 1970s, epitomized by Ramesh Sippy's *Seeta aur Geeta* (Seeta and Geeta, 1972).[21] *Seeta aur Geeta* is unique in its combination of comedy, stunts, and pleasurable revenge fantasies, which anticipate the 1980s' female avenger films—a response to the public discourse on women's issues.[22]

The film is a robust comedy-cum-action film about twin sisters separated at birth and subsequently by their class location, which casts them as polar opposites: Seeta is quiet, demure, and repressed, while Geeta is loquacious, tough, and street-smart. Their class difference is marked in their persona: Geeta's low-class status allows her free mobility beyond the home, while Seeta's bourgeois upbringing confines her within an isolated domestic space. However, the distinction between the poor rich girl and the happy poor girl—a classic antonym played out in Hindi films—is embellished to combine the classic features of class and gender. Seeta's repressed upper-class persona and Geeta's vaudevillian free spirit become the narrative alibi for confusion, mayhem, and levity. Geeta's class location is celebrated in the film: her exposure to the public world toughens her to deal with its vagaries and also to challenge the rules of bourgeois domestic oppression.

The prologue depicts a brief event: a well-to-do couple traveling on the highway takes refuge in a small village due to inclement weather. The young woman, going into labor, receives assistance from a childless gypsy couple. After the baby is delivered, the departing father, grateful for the help, wistfully announces that had they had twins they would have gifted one to the childless couple. As the car pulls away the gypsy woman reveals a baby girl she had hidden: the mother had in fact given birth to twins. Admonished by her husband for depriving the child of life's creature comforts, she pledges to make good this lack by loving her more than "people raised in palaces."

The opening credit roll ends with the prologue, and the main narrative of the film begins by revealing an exhausted Seeta (Hema Malini), mopping the floors of a large wealthy house. On the wall hangs the picture of her deceased parents, the rich couple from the prologue. We soon learn that Seeta, their grown-up daughter and heiress, was orphaned at a young age and lives with her loving but helpless grandmother, wicked aunt (*chaachi*, father's younger brother's wife), the aunt's dominated husband (*chaacha*, uncle), their spoiled college-student daughter, and the aunt's villainous brother, Ranjit. Seeta's *chaacha*, her legal guardian until she gets married, cannot keep his wife from stealing Seeta's money, which is delivered every month by the family lawyer. The aunt uses Seeta, a pitiable defenseless victim, as a slave in her own home. Her only allies are her uncle and her grandmother.

The twin, Geeta (Hema Malini again, performing a double role) has grown up in a rough street life environment and lives with her loving mother, the now aged gypsy woman from the prologue. Geeta is the family breadwinner, a talented street performer who can sing, juggle, and walk tightropes. She splits the proceeds from the street show with her male coworker, Raka, and their child assistant, both members of her gypsy community. Geeta is the antithesis of Seeta: gregarious, outgoing, and clever.

The complication begins when Seeta and Geeta, unaware of each other's existence, exchange each other's life situation through a chain of hilarious accidents. Seeta escapes her abusive family to land in the gypsy community, experiences a family's affection for the first time and develops a romantic interest in Geeta's work partner, Raka. Geeta, in turn, ends up in Seeta's well-to-do household. It is here that the revenge story plays out. Strong, bold, and accustomed to the rigors of street life, Geeta transforms the once-terrorizing household into a terrorized one. She falls in love with Ravi, a doctor, who proposes to her thinking she is Seeta. In the new, reversed situations of both sisters, friends and family are flummoxed by the change in their personalities.

Ranjit, the aunt's villainous brother, is incensed when Geeta resists his physical abuse. Then Ranjit spots Seeta in the bazaar and later overhears Geeta repenting for being an impostor. With an eye on Seeta's inheritance, Ranjit arranges to kidnap her. Meanwhile, Geeta's marriage with Ravi is finalized, and she vacillates between revealing her identity or marrying under false pretenses. On the wedding day a drunken Geeta lurches in, dressed in revealing clothes and boasting about her fondness for alcohol in a song-dance number.

This is Geeta's way of breaking off her relationship to avoid marrying under false pretenses. But the pretense is shattered anyway when her former colleague Raka and her gypsy mother arrive on the scene. Accusations from Ranjit and Raka mount against Geeta: that she masqueraded as Seeta to extract the family inheritance, and that she is in fact an ordinary street performer. Geeta embraces her mother, confesses her identity, and turns to explain herself to her fiancé, Ravi, who, shocked and disgusted, turns his back on her. The police arrive and place Geeta under arrest.

Geeta's overwrought mother recognizes Seeta's dead parents' photograph hanging on the wall and confesses to Raka that Geeta is Seeta's twin, whom she had once stolen. But the narrative denouement is deferred by another complication: the discovery that Ranjit has taken Seeta hostage. Raka rescues Geeta from the police and, several hilarious but volatile incidents later, Geeta rescues her sister Seeta, gets rid of the bad guys, and all is well that ends well.

The film takes its cue from *Ram aur Shyam* (Ram and Shyam, 1967), which plays out a similar plot of twin brothers separated at birth (with Dilip Kumar taking the double role). *Ram aur Shyam* explores two male archetypes: the effeminate, shy, and introverted Ram, who grows up in a palatial feudal home under the aegis of his cruel uncle, and his twin brother Shyam a robust and extroverted village peasant. A similar mixup of identities and a rich/poor inversion makes for entertaining comedy. Fashioned after *The Prince and the Pauper* paradigm, the end celebrates the victory of the good and weak over evil, powerful forces that universally mark popular culture.

But with a shift in the protagonist's gender, the entire semiological balance of the film entails a critical transformation, evoking an entirely different array of issues in the social text. In the world of commercial Hindi cinema, where financial success supposedly relies on formulaic narratives, displacing the male lead with a female one spawns a whole new set of meanings. Geeta, for instance, punishes Seeta's tormenters for the abuse inflicted on both sisters. Playing off polar masculine archetypes, the film foregrounds an altogether different dimension. These new meanings derive from challenging patriarchal control and burdensome domestic work.[23] Seeta's position, rather ominously, resonates with the bourgeois housewife's precarious and conditional access to family wealth. Losing tolerance for domestic oppression costs her total dispossession.

As in many comedies, a long string of situational gags and inversion of traditional gender relations shape the film's comic moments and affect complications. Noël Carroll's elaborate "sight gag" taxonomy underscores the importance of multiple interpretations derived from visual incongruity. As such, Carroll makes a case for films reconstituting and reinterpreting reality, rather than slavishly reproducing or recording it.[24] The comedic aspect enables possibilities, such as the heroic stunts Geeta pulls off, dodging the incompetent police who try to arrest her. Equally humorous are the deliberate misunderstandings. When Seeta's uncle calls the police to report her as a runaway, the aunt points a forefinger to her temple, prompting him to proffer the girl's mental instability as reason for her flight.

By making Seeta's craziness the alibi for her walking out, the aunt keeps Seeta's mistreatment a well-guarded family secret. But when they find Geeta instead at the police station her behavior does in fact tally up as Seeta having "gone cuckoo": a worn-out catatonic cop sits in a ruined office, and in response to the aunt's query about Seeta's whereabouts, he points toward the ceiling. The camera tilts up to reveal Geeta straddling the ceiling fan. Much to the audience's satisfaction, the family's effort to keep up the charade of concern requires that they make the police believe she is crazy. The pleasure lies in watching Seeta/Geeta's alleged "madness" and the ensuing misunderstanding when she

19. Seeta straddles the fan. *Seeta aur Geeta* (Seeta and Geeta), Ramesh Sippy, 1972.

puts both the family and the police in their place. Once Geeta lays down her terms, she reverses the domestic tyranny by intimidating the aunt, her daughter, and villainous brother.

Spectatorial pleasure and humor lie in the knowledge the audience is privy to that the characters are not: the tyrannical family mistaking Geeta for the demure, suffering Seeta. But beneath the comic surface, Seeta's reality resonates with Indian women's loneliness in their in-laws' homes, a world of domestic work and sometimes physical abuse. Avoiding melodrama, the film to its credit picks a phantasmic scenario. Geeta's performance becomes a story of avenging the condition of all women—or at least offering pleasurable fantasies of revenge. In this it is a variant of other popular depictions of women in comedy—for instance, Lucille Ball in the *I Love Lucy* show, whose desire to escape domestic confinement converts her anger into humor. Patricia Mellencamp notes that "this desire is caricatured by her unrealistic dreams of instant stardom in the face of her narrative lack of talent: her wretched, off-key singing, her mugging facial exaggerations, and her out-of-step dancing. Her lack of talent is paradoxically both the source of audience pleasure and the narrative necessity for housewifery. . . . Situation comedy avoids the unpleasant effects of its own situation."[25]

Seeta aur Geeta also echoes familiar religio-mythical references. Geeta learns about the teachings of the holy book the *Gita* from her grandmother: a lie, it says, is justifiable if proffered in the service of people and to fight oppression. Geeta's masquerade, the grandmother reiterates, is justifiable because Geeta subverts the power balance and introduces a new just order in the household: the grandmother gains her rightful authority; the unkind aunt is put to work in the kitchen; and Ranjit, who habitually roughed up and even molested Seeta, is single-handedly beaten by Geeta, forced to defer to the elderly domestic servant, and put to work in the household's service. Servants and elders get their due respect while the parasites and bullies now serve them.

The suffering Vandana in *Aradhana* and Seeta in *Seeta aur Geeta* stand in contrast to Geeta, a powerful woman, the dispossessed "subaltern" figure, yet the ultimate avenging heroine liberating her hesitant, repressed upper-class sister. This tale resonates clearly with the epic *Ramayana*, in which Ravana kidnaps Seeta and Lord Rama's loyal follower, Hanuman, rescues her. There is one outstanding difference between the two: In the film, Seeta's sister is the one to stage the rescue. Even more interesting is the symbolic empowerment the narrative accords to the lower-class woman. The street-savvy Geeta's physical agility and prowess as a performer comes handy in rescuing Seeta, whose upper-class restraint prevents her from helping herself.

The climactic fight scene is enacted toward the end of all Hindi films, and depicts the classic showdown between good and evil. In *Seeta aur Geeta* the battle pits Geeta, Ravi, Seeta, and Raka against Ranjit and his hoodlums. Choreographed as comedic, Geeta handily defeats Ranjit's hoodlums, who hold Seeta in captivity. Tellingly, in the final showdown Ranjit is overcome not by Raka, as would be traditionally expected (two males fighting over the woman), but by Geeta. It is an interesting reversal of the conventional Indian feminist self-aggrandizing historical narrative, wherein the bourgeois woman "saves" lower-class women from social evils such as illiteracy, coercive reproductive control, and abusive marriages.[26] It is easy to appreciate the appeal of such a reversal, even as a symbolic gesture toward what contemporary discourse might term "political correctness."

Ella Shohat and Robert Stam discuss the "carnival-like tradition" as "overturning good order and respectable ethics," an aesthetic of resistance to unity and harmony favoring asymmetry, heterogeneity, embracing the grotesque, and standing in for the anticanonical, the counterhegemonic.[27] Although they discuss this in the context of alternative cinema, they admit that "the appeal of mass media . . . derives partly from their capacity to relay, in however compromised a manner, the distant cultural memory (or the vague future hope) of an egalitarian carnival-like communitas."[28] Useful also in considering this effect in Hindi cinema is Rabelias' concept of a "laughing grammar," which is invoked as an "artistic language . . . liberated from the stifling norms of correctness and decorum."[29] Strains of this are visible from time to time in mainstream popular Hindi cinema. In *Seeta aur Geeta*, Geeta's stunts defy the laws of gravity and of spatial and temporal determinacy. Even as a successful trapeze artist, Geeta's physical prowess is scarcely credible: fencing, wrestling, and jumping down and then back up three flights of stairs in reverse motion all exemplify the "laughing grammar," the film's celebration of the carnivalesque, while adhering to popular Hindi cinema's traditional narrative structure. Such carnivalesque principles can go beyond inverting existing power relations, although Shohat and Stam note that "we need not scoff at 'mere' inversion. Oppressed people might have difficulty in imagining the exact contours of an alternative society . . . but they have no trouble at all imagining a reversal of the existing distribution of status and rewards within a 'counterfactual social order.'"[30]

The denouement of Hindi film, however, is of course never complete without the heterosexual couple's union marked by their proverbial ride into the sunset. In *Seeta aur Geeta*, Geeta resembles the bigendered positions available to heroines in Harlequin romances. According to Teresa L. Ebert,

> The romances conceal and narrativize the difficulties and precariousness inherent in the position of being constructed as what is *not*—not male, not having the phallus, not privileged— and effect a narrative resolution of contradictory gender identities, thereby suppressing the ideological incongruities that threaten patriarchal hegemony. Harlequin romances (as well as other romance narratives) represent this ideological recuperation in the form of a narrative dilemma: the heroine, the

subject of the text, is not sufficiently a woman; she has not fully
realized her sexuality, which in patriarchal ideology can only be
her heterosexuality and which is synonymous with her gender.[31]

Geeta's gendered female subject position is indeed recuperated at the
end of the film. However in her case it is *not* the errant heroine "not
yet a woman, . . . 'a child'," that is brought into line by a masterful, domi-
nating privileged, wealthy, and propertied" hero's "overpowering virility."[32] If anything, in the final comic gag the two new husbands—bashful
lovers—are "had" by the twin sisters, who enjoy confusing them by send-
ing them scurrying between bridal suites to claim their rightful wife.
All, of course, much to the delight of an equally confused audience.
Geeta's bigendered position is recuperated and confirmed in her heterosexuality, by demonstrating that she is after all entirely exchangeable with the passive, feminine Seeta; while Seeta is permitted to claim
a playful persona, in what viewers are left to speculate might be a new
beginning.

It is unfortunate that such creative, lively, satiric, and comedic representations of women of the kind seen in *Seeta aur Geeta* did not ultimately seem profitable to the Bombay film industry. Seduced by the rise
of superstar Amitabh Bachchan, whose success promoted a distinctive,
Bachchan-style "angry young man" persona, heterosexual romance in
film underwent significant attrition, leading to a steady eclipse of women's
roles. Outside the success of the Bachchan films, there were a few
woman-centered films—*Julie* (1975), *Jai Santoshi Maa* (Hail Mother
Santoshi, 1975), and *Noorie* (1979)—that did well at the box office.

Rape and the Rape Threat

It was not until the early 1980s that the ferment surrounding women's
issues and its unsettling impact on gender relations was featured in popular films. From this point, women were portrayed either as masculinized creatures or eroticized figures—sexual and violent, capable of
wielding guns and taking control. One film in particular marks the resurgence of this second wave of the women's movement, dormant since
the period before independence. During this phase women organized
spontaneously, rather than under men's tutelage. A "grassroots female
militancy" forced itself onto the national agenda.[33]

Two films in particular are worth examining. *Insaaf ka Taraazu* (The Scales of Justice, 1980) tackled the subject of rape, and *Teesri Manzil* (Third Floor, 1966), an extremely popular 1960s-style thriller film, ostensibly a murder mystery, staged rape more covertly. In the early 1980s women's groups all over India coalesced for the first time as a distinctive feminist voice and demanded changes in the laws dealing with rape, and this structures *Insaaf ka Tarazu's* narrative. *Insaaf ka Taraazu* arrived at the historical moment that the infamous Mathura rape case outraged women across the nation. In 1979 the Supreme Court overturned a High Court ruling and freed two police constables accused of raping Mathura, a minor, in police custody. Nationwide agitations by women's groups coalesced into demands to revisit the court's ruling and enact changes in the rape laws. In 1978, a Muslim woman, Rameeza Bee, was raped in police custody in Hyderabad and her husband, a rickshaw puller, was murdered for protesting this. In 1980, Maya Tyagi was raped in Baghpat, Haryana, then stripped naked and paraded through the streets by the police.[34]

The director of *Insaaf ka Taraazu*, B. R. Chopra, a reigning auteur in the film industry since the 1950s, has carved a special niche in Hindi cinema in his explorations of gender politics through the vicissitudes of heterosexual love. Chopra's films often trace the liminal social space women occupy, questioning permissible moral boundaries even as he carefully reinstates them. His other films that stand out in this respect are *Gumrah* (Deception, 1963), *Dhund* (Fog, 1973), and *Pati Patni aur Woh* (Husband, Wife and the Other, 1978). *Insaaf ka Taraazu*, arriving on the heels of the demand to reopen the Supreme Court's judgment in the Mathura trial, bears more than an incidental relation to the public discourse the verdict set off. Historically, the event marks the beginning of the reentry of a discourse on women's place in the private and public spheres framed in terms of women's *rights*—not reform, "uplift," or the need to nurture special "feminine" (read: Indian) virtues.

The nation was undergoing a long consciousness-raising process as women were challenging and rewriting discriminatory laws on domestic violence, rape, dowry, and the growing incidence of dowry deaths. Family courts, instituted solely to relieve conventional courts from the burden of domestic disputes, along with the soaring divorce rates, were testimony to the serious gender trouble stirred up by women's grassroots militancy. This ferment in gender relations features in popular films: women, albeit feminized and sexualized, were once revered for their suffering. As the decades go by, however, they retaliate with violence.

In *Insaaf ka Taraazu* the film's eponymous heroine, Bharati (Zeenat Aman), winner of the Miss India title, is an independent career woman, working as a model and making good money to support herself and her schoolgirl sister, Nita (Padmini Kolahpure) in an apartment in Bombay.[35] The film begins with Bharati winning the popular vote in a beauty contest. The man who awards her the highest score, Ramesh Gupta (Raj Babbar), receives the honor of placing the crown on her head.

Ramesh, a longstanding admirer of Bharati, uses his wealth to his advantage and makes seemingly casual efforts to be with her, while she, self-absorbed and preoccupied with her fiancé Ashok, obliges Ramesh in the routine fashion that a star obliges fans. Slighted by her lack of interest one day when he visits her, Ramesh barges into her room and, in a protracted sequence, attacks her, ties her down and repeatedly rapes her. Bharati falls unconscious, and somewhere toward the end of this sequence her sister Nita comes home, sees Ramesh on top of Bharati and flees the house, fearful and confused.

When Bharati reports the incident and presses charges, her lawyer warns that loopholes in the anti-rape laws make it virtually impossible to prove the rapist's guilt. In fact the defendant's lawyer easily reinterprets the sequence of events, casting severe doubts on her lack of consent—the critical issue in all rape litigation. Bharati loses the lawsuit even though her lawyer is a committed and competent woman, and despite the trial's widespread publicity. Shunned by advertising companies that can no longer afford to have her name associated with their products, and by her prospective in-laws, who cannot cope with the adverse publicity, Bharati leaves Bombay.

Dispirited and depressed, she relocates with her sister in Pune (a city close to Bombay) and takes up a low-paid job as a secretary in a store selling firearms. Meanwhile, Nita's job interview with a prestigious firm turns into a nightmare when the firm's proprietor—Ramesh again—traps her in a room and rapes her as well. Bharati responds by taking a gun from the store, following Ramesh and killing him at close range, in cold blood, and in full view of his colleagues.

Bharati is arrested and tried. She refuses to hire a lawyer, choosing instead to defend herself. The court fails to recognize her due to the transformation in her appearance. In an impassioned speech about the miscarriage of justice for women, she reminds the court that she is Bharati, the model who was once raped by Ramesh Gupta. The failure to punish her rapist then, she argues, had only abetted him in victimizing another woman. In a dramatic end to the court proceedings, the judge, impressed by Bharati's arguments, sets her free.

In *Insaaf ka Taraazu* the victim becomes vengeful and victorious not only against the man who victimizes her but against the entire misogynist juridical system. The film examines the ramifications of rape: the fact that it is nothing but an assertion of male aggression and power; that the rape gets rehearsed both literally and figuratively in a court trial meant to punish the rapist; that the rapist gets off due to lack of conclusive evidence; that the victim faces social ostracism along with acute depression and trauma in the aftermath; and that the crowning act of injustice is the court setting the rapist free. The film truly centers on the woman's narrative; the rapist's character is not elaborated on beyond the fact that he is a well-to-do, "normal," even pleasant person, someone whose violence leaves an unsuspecting Bharati and the audience shocked and dismayed.[36]

The narrative structure explores two possible responses to rape that popular films have deployed. First, recourse to the legal process turns out to be a farce that leads to yet another woman becoming a rape victim. Second, the film valorizes a revenge fantasy: direct action and punishment followed by success in court. In the first courtroom proceedings *Insaaf ka Taraazu* is unequivocal in condemning the juridical-legal system. As the woman lawyer tells Bharati at the outset, "It is very hard to establish rape. That is why so many rapists go unpunished. And whether or not the rapist is punished, one thing is certain, the woman definitely gets a bad name. . . . You may not know this, but for a woman, a court case involving rape is not very different from rape." The lawyer invokes shame and honor, qualities at stake for the *shareef aurat* (good woman).

Bharati's response is firm—"I now neither care about society, nor about getting a bad name"—but she is less tough than she thinks. The defense attorney's reinterpretation of outtakes of her as a model, along with a photo series of her with Ramesh, resembles Barthes' principle of writerly texts. Her photographs, he argues, demonstrate the inner logic of an alluring sex object and a modern woman's permissive lifestyle. The defendant's lawyer badgers her for her "improper" conduct demonstrated by her choosing a profession in which she displays her body. When Ramesh is set free for lack of sufficient evidence, Bharati sinks into a depression, unable to cope with the publicity following the debacle in court, or with a job requiring she suffuse consumer products with her charm.

It is the second time around, when Nita gets raped by Ramesh Gupta for daring to testify against him in court, that Bharati takes direct action. Nita, making a career as a stenographer, is no model selling her body. As Bharati's lawyer states before she takes up the case, "A woman has to stand up some day and say she has the right to say, 'No,' and no man can touch her without her consent." Yet the first half of the film obfuscates this point, particularly through Ramesh's lawyer's vociferous argument in court. By posing extraneous issues such as Bharati's professional career as a model and the sexualization of her body that inheres to that career, the film implies a difficulty in demarcating consent from a woman's prior conduct.[37]

Compared to the brutal rapes of Bharati and Nita—involving terror, pain, humiliation, and a tortured aftermath—Bharati's swift action against Ramesh seems painless. The film does not escalate to the horror and cruelty that Hollywood slasher films and, to a lesser extent, latter-day rape-revenge Hindi films indulge in.[38] What the film carefully implants, however, is a woman character who is once a victim, but now ready to fight back. It is she (initially through a female lawyer) who takes up the fight—not her boyfriend, the police, or her father.[39]

The weakest point in the film is the last sequence, when Bharati makes her impassioned speech in court against rape. She likens women to temples of worship; each time a woman is violated, she says, a religious shrine is desecrated. In the montage of visuals that accompany her soliloquy we witness a church, a Hindu temple, and a crumbling mosque. The allusion to women as symbols of men's religious communities is disconcerting, if not downright dangerous. While the film text elsewhere attempts to undermine patriarchal ideology, here it suddenly falls into the trap of rejecting rape not because it is a uniquely perverse assertion of men's power but because women, the victims, are likened to religious shrines. The film suddenly and unexpectedly concludes with an insidious thesis on rape. Rather than laying bare the connection between rape and patriarchy, it ends up invoking extant patriarchal discourses within Hindu tradition that place women in binary *devi* or *dasi* (goddess or slave) positions. Holding women up as objects of reverence is posited as a counterpoint to rape, rather than as a continuum within patriarchal discourse. This aspect of the film is more reprehensible than the depiction of rape protested by Indian feminists.

Despite the film's ending with a tirade about reverence for women, what was new in *Insaaf* was that the woman, a victim such as those in the genre of Hindi films from *Mother India* to *Aradhana*, turned into a vigilante. Throughout the 1980s the avenging woman figure became a trend: the "angry woman" replacing the "angry man" of the 1970s. The appearance of "rape-revenge" films in other cultures has been described as feminism's gift to popular culture: "The marriage of rape to revenge was made in movie heaven. . . . Ironically enough, it was a marriage for which the matchmaker was the women's movement, for in terms more or less explicitly feminist, rape became not only a deed deserving of brutal retribution, but a deed that women themselves (not cops, boyfriends, or fathers) undertook to redress."[40]

It was perhaps this innovation—the introduction of rape to the revenge schema, already a staple of popular Hindi cinema—that made *Insaaf ka Taraazu* so popular, creating a veritable new subgenre. It led the way to fusing the themes of sexual violence and rape—a handy (though not exclusive) trope to excoriate and expose the pervasive violence between classes and corruption within institutions.[41] Although rape appeared in earlier films it was never at the center of the narrative, and even when it was salient, allusions to its reality were carefully repressed. The rape *threat* is seized upon and made central in the 1980s, instead of just hovering in the margins. Women exterminating men appeared in earlier films such as *Mother India* and *Mamta* (Maternal Love, 1966).[42] However, in these films women's fury and power service conservative patriarchal ideals apotheosizing motherhood. In these earlier films, women are objects of reverence rather than agents exacting revenge in the name of womankind.

Judged by its production values *Insaaf ka Taraazu* is unusually poor, which comes as a surprise, given that B. R. Chopra is a seasoned director. Zeenat Aman's method acting, meant to convey a post-rape depressive stupor, lacks credibility. The song sequences fill out a parsimonious storyline, in contrast with Hindi cinema's usual well-woven multiple subplots. Furthermore, the long takes, virtually static camera, and flat, three-key lighting make the film visually uninteresting.

Teesri Manzil (Third Floor, 1966) offers a remarkable comparison with *Insaaf ka Taraazu*, different both in terms of its production values and its articulation of rape, or rather, the rape threat. An entertaining thriller by Vijay Anand with a superb cast, excellent pacing, and enthralling story line, it differs from later films like *Insaaf ka Taraazu* in the way it stages and then represses the rape threat.[43]

As the opening credits roll a car pulls up in the darkness of the night. The camera tracks a woman's footsteps as she runs up several flights of stairs, jumps off the third floor, and dies. When the main narrative begins Sunita (Asha Parekh) announces her resolve to avenge her sister Rupa's death and travels to the hill resort Mussorie where her sister, she believes, was murdered the year before. Reconstructing Rupa's letters as evidence, Sunita is convinced that Rocky, the rock-'n'-roll musician at the hotel there, is responsible for her death. Sunita meets Anil (Shammi Kapoor), enlists his support for her mission, and the two fall in love. Anil conceals his alias—Rocky (his band name)—and the fact that he knew Rupa, who was once his admirer and infatuated fan. When Sunita discovers his chicanery she rejects Anil/Rocky. Meanwhile, several abortive attempts on Anil's life compel him to get to the bottom of the mystery. The presence of Ruby, a nightclub dancer and also Rocky's admirer, intensifies suggestions of sexual intrigue. Rocky single-handedly finds his assailant, Kunwar Sahib, and as he uncovers the connection between the deaths of Rupa (and later Ruby) and the attempts on his own life, another subplot unfolds: Rupa, accidentally an eyewitness to a murder implicating Kunwar Sahib, was pursued to her death and Rocky, a suspected eyewitness to that death, becomes the next target.

The rape threat is an unmistakable subtext of the film. Sunita's goal to avenge her sister's death motivates the action in the first half of the film. Convinced that her sister was raped, her goal is to find the perpetrator. The text is, however, equivocal about the exact circumstances of Rupa's ostensible rape and death. This equivocation stems partly from the fact that the crime is reconstructed through second- and third-person accounts a year later. Apart from the prologue, which establishes the crime scene—a long shot of a woman running up three flights of stairs, her fatal fall, followed by a cut away of a man's footsteps fleeing the crime scene—the scenario surrounding her death is revisited several times in the film. *Rashomon*-style, we get varying accounts of the event: we are given Sunita's version twice, Anil's fragmented description once, and in the denouement, the villain's nameless lover fills in the missing pieces.

The difficulty is in fixing and naming with certainty what happened to Rupa. Sunita's reconstruction, along with other narrative accounts, moves restlessly between explanations of unrequited love, a spurned lover, desire, shame, honor, homicide, suicide, and rape. Sunita infers from Rupa's account (wrongly, it is later proven) that she was driven to commit suicide. Rupa's own letter, apart from expressing her desire for Rocky, is ambiguous. Rocky's later account quite plainly states that he consistently rebuffed Rupa's overtures. But one thing is clear, according to Sunita: when a girl crosses the boundaries, she must die. Rupa, Ruby, and Kunwar Sahib's nameless mistress all meet this fate. When Ruby dies, she lies in Rocky's arms and says it in as many words: "My only crime, Rocky, has been that I've desired you."

There are moments in the film when the rape threat buried within the subtext is openly enunciated. Sunita's initial discomfiture with Anil when she journeys with him to locate Rupa's killer turns into romantic love after he makes short shrift of a marauding gang threatening to rape her in the woods. In an earlier scene, Meena, Sunita's friend, is accidentally separated from Sunita and Anil on the same journey. The camera tracks Meena's lonely figure walking through the woods, tightening the frame around her as she looks fearfully beyond its edges—a classic cinematic signification of the rape threat.

Yet the quest for Rupa's rapist, which initially propels the narrative, stops abruptly, changes its course, and becomes a tale of persecuting an innocent man and his redemption. Certainly the female protagonist, Sunita, is no defenseless woman. She sets out from her home as a woman with a purpose, a mission to avenge her sister's death. *Teesri Manzil*, however, becomes an exploration of male anxieties of wrongful accusations—anxieties that constitute the founding principles of English common law transferred to the Empire's colonies.[44]

Representations of rape in myths and literary texts are at once a structuring device and a gaping elision, "an obsessive inscription—and an obsessive erasure—of sexual violence against women (and by those placed by society in the position of 'woman'). . . . Over and over . . . rape exists as an absence or gap that is both product and source of textual anxiety, contradiction, or censorship."[45] Classics such as Samuel Richardson's *Clarissa* and E. M. Forster's *Passage to India* are cited most frequently as examples.[46] With the arrival of the women's movement in the United States, signifying rape displaces its erasure. What mainstream Hollywood glossed up to Oscar standards in films like *The Accused* (Jonathan Kaplan, 1988) had already been said a decade earlier in the lowly horror/slasher genre, only "in flatter, starker terms, and on a shoestring."[47] This suggests a temporal lag between high and low culture's representation of rape; in folkloric terms, "a motif graduated into a tale-type."[48]

The silence and elision on this topic was a mark of popular Hindi cinema's tradition, notwithstanding its "obsessive inscription" of rape.[49] *Teesri Manzil* exemplifies this simultaneous inscription and erasure by at once using rape as a structuring narrative device and adeptly repressing it.

The Sexed Body and Specular Pleasure

It is interesting to note that the figure of the vamp—a liminal figure, favored for decades in Hindi cinema—that significantly attenuated in the 1970s had disappeared by the 1980s, coinciding with the emergence of the avenging woman. In a plot involving mystery and intrigue, the chicanery Sunita and Anil perform in *Teesri Manzil* differs only in degree from the subterfuge in which Ruby engages. Yet Ruby is singled out as Sunita's opposite: the vamp. Ruby makes her living as a nightclub dancer. The "difference" between Ruby and Sunita is that Sunita is the object of desire. Ruby, however, transgresses the line: a sexualized subject with a desire of her own, she aggressively pursues the man she loves. She appropriates "phallic power" and must pay for it with her death.[50]

The actress Helen, who plays a Ruby-like figure in scores of films, is iconic of the vamp. In the roles she repeats time and again, Helen portrays not so much the "wicked" woman as the "naughty," sexually alluring, immodest one, coded by her erotic and nimbly performed dance numbers—a wonderful medley of flamenco, jazz, modern, and belly dance movements set to adaptations of rock'n'roll or jazz rhythms. Located in the public sphere, in the world of men, she is somehow bereft of a man of her own. Desired by all, yet loved by none, she inevitably zeroes in on the hero in her search to be loved by one man.

Yet within the pleasures and dangers of a liminal but exciting nightlife, the role enacted by Helen is that of the "bad," undomesticated woman. For this she is punished with death, always an accident of fate. Not altogether insignificant are the communal overtones of Helen's offscreen minority status as a Christian. Perceived as part of the Anglo-Indian community, an "impure" breed that could never gain legitimacy in a society acutely conscious of origins, Helen plays with the pleasure and anxiety the otherized westerners' lifestyle elicits.

20. Helen playing Ruby, the alluring woman. *Teesri Manzil* (Third Floor), Vijay Anand, 1966.

Double-Speak about the Body

Between the moral authority of the state's censor board and preoccupation with women's bodies through strategic camera angles and movement is the gratification and scopic pleasure filmed bodies, especially those of the vamp, offer to both male and female viewers. The vamp is presented as the sexualized woman, craving men and their attention by inviting their gaze upon her body, her eroticized gestures, and movements. This exhibitionism, pleasurable to the audience, is simultaneously condemned as immodest and prurient. Thus the audience can enjoy the visual pleasure, the spectacular and erotic dance numbers, while morally condemning the woman in unison with the narrative.

This double-speak is evident not only in films but in the entire discursive culture surrounding films. It operates no differently in associated texts such as film magazines. The industry positions itself as demanding freedom of expression and opposing censorship, and at the heart of this wrangle is the contentious issue of how much the films can show—a debate that is really about nothing more than the right to show and see the woman's body. In film magazines the major preoccupation in the years since independence is the reproduction of stills, centerfolds, pin-ups, and close-ups of physical details of female stars. At the same time, the accompanying written text virtuously repudiates the industry and the stars for their declining values. The visuals show the reader exactly what is being decried. Such double-speak continues in the text of the films themselves, which invite us to see and then condemn the figure of the vamp.

One film fan from the 1940s reminds us in an unusually plainspoken way of the intrinsically and organically linked pleasures of voyeurism and scopophilia related to film viewing. This fan wrote unselfconsciously to the magazine *Film India* about his admiration for a new actress, Begum Para, marveling at her diaphanous sarees that enabled him to gaze at her magnificent breasts. In a similar vein, the critic Pandit Indra makes a case against the censorship advocated by *Film India's* editor and the state. The open depiction of sex and the body are, he argues, part of India's classical poetry. He quotes at length from various Hindu poets, including the fourth-century poet Kalidasa's poems in *shringaar rasa*, full of descriptions of gods and goddesses, their bodies, details about their lovemaking, and frequent references to the breasts and buttocks of the amorous women.[51] Analogously, he goes on, films ". . . without romance will be as tasteless as food without salt!. . . . The editor should not try . . . to destroy the sweetness of our life leading us towards [the] darkness of so-called purity."[52]

While the discourse on the extent to which films can or should show women's bodies continues to this day, the figure of the vamp has become conspicuous by its absence. We can only speculate about the changes that prompted this. The distance traveled can be measured by the extent to which the heroines substitute for the vamps. As the Helen-type figure atrophied in Hindi films during the 1970s, the female lead by the 1980s was transformed from a childlike innocent into a sexually alluring creature. In short, if heroines could satisfy what Begum Para's admirer sought in the movies, the vamp was redundant. Much of this had to do with changing boundaries within rules governing sexuality: the boundaries "good" women could occupy expanded slightly. Eroticizing the heroine marked a new trend; the vamp's figure thereafter was banished from Hindi films.[53]

Unsettled Scores

The film *Insaaf*, with its enactment and repression of rape, epitomized broader discursive contexts on the topic. Indian feminists, for example, leveled the charge that it eroticized rape for the male gaze.[54] How do we refuse to erase the palpability of rape and negotiate the splintering of the private/public trauma associated with it? *Insaaf* came under fire from Indian feminists because the fictional representation of rape elided the reality of underclass women's rape by the state (e.g., the police or warring armies). Further, a commercial filmmaker's intervention in a discourse forced upon the nation by women was viewed as opportunism, which feminists found particularly odious. Equally, feminists who had seen (or not seen) the film condemned the filmic depiction of rape, arguing it could only titillate and entertain male viewers.[55]

Some of these criticisms are valid; still, too much gets thrown out with the bath water. It is no accident that *Insaaf* chose an upmarket model as the victim of rape. By showing a woman voluntarily "selling" herself in the world of advertising, the film operates through the same double-speak discussed earlier. Popular cinema in general focuses on the lives of the rich and famous, just as alternate cinema is conversely obsessed with portraying the lives of the poor, the subaltern. By focusing on Bharati (played by Zeenat Aman, who herself won the 1969 Miss Asia title), the film plays on the extra-textual information the audience has about the star, situating itself in the space between the star's real life and the character she plays on screen. *Insaaf*, unlike *Teesri Manzil* or *Aradhana*, set the new trend of eroticizing the heroine's body. Bharati's job of striking poses and openly flaunting herself before the camera centers attention on her body. The centrality of Bharati/Aman's body has the effect of misleading the audience into drawing incorrect conclusions regarding beauty, desire, lust, and rape. The subtext of this is the most insidious of rape myths: "she asked for it." While such a critique rings true, it is equally pertinent that the film's second half subverts the argument of the first half.

When a humdrum, low-paid existence replaces Bharati's glamorous lifestyle after the courtroom fiasco, her younger sister Nita gets a hard-won interview with a prestigious firm. It is of course a set-up, an occasion for Ramesh Gupta to assert his personal vendetta against Nita for testifying against him in court. If initially the film makes confused connections between lust, desire, and rape on the one hand, and women's culpability on the other, this latter part of the film clearly deflects such a thesis. Nita represents legions of women in lowly, underpaid positions, acutely vulnerable to men with power.

Regarding the rape scene's imbrication in representations of the already sexually coded woman's body, Indian feminists who argue that the rape sequences in *Insaaf* are titillating are off-base. Although protracted, the scenes convey nothing but pain, horror, and naked male aggression. The rape is unquestionably gruesome. When Ramesh enters Bharati's bedroom he intimidates her and his intentions are clear. As Bharati protests, "No, no," Ramesh responds, "Yes, yes, . . . beauty queen . . . Now kiss me. . . . " Bharati first fights back, then breaks down and finally passes out. She lies on the floor on the other side of the bed; in view are her feet tied to the bed, her head thrown back in an expression of terror and, eventually, exhaustion as Ramesh stays on top of her. When Ramesh is done with Bharati, he cuts the cords used to tie her to the bed, dresses and leaves.

21. Bharati's rape. *Insaaf ka Taraazu* (Scales of Justice), B. R. Chopra, 1980.

Mary Ann Doane discusses the impasse confronting feminist filmmakers (or theorists for that matter) that stems from a "theoretical discourse which denies the neutrality of the cinematic apparatus itself. A machine for the production of image and sounds, the cinema generates and guarantees pleasure by a corroboration of the spectator's identity . . . [an] identity . . . bound up with that of the voyeur and the fetishist." She points to essentialist and anti-essentialist theories wherein the former presume and aim to restore representation of the female form in "images which provide a pure reflection of woman," while the anti-essentialist refuses "any attempt to figure or represent that body," since the female body is always already and inescapably coded, written, overdetermined.[56]

In her attempt to go beyond this impasse Doane identifies the stakes involved as "not simply concerned with the isolated image of the body . . . rather, the syntax which constitutes the body as a term." In *Insaaf*, the rape scene, attacked so vociferously by feminists, refuses to indulge the voyeur's fetishistic gaze; it does not shy away from showing the brutality of rape. Its "syntax" distances it from the "mandatory rape scenes" reviled in Hindi films. Displacing elliptical references to rape—pushing rape into the public domain and refusing its status as a private matter—are unequivocal gains made by the women's movement.[57]

Yet scopophilic pleasure in rape representations is still a tangled issue. Linda Williams offers a psychoanalytic explanation of melodrama, horror, and pornography, three "body genres" that she classifies by their convulsive impact on the body—tears, fear, and orgasm, or the "tear-jerker," "fearjerker" and texts "some people might be inclined to 'jerk off'" to. Williams draws attention to the perversions that these genres draw upon: masochism in melodrama, an oscillation between sadism and masochism in horror, and sadism, at least in the antipornography group's perception of pornography. Williams, however, urges us to see

> the value of not invoking the perversions as terms of condem-
> nation. As even the most cursory reading of Freud shows,
> sexuality is, by definition, perverse. The "aims" and "objects" of
> sexual desire are often obscure and inherently substitutive.
> Unless we are willing to see reproduction as the common
> goal of sexual drive, then we all have to admit, as Jonathan
> Dollimore has put it, that we are all perverts. Dollimore's goal
> of retrieving the "concept of perversion as a category of cultural
> analysis," as a structure intrinsic to all sexuality rather than
> extrinsic to it, is crucial to any attempt to understand cultural
> forms . . . in which fantasy predominates.[58]

Shohini Ghosh points to the difficulty of fixing (gender) identification among viewers, and Lalitha Gopalan concedes the viewer's oscillation between masochism in rape and sadism in revenge sequences.[59] Even if we do admit to a variety of permutations and combinations in the masochistic/sadistic viewing positions—masochistic identification with rape, sadistic identification with revenge, a masochistic identification with rape and revenge, or a sadistic incitement in the rape and revenge sequences—it is not clear what is at stake for us as feminists. What are our anxieties about the effects of spectatorial arousal?

We might reconsider our own anxieties about the rape scene and focus instead on various other moments in the first half of *Insaaf* (especially the advertising agency's filming) that fetishize the female body as an object of the male gaze. The onus of such a construction shifts to a different filmmaking mode—advertising—that plays with its recipient, the generalized consumer, rather than exclusively the male gaze and desire. Bharati's post-rape depression interrupts her ability to glow at the camera and infuse consumer products with her radiance, motivating the second half of the film. Racialized beauty myths and proliferating beauty pageants, currently offering women dramatic upward mobility from India's small towns to metropolitan penthouses, are trends *Insaaf* clairvoyantly signals.[60] This naturalized body/beauty myth combines far more pernicious aspects of patriarchy, capital, and commodification than the rape depiction.

I draw a distinction between the fetishization and sublimation of women's bodies for consumer commodities in advertising, and felicitations of the body as a site of intimacy, pleasure, and desire. In the 1980s the sexualized Hindi film heroine was no longer punished as was the phallic vamp for satisfying specular desires. Female stars' feigned lack of awareness about their bodies gave way to teasing consciously the limits of, and the pleasure in, "showing." In the 1990s, bawdy film songs pushed the boundaries of sexualized public discourse further. Playing off the ribaldry in the *rasiya* festival song tradition, these songs celebrate the risqué once associated with the peasantry and folk music. Displacing earlier decades of film music's lilting poetry fashioned by a refined urbane sensibility, these tongue-in-cheek lyrics reflect trouble between the sexes, as well as women's pleasure in being both the objects *and subjects* of desire.

Bharati's courtroom tirade at the end of the film results in more than a symbolic victory. The judge ruefully admits the court's (read: the Indian state's) failure toward women and sets Bharati free. The sequence's extreme lack of credibility undermines it and fails to vindicate the original indictment of the judicial system. Yet a lot has changed in the decade since the self-punishing Vandana in *Aradhana* quietly acquiesced to a twelve-year incarceration for defending herself against rape. If melodrama condenses profound public/private conflicts, at once exposing and reaffirming power relations, it is also a vivid emotional register in Hindi films.[61] In *Aradhana*, the centrality of affect shored up by the pro-filmic masculine fantasy acknowledges patriarchal oppression and proffers reverence in the form of a grand award from the state (fusing mother/nation/state)—an awkward and phantasmic compensation. In the post–1980s woman's film, however, nothing short of "sweet revenge" compensates for women's suffering.

The 1980s rape revenge film, fuelled by women's rage, dramatizes a public discourse that repudiates victimization and patriarchy—and is distinct from the pre–1980s obsessive "inscription" and "erasure" of sexual violence, *Teesri Manzil*-style. The topos of rape, a weapon against the weak, is used by filmmakers as a rhetorical trope to conjure images of power, coercion, and humiliation in conflicts between the culturally powerless and powerful.[62] The historical context is crucial to understanding the arrival of the avenging women's film and its role in the circulation of discourses between representation and reality.[63] From the 1960s through the 1980s, Hindi cinema's discourse on womanhood has traveled an orbit—from reverence to rape, and then revenge.

As we realize more than a decade later that the all-inclusive category "women" is splintered by other hierarchies—caste or community—rape is again a handy trope to reveal the topos of oppression. Shekhar Kapur's controversial film *Bandit Queen* (1994), for example, chronicles the life of Phoolan Devi (1957–2001); a low-caste woman, her repeated rape depicts the pervasive violence against low-caste *dalits*—whose political consolidation today is unprecedented.

The news of Phoolan Devi's assassination on July 25, 2001—gunned down by three hit men during lunch hour in New-Delhi, a story still unfolding—might just put an end to the saga of this most extraordinary figure's life, on which the film is *based*, even though the words across the screen: "This is a true story" appear in the opening shot. One can expect speculations about the motive behind her assassination to proliferate and the truth about her death to be as elusive as her life. Yet the film captures some incontrovertible facts. Phoolan Devi was a low-caste woman, married when she was only age ten to a man three times her age (a marriage that did not work out). The rest of her story as it unfolds in the film reveals that Phoolan Devi was raped by upper-caste men in the village, after which she joined a gang of bandits in the Chambal Valley in central India. There she falls in love with Vikram Mallah, a low-caste bandit like herself, when he rescues her from an upper-caste boss. Mallah's subsequent murder for challenging upper-caste authority in the gang, Phoolan Devi's gang rape, and her public humiliation by the gang's upper-caste leaders (she is paraded naked at the village well as a lesson to lower castes who might forget their place) result in her establishing her own gang of low-caste bandits. She is held responsible for killing twenty-two upper-caste men (one of the fifty-two charges pending against her at the time of her assassination) in Behmai, the village where she was raped, and her "wanted" status as a woman bandit gives her mythic status: a goddess to the lower castes, a "bandit queen" to the English press. The film ends with her surrender, negotiated by the Chief Minister of Madhya Pradesh (a nationally televised event in 1981). It was a surrender in which she negotiated a goat and a bicycle as part of the deal to rehabilitate her parents.

Phoolan Devi was incarcerated for eleven years (even though she had negotiated for less), and her release from prison coincided with HarperCollins' publication of her biography, *India's Bandit Queen*, written by Mala Sen. It relied on prison interviews with her and was the basis for Shekhar Kapur's film produced by Britain's Channel 4. Legal wrangles ensued when the film was released, between Phoolan Devi and Channel 4 on the remuneration from the deal, and between Shekhar Kapur and the Government of India over censoring the scene in which she is paraded naked. These were settled with amazing alacrity (Phoolan Devi was given a fixed sum of £40,000 by Channel 4, rather than a percentage of the film's profits) and the Supreme Court ruled to release the films without cuts. She was subsequently elected to parliament in 1995, as a candidate of the Samajvadi Party, which has consolidated lower castes as an electoral force. In Phoolan Devi's last six years the English press sneered at her newly won legitimacy as a member of Parliament, finding closure to her story by writing her off as a Machiavellian opportunist.

Hence it is that Phoolan Devi's spectacular life story perhaps makes the film about it pale, confusing ideas about art imitating life or vice versa—and in her unique case, a strange interpenetration of the two. The film lays down clear-cut lines in which gender and caste, the intersecting vectors shaping Phoolan Devi's life, make her a victim of rape—the trope for oppression and the reason for her rebellion and revenge. However, her status as a parliamentarian, not to mention the international attention the book and film brought her, were assumed to inure her from her upper-caste enemies even as it further fuelled their

ire. And if the book, the film, the attendant forces of international media publicity, her life, and her eventual assassination tell us something,
it is that any symbolic representations and fantasies of avenging rape
offered up in films dare not cross into reality—particularly not for
women born on the wrong side of the Indian caste divide.

Chapter 6   *Re-reading Romance*

In the Nehruvian era romance generally featured as a narrative subplot, and was used along with other devices to explore the cartography of social tensions. However, in the 1970s romantic love became less central as Hindi cinema took a turn toward gangster films. Stories of individual revenge against social injustice, mediated through elaborate family melodramas, proliferated. In the late 1960s repression of student-peasant uprisings, followed by a crisis-ridden economy and a corrupt, repressive government during the notorious 1975 Emergency, infused the cinematic imagination of the 1970s with themes of cynicism and violence. Amitabh Bachchan's rise to superstardom—emblematic of that historical moment and portraying a new kind of heroism—gave voice to the disenchanted working class, which, compared to Raj Kapoor's 1940s' and 1950s' films, is far more strident.

Amitabh Bachchan's preeminence eclipsed women's roles: the attrition of the romance subplot limited the space for women characters, turning them into liminal figures in narratives centered on a newfound masculinity. The proliferating gangster-cum-action films revealed corruption in high places, avaricious "antinational" elements, and profiteering by wealthy smugglers and were eagerly consumed by audiences throughout the 1970s and 1980s, becoming integral to Hindi cinema (see chapter 3).

Romance, however, returned as a dominant element in the late

1980s, perplexing critics who viewed adventure films projecting angst and violence as a staple that was there to stay. The generation that had come of age in the early 1980s was in its pre-teens when the cult film *Bobby* (1973), a precursor to the late 1980s' romance films, was released. *Bobby*, a teen romance, was but a faint memory for this generation. The later romance films repeat the transgressions heterosexual romance performs in *Bobby* (and earlier films), but a significant unarticulated contest surfaced for the first time between generations—or rather, the films reframed representations of intergenerational conflict.

The romance films were conditioned by a new factor: economic liberalization. The topos of recent romance narratives remapped social institutions in the nation, focusing on heterosexual romance's place in Indian culture, its tryst with the nuclearization of the family, and redefinitions of the self and subjectivity in relation to the family and community. The topography of heterosexual romance is not only a site of obsessive pleasure; it also throws into relief the crisis in the family and community, departing from Hindi cinema's traditional agenda—of using romance to explore social hierarchies.

Transgressions of "True Love"

In *Bobby*, puppy love confronts patriarchal authority. The teen lovers face parental authority's power to summon privileges of class and the support of the state via its restrictive age of consent laws. Raja (Rishi Kapoor), the only son of the wealthy Mr. Nath (Pran) and his wife Sushma (Sonia Sahni), is sent away to a boarding school because his parents cannot spare the time for child care, and Mrs. Briganza, the governess, cannot discipline him. He returns after graduating from high school, meets and falls in love with Bobby, Mrs. Briganza's granddaughter, and wants to marry her.

Bobby's father, Jack Briganza, has unschooled manners and comes from a "plebeian" rum-drinking culture that appalls the class-conscious Mr. Nath. He accuses Jack of setting Raja up. The young lovers are separated, and Raja is warned that marrying Bobby before turning twenty-one violates the law. Raja defers his marriage, but when he discovers that his father is arranging his marriage to enhance his own financial prospects, he elopes with Bobby. Nath suspects Jack Briganza is behind

22.   Bobby and Raj escape. *Bobby* (Raj Kapoor, 1973).

this despite the fact that Mrs. Briganza calls the police to trace Raja. The young lovers, speeding down the highway to their freedom, are chased by their fathers, the police, and hoodlums interested in the handsome reward on Raja's head. Raja and Bobby are rescued from the hoodlums by their fathers, but, feeling no safety with their families, they jump into the river in a joint suicide bid. Jack and Nath jump in after them, with the result that Jack rescues Raja and Nash rescues Bobby. All is well in the end: a reformed Nath accepts Bobby and Jack Briganza.

The narrative in *Bobby* is curiously ambivalent about many issues it raises. Nath's authority and state laws are brought to bear on Raja for daring to marry Bobby when they are still minors. Yet Nath goes on to arrange the marriage between Raja and Alka, a business colleague's daughter who is a minor like Raja, and mentally a child. It is through Alka's childlike prattle that Raja discovers he is a pawn in a business deal: her father has guaranteed Nath "plenty of business" after the marriage. The prohibition of the marriage of minors is used only to consolidate parental authority *against* the minor's will. Of course, the age of consent is a mere narrative ploy, the complication leading to the climax.[1]

Perhaps the most unusual aspect of *Bobby* is its device of center-staging India's underrepresented minority Christian community. Jack Briganza's endearing personality combines a robust working-class sensibility along with his identity as a Goan Christian. However, cultural differences are flattened and diminish in importance as the central conflict condenses along class lines. Differences between the Christian community and Raja's obvious Hindu background remain buried. Nath's willingness to negotiate Raja's marriage with Bobby so long as her father is a well-to-do businessman represents an emergent cosmopolitanism concerned exclusively with financial success. Bobby's affiliation with the Christian community becomes the narrative's excuse for the scanty outfits she wears—especially the bikini scene that made the film famous.[2] The film ultimately favors a sentiment privileged by Hindi cinema—romantic love transgressing class—captured in the film's very popular theme song:

> *Na mangum sona chandi, na chahun hira moti, ye mere kis kaam*
> *ke? Deti hai dil de, badle mein dil ke . . . pyaar mein sauda nahin,*
> (I don't want silver or gold, I don't want diamond or pearls,
> what use are these to me? Give me your heart in exchange for a
> heart . . . there's no bargaining in love).

Curiously, *Bobby*'s astonishing success was not replicated for almost two decades, when the narrative elements of young love and defiance of parental authority became established genre conventions. The 1990s' romance films assert the individual's rights against feudal strictures associated with vested familial interests: the authority of the father, the state, and the unwritten rules of endogamy operating within class and community. To this end the films are remarkably secular, and elicit antipatriarchal sentiments. Audiences root for the young lovers—momentarily blinded by sentiments of "true love" that papers over religious community, caste, or class difference—and cheer on, for instance, a Hindu-Christian union.

If *Bobby* naturalizes interreligious love without making much of the cultural difference, *Qyamat se Qyamat tak* (From Eternity to Eternity, Mansoor Khan, 1988), produced at the height of the Hindu revivalist movement in India, focuses on intrareligious strife. The film is metonymic for the endogamous rules patriarchal authority enforces to ensure the community's "purity." The *Romeo and Juliet*–style love story is set against the backdrop of a bloody war between two feuding Rajput families. Brothers Dhanraj and Jaswant become Ranbir's lifelong enemies when their sister commits suicide after she is impregnated by Ranbir's brother, who then refuses to marry her. Dhanraj kills Ranbir's brother on his wedding day in full view of the invited guests. This prologue is followed by a voiceover summarizing intervening events. Dhanraj serves a fourteen-year sentence while his brother, Jaswant, sells the family property, migrates from the village, and relocates in Delhi, where his cloth trade does booming business. He raises Dhanraj's son Raj (Aamir Khan), the protagonist. The main narrative of the film begins when Dhanraj returns from prison and joins his brother's enterprise.

Raj and Rashmi (Juhi Chawla), Ranbir's daughter, meet when they are vacationing with their parents. Knowing Rashmi's family background, Raj at first avoids her. But following her persistence and a series of chance encounters, they fall in love. Ranbir discovers the affair, which continues through clandestine phone conversations and meetings at the college library. He banishes Rashmi from college and arranges her marriage with another man. A month later, on her wedding day,

23. Dhanraj arriving at the wedding to avenge his sister's death. *Qyamat se Qyamat tak* (From Eternity to Eternity), Mansoor Khan, 1988.

Rashmi escapes from home with the help of a friend, hidden behind a long veil (*purdah*), passing for one of the singers performing at the wedding.

Rashmi and Raj elope and build their nest in the wilderness, prompting Ranbir to hire hit men to get rid of Raj without witnesses or evidence of his body. Ranbir's mother, the matriarch of the family (*dadima*), urges her son to relent, stop the cycle of violence, and accept his daughter's wishes. Ranbir is intransigent. Fearing the worst, she goes to Dhanraj, the family's enemy, asking him to intervene. When the two families converge at the young lovers' nest Rashmi dashes out to warn Raj and finds him wrestling with the hit man. In keeping with his orders to avoid witnesses, the hit man guns her down. As the families rush forward to protect their children, Raj, in a final act of defiance and self-punishing rebellion, stabs himself. The victory and defeat of the lovers, united in death, ends the family feud.

The film traces the resilience of a strong feudal ethic that remains unchanged even as families move away from their agrarian roots to urban big business. Unlike the 1950s' films that marked the trauma of migrating to the city, this film traces mobility, success, and the emergence of a new generation for whom connection with the country and its feudal values is nothing more than fascinating family lore. It captures a transition in values. The trajectory of upward mobility from rural wealth to trader in the metropolis is marked by the promise of western-style consumption. The feudal landlord is transformed into an urban businessman with links to the criminal underworld. It is this feudal-cum-bourgeois world's patriarchal order the innocent lovers challenge, underestimating the wrath lurking beneath the veneer of parental love.

Raised in a cosmopolitan environment removed from village life, the younger generation fails to internalize the intensity of the family feud and refuses to abide by the older generation's ban. Individual will, an aspect of bourgeois sensibility, clashes with patriarchal strictures. In the intergenerational war heterosexual love signifies freedom, choice, and individual agency. But what of the agency granted to women? The space for women is circumscribed by the patriarchal teleology that traditionally valorizes Rajput honor and courage. Death—the final sentence meted out to both Dhanraj's sister and Rashmi, situated two generations apart—indicates that nothing much has changed. The narrative, however, betrays another story, even inverting gender roles in the heterosexual romance. In their first encounter Rashmi gazes voyeuristically at Raj's athletic body running toward her against the setting sun. She initiates their relationship and comes across as a "new" kind of heroine: demure and assertive, childlike and smart, terrified of her father yet willful enough to put up a fight to have her own way. She elopes with her lover after she is betrothed to a man of her father's choice. For all the stifling control, surveillance, and patriarchal authority that Ranbir exerts over his daughter, Rashmi, with a little help from a resourceful friend, flees as one of the performing artists at her own wedding. Her face veiled, body bowed deferentially, she walks past her father's threshold. Signs of female subordination are transformed imaginatively into instruments of subversion.

This is the change that has intervened since the times when Dhanraj's sister lived and died. Rashmi enjoys new privileges: a supportive peer group with cars, telephones, and the "liberal zones" of a college and library that enable limited freedom from parental control. Of course, access to these advantages is tenuous and ultimately controlled by paternal authority: Ranbir, after all, terminates Rashmi's college education days before her wedding. Banishing her to her room, he invokes family tradition and invests her future husband with the authority to continue her education. Rashmi questions her father's decree even as she obediently recedes to her room.

Openly repudiating pride in rigid Rajput feudal norms, the film runs contrary to a hugely popular tradition of songs, folk tales, and legends venerating masculinity, unequivocally rewriting such approbation as patriarchal excess. The most vocal dissent comes from the surviving wife of the grand patriarch, Rashmi's *dadima*. After accidentally witnessing an exchange between her cowardly son and Dhanraj's sister, she courageously prevails on her husband to accept their marriage and make their son take responsibility for fathering the child. But her husband's response is stern: "No woman carrying a child before she marries fits as a daughter-in-law in this house." Helpless, she appeals to her son Ranbir, who does not dare challenge his father.

Years later the matriarch advises Ranbir not to ruin his daughter Rashmi's life by arranging an unwelcome marriage, and to gracefully ac-

cept Raj as his son-in-law. Ranbir sneers at her, asserting his vengeful-
ness for his brother's death, even if his mother is reconciled with the
family responsible for this. *Dadima* alone is clairvoyant: she foresees the
tragic outcome and tries to stop the violence about to repeat itself. Un-
heeded earlier by her husband, and later by her son, she is powerless
against the authority of the men in her home. She goes to Raj's family
to inform them of her foreboding. Of course, the planned machinations
are beyond her control. Significantly, an older woman, made powerless
and marginal by Rajput values, is the one to challenge its celebrated
chauvinism.

Qyamat se Qyamat tak accepts the impossibility of the romantic notion: heterosexual romance combating feudal/patriarchal authority. The
lovers' deaths mark assertive individualism's moral victory but also its
defeat in a "real" sense. Yet intergenerational conflict, a powerful theme
with protean dimensions, captured the imagination of the cinematic
world. *Dil* (Heart, 1990), following close on the heels of *Qyamat se
Qyamat tak*'s success, tapped into its successful theme.

Vinod Doshi's *Dil* is a sharp satire, a politicized representation of
capitalism and patriarchy's imbrication in a new phase of capitalist development in India. It was a roaring success at the box office. Hazari
Prasad (Anupam Kher), the male protagonist's father, is the miserly
owner of a small *kabari* operation who nurtures get-rich-quick fantasies.[3] More than anything else, he wants to arrange his son's marriage
with a wealthy family and fetch himself a handsome dowry. He turns
down a proposal from the wealthy businessman Girdhari Lal, only because Prasad is looking for a wealthier match. The opportunity for huge
capital gain presents itself when he spots Mehra (Saeed Jaffery), a tycoon with local and overseas business interests in hotels and industries.
When Prasad learns that Mehra's daughter is eligible, he is determined
to arrange his son's marriage with her.

But the young protagonists, Prasad's son Raja (Aamir Khan), and
Mehra's daughter Madhu (Madhuri Dixit), are strong-willed youths
whose run-ins at college have led them to despise each other. Prasad,
feigning to be in the same league as Mehra, befriends him and airs his
anxiety over their children's mutual animosity. Meanwhile, Raja and
Madhu go on a college trip, fall in love, and when they return two glee-
ful fathers set a date to celebrate their engagement.

As the local city's luminaries arrive to grace the engagement party, the young couple dance with gay abandon while Mehra introduces Prasad to his guests as a business magnate. But Girdhari Lal, Mehra's friend, recognizes Prasad for who he is and exposes his charade. Enraged, Mehra disrupts the party, humiliates Prasad, mocks his pitiable "garbage" business, and calls off the engagement. Raja and Madhu are torn from each other against their wishes while Prasad swears to avenge this humiliation.

When Raja and Madhu run into their fathers' intransigence they turn defiant. They finally succeed in breaking Mehra down by conducting a mock wedding before his eyes. A beleaguered Mehra resigns himself to severing connections with his defiant daughter. Raja and Madhu live in an isolated farmhouse, a studio set suspended in an unfamiliar time or space. Raja becomes a construction worker and has an accident; to raise money for his surgery, Madhu goes to Prasad because her father is away traveling. He agrees to help on the condition that she forsake Raja.

Prasad goes on to arrange Raja's marriage with a mentally retarded girl in exchange for a hefty dowry. Through a circuitous chain of events Raja discovers his father's misdeeds and his machinations to drive Madhu away, and in the nick of time learns Madhu is about to relocate to England with her father. He hurtles through city traffic to the airport and discovers the flight has left—but finds that a reformed Hazari Prasad has persuaded Madhu and her family to stay.

Dil presents the best combination of technical skill and artistic talent that the Bombay film industry has come to represent. Combining the comedic with the serious in an intelligently scripted, well-acted, and brilliantly crafted film, it creates new possibilities within the world of commercial cinema. The opening sequence reveals Baba Azmi's spectacular cinematography. A man lies on a bed in a bare room encircled by windows thrown open by a storm. As sharply angled rays of light stream in, the camera swoops up from the side of the bed to a high angle and then to an aerial shot. Slowly, pieces of paper drift in from the window. Money, heaps of money, fall on the floor, gradually flooding the room. The camera pulls closer to the man as he mutters incoherently, grabbing at the sheaves of money. The image slowly dissolves to the man standing on his bed pulling tufts of cotton from the pillow and speaking excitedly. The punchline comes when the door opens and a woman walks into the room. "He's having his dreams about money again," she says, ordering the servant to fetch water. As she shakes her husband out of his stupor the servant pours a pitcher of water over the delirious man's head, shocking him out of his pleasurable manna-from-heaven dream. This is the viewer's introduction to Hazari Prasad. Other equally humorous scenes add to the exposition of his incorrigible personality—a miser whose favorite fantasy is accumulating money and worst fear is spending it.

Unlike other Hindi films that play up a binary rich-poor opposition, *Dil* zeroes in on a rich and richer class, the sign of an expanded and variegated bourgeoisie that has grown over fifty years of independence. Differences within the bourgeoisie, between the traditional *bania* (trader) and the new multinational corporations, point to a broad middle- and upper-class cultural economy. The distinction between new and old money is in their cultural capital and social standing. Mehra goes jogging on the beach with his pure-bread Doberman, representing the cultural lifestyle of a new elite tied to multinational corporations. He is distinguishable from Hazari Prasad, whose occupation as a *kabarigaar* is a reminder of that which is traditionally inherited—an inert feudal culture.[4] This makes Prasad's attempts to buy a cosmopolitan appearance humorous: he jogs on the beach with dogs he rents and with unemployed actors from the Bombay film industry who pose as his managers.

Although superstar Amitabh Bachchan was an angry, defiant hero in the 1970s, the youth represented in Hindi cinema have typically been pliable and deferential toward their elders, a cherished value in Indian culture.[5] When the Brahmin priest, the traditional matchmaker in *Dil*, suggests that Prasad seek his son's opinion, he imperiously waves him aside: "My son will do as I tell him. That's the way it's been for seven generations in my family." But viewer confidence in unchanging family codes and bonds is undercut by the next scene: a dapper Raja, a young college boy, throws an extravagant birthday party. When Prasad confronts his son about the expenses incurred, a nonchalant Raja, brushing his hair before a mirror, insolently corrects his father for rounding off a 17,000-rupee bill to 20,000 rupees. If Prasad is miserly to a fault,

Raja is an audacious, egotistical, and willful narcissist. But Prasad puts up with his son Raja because he is, after all, a financial opportunity.

Dil projects anger, building on a feisty youth culture defying the law of the father, unwilling to play by old rules and assertive enough to make its own. The most audacious challenge to authority is in the fantasy/song sequence when the young lovers, incarcerated for eloping, embrace in the jail cell and mock their fathers, who look at them helplessly through the prison bars. The reverse shot implies that the old men are imprisoned by patriarchal values.

Hindi cinema's song and dance convention is often a license for a fantasy sequence, and the number in *Dil* is no exception: it shows Mehra and Prasad dressed as hangmen, gods of Death, ghoulish creatures wearing black capes, dark glasses, and carrying hatchets as they hound their children. Elements of surrealism and humor mark this sequence. The empty, unidentifiable space is enclosed by a dome-like structure constructed with metallic bars. A phalanx of cadaver-like bodies clothed in white bow to Madhu and Raja, moving in carefully choreographed steps as they all walk through clouds. Raja and Madhu are dressed in spectacular western fairy-tale-style prince and princess outfits: Madhu in flowing blue robes and glistening diamonds, and Raja in a white frilly shirt.

In Hindi cinema songs perform various functions within the narrative; a song can be marshaled to advance the story at a rhapsodic junc-

24. Fathers are hangmen in the lovers' fantasy song-dance. *Dil* (Heart), Vinod Doshi, 1990.

ture within the narrative or to convey moods—love, passion, separation, longing—or the lyrics may simply be part of the extra-diegetic
music overlaid upon a montage sequence summarizing the narrative.
The specific number performed in *Dil* is unusual because it does not
appear as a dream sequence, fantasy, memory, or a flashback. Rather, it
provides a third-person rendition, a commentary within the narration
using death and hangmen figures to satirize patriarchs. It is part of the
general strategy of lampoon adopted in the film.

The hangmen sneak into the corners of the frame, harassing the
young lovers. The sequence draws upon a fantastic potpourri of traditions and forms: amateur dance drama; music video-style effects of clouds
and smoke; western fairy-tale-like costumes; surreal, unspecified, and
unidentifiable spaces; and, of course, Hindi film-style song and music,
itself a hybrid of various traditions. As the lovers run from the ghoulish-
looking creatures, they pass through a labyrinth of prison gates that open
onto arched hallways and more prison gates. They walk on clouds in a
cold, death-like white, blue, and metallic-gray setting. The hangmen
are constantly outmaneuvered, frustrated by the fleeing lovers. The spectacle condenses intergenerational hostilities by parodying the fathers—
conniving, mean-minded men out to foil innocent, primal, "true" love.
The sequence ends by returning to "real life," moving from the narrator's
commentary to plot development. In the next scene Madhu and Raja
take flight, speeding away on Raja's motorcycle.

When Mehra drags his runaway daughter home after bringing hoodlums to beat up Raja, Madhu shows fiery defiance. "I'll break your legs
if you step out of this house again," Mehra threatens. "Do what you
will . . . If you break my legs, I'll walk to Raja on my arms, and if you
cut my arms off, my body and soul will still desire him," she spits back.
The film—or rather this type of film, some have argued—went too far
in castigating parental authority, vilifying the family, applauding teenage rebellion, and making a mockery of the father figure, as in the portrayal of Hazari Prasad, a *kabarigaar* lacking the sophistication and grace
the younger generation are fortunate enough to acquire through the education and cultural capital their parents' wealth can buy.

This sense of injury some viewers felt came through clearly in several interviews I conducted in the summer of 1992 in a middle-class
neighborhood in south Delhi. Viewing films on video is now common-

place in middle-class homes, yet such viewings often heighten intergenerational tensions. In one instance, a gentle elderly man with col-
lege-going teenagers of his own said that he was saddened by such
portrayals.[6] While depicting youthful arrogance and the younger
generation's pranks was deemed acceptable, caricaturing and ridiculing
parents was not.

The parody and humor used to satirize the figure of Hazari Prasad
certainly sharpened the film's edge in lampooning paternal authority.
Admittedly, this assault has much to do with the younger, westernized
generation's misplaced sense of superiority over their nonwesternized
parents. But it has as much to do with the very nature of intergenerational conflict, the rebellion against parental control and values
that are transposed onto a culture war. As for the attack on petit bourgeois culture, the film, is even-handed about chastising the inordinate
power father figures assert.

Mehra's cool cosmopolitanism vanishes, for example, when he realizes the truth about Prasad's status—and when his daughter dares to
pledge her allegiance to a man beneath their class. And when a grim
Raja defiantly walks into Madhu's house, past the guards and servants,
straight to Madhu's room, lights a little fire, ties himself to Madhu's scarf
and circles the fire four times signaling the Hindi marriage ritual, we
see Mehra mouthing the worst profanities. Shot in slow motion, his
words are drowned by the extra-diegetic wedding music played to sanc-
tify the "sacred" moment.

The film not only mocks patriarchal authority but also the ritualized dowry exchanges in marriage alliance among the "enlightened"
bourgeoisie. In fact, the entire narrative springs from and is spun around
the ubiquitous acceptance of dowry despite progressive legislation outlawing it. The film exemplifies the reinvention of tradition—adapting
marriage customs to pseudo-cosmopolitanism, new modes of production,
consumption, and business alliances.[7]

Early in the film, in a sharply satirical sequence where Girdhari Lal
first meets Hazari Prasad, the mise-en-scène compares the marriage arrangement process to business dealings. Prasad is haggling with laborers over the price of recycled newspaper when the matchmaker and
Girdhari Lal arrive with a marriage proposal. Prasad shamelessly quotes

his dowry demand, turning down a generous bid as insufficient. An irate Girdhari reminds Prasad of his own status: a mere *kabarigaar*, an entrepreneur in the garbage business. Their exchange occurs not at home but in the bazaar, at the threshold of Prasad's store where he has just haggled with laborers—parodying arranged marriage transactions.

Though accumulating a large dowry is the primary engine in the narrative, it gets buried in the subtext, unexplored and subverted by the young lovers' independent choice to marry without a penny changing hands. The couple celebrate their victory in a song that is unusual for openly referring to this anachronistic social practice. Escaping in an open truck, they sing "*Hamre rasme tore hein* (we have broken norms)," making an elliptical reference to dowry.

Heterosexual romance in *Dil* is indeed radically transgressive. Not only does the couple resist the patriarchal order by breaking social norms, the woman exhibits new aggressiveness in the couple's relationship. Madhu walks up and kisses Raja openly before her peers and college authorities: she initiates their relationship. But that radical moment is also recontained within heterosexism's limits. In the world away from the world that the young couple create, a strictly conservative paradigm rules: he goes to work, while she waits long hours for him to return. Even more interesting is the vacuous, imaginary space the lovers occupy. If Raja's "real world" job is a construction worker's, his home certainly is not. Far from other working-class families living in the congested city, Raja and Madhu live in a studio-constructed cottage—an ambiguous sign, representing on the one hand poverty and downward mobility (compared to their lavish parental homes), and bucolic charm, which is now Indian advertising's cachet, on the other. "Rural chic" is added to "ethnic chic" and romance exists outside the real world, beyond the familiar city limits.

Romance in the 1980s and 1990s films make college campuses the institutional site, the locus where the boy meets girl in "real" time and space. Urban centers registering an increasing number of women in higher education partly reflects the pressures of inflation forcing women into the work force. For the majority of the population dwelling in small townships and rural areas, higher education is still a sign of privilege—thus making college campus scenarios pleasant fantasies of the possible.

In other romance films of the 1990s the locus of romance shifts to the secure environs of the home as the films come to rest on more conservative ideals.

In *Dil*, during a life-threatening crisis, without a thought Madhu falls back on her family, still an indispensable safety net in Indian society. The moment of romantic transgression transforms into temporary dissidence: the film exposes the impossibility of dislodging the sturdy relation between family and class. In some ways even the intergenerational conflict was not entirely new.[8] What was original was the film's irreverence, which gave an edge to the defiance with which the new generation went about having its way. It is no surprise that other romance films of the time center on and renegotiate the couple's relationship with the family, such as the enormously successful Rajshree Production films *Maine Pyaar Kiyaa* (I Have Loved, 1989) and *Hum Aapke Hain Kaun* (Who Am I to You, 1994). These films soften the blow against patriarchy. The narrative axis shifts, evades the issue of individualism, and wrestles instead with new arrangements within the family.

Reinstating "Family Values"

The decline of "family values," popularized by the Right as a diagnosis of social ills in the United States, is also invoked by Indian religious groups, particularly the Hindu Right. Such revivalism responds to the challenge of the women's liberation movement by promoting its own convoluted brand of neotraditionalism: "tradition" with a "modern" face. The appeal of neotraditionalism, with its promise to empower women, is overwhelming.[9] It offers an old nationalist argument, one that urges equipping the nation with scientific know-how and technological modernization while retaining an intrinsic Indian spiritual essence. The Hindu Right builds on this argument to sweep women into the nation's strides toward scientization and progress. Women, it mandates, should become doctors, engineers, and scientists, positions traditionally the preserve of men, along with their primary role as nurturers and homemakers—thus bringing together the "world" and "home."[10]

Maine Pyaar Kiya (I Have Loved, 1989), the debut film by Sooraj Barjatya, the youngest entrant in the well-established Barjatya family enterprise Rajshree Films, skillfully tempers the culture war in romance films, drawing instead on neoconservative discourse. The film's tremendous success was outdone by Sooraj Barjatya's second film, *Hum Aapke Hain Kaun*, which grossed more than any other film in the previous fifty years. Interestingly, it also defies Hindi cinema's conventional narrative structure. These films are striking for the ways in which they deflect the contradictions posed by heterosexual romance, and the deftness with which they reconcile warring elements (the romantic couple and patriarchal authority) and contain intergenerational conflict, protest, and transgression. The resounding approval these films received at the box office in a general climate of right-wing resurgence attests to the strength with which conservative values uphold the family as the final bastion of stability and security in a rapidly changing world.

In *Maine Pyaar Kiya*, Karan (Alok Nath), a diesel mechanic and widower, leaves his daughter, Suman (Bhagyashree), with his childhood friend-turned-tycoon Kishen and his wife Kaushalya, when he goes to make his fortune in the Middle East. Suman falls in love with Kishen's son, Prem (Salman Khan), but Kishen's upward mobility changes his affections and he finds the alliance unacceptable. Moreover, his business associate, Ranjit, has designs on Kishen's wealth and poisons him against his old friend Karan.

Kishen accuses Karan of setting Prem up using his daughter. Prem rebels against his father and leaves home, but can marry Suman only after he proves to Karan he is a capable householder by raiding 2,000 rupees in a month. Prem takes up construction work and earns the money, but in the climactic moment en route to meeting Karan, Ranjit's villainous nephew ambushes him. In the final resolution Kishen discovers his business associates' motives, apologizes to his son, accepts Suman, and the lovers are married.

In *Hum Aapke Hain Kaun* once again two long-lost friends meet when their children are grown and negotiate a marriage between them. Pooja (Renuka Sahane) and Nisha (Madhuri Dixit) are the daughters of a professor (Anupam Kher) and his wife (Reema Lagoo). Pooja marries their old family friend's (Alok Nath) adopted son, Rajesh (Monish Behl). During the protracted North Indian wedding celebration which dominates the film, the groom's younger brother, Prem (Salman Khan), falls in love with the bride's sister, Nisha. Meanwhile, Pooja's father-in-law entrusts her with finding a marriage alliance for Prem, prompting Nisha and Prem to confide in her. Pooja dies suddenly before sharing this information with anyone.

The family elders suggest that Rajesh, a young widower now with an infant, remarry. They propose the infant's aunt, Nisha, as the appropriate match. Rajesh agrees on the proviso that Nisha accepts the proposition. Nisha does—assuming the proposal is from Prem—only to later discover the mix-up. For the baby nephew's sake, a guilt-ridden Nisha goes along with the betrothal despite her unhappiness. On the wedding day Rajesh miraculously intercepts a letter Nisha writes to Prem and learns of their relationship. Rajesh announces Prem's marriage to Nisha in place of himself moments before the wedding ceremony.

In both Maine Pyar Kiya and Hum Aapke Hain Kaun the romance is not set in the traditional holiday resort, but in large homes in which lovers maneuver to maintain their privacy, keep the relationship a secret, and gain relative autonomy from parental figures. The secret is shared between the couple and their peer group within the diegesis— and the audience. Complications arise due to a malevolent patriarch (Maine Pyaar Kiya) or because the benign family elders fail to discover the romance (Hum Aapke). In earlier films secrecy was ensured by the anonymity of the location where the boy and girl met coincidentally. They promise secular possibilities: individuals unencumbered by their caste and clan origins fall in love. In the conservative romance films anonymity is displaced by family connections. Within the family a thin line separates privacy from secrecy, which relies on an unspoken assumption much like "Don't ask, don't tell."

Perhaps part of the viewing pleasure lies in seeing how the couple forges a private space for themselves by, for instance, exchanging surreptitious glances. In both Maine Pyaar Kiya and Hum Aapke the couple express their desires in the midst of revelry—occasioned by an engagement, wedding, or the birth of a child. In Hum Aapke the protracted wedding celebration maximizes the pleasure in ritualized articulations of filial and sexual tensions through folk songs, dance routines, and anthakshari sessions.[11] These moments of revelry in Hindi film are occasions to celebrate its own musical tradition. Embraced by all classes and communities, this music is truly the insignia of national popular culture. Film culture and filial festivity intersect: Hindi film music, a

25. Nisha and the woman in drag in women's space. *Hum Aapke Hain Kaun* (Who Am I to You), Sooraj Barjatya, 1994.

part of urban familial celebrations, becomes self-referential—invoking collages of songs from other films.

In *Hum Aapke* a prolonged song-and-dance sequence in a strictly demarcated women's space marks the celebration of Pooja's first child. In the all-women's gathering a woman in drag (dresses identical to the male lead) pairs with the leading lady, Nisha, playing an oversized pregnant woman. Together they parody "private scenes" between heterosexual couples, regaling everyone. The lead male star and his buddies are voyeurs, gazing at the performance meant for women only—the woman in drag enacting scenes a man could never perform publicly with his lady love. This strategy serves a dual purpose. It recreates women's space where women traditionally relax together, enact heterosexual encounters, act as sexual teases, and mock men and the codes of intimacy. As well, the cross-dressed woman enacts the leading man's eroticized relationship with his lady—the very thing the performance parodies.[12]

This celebration of women's space is akin to what Lisa Lewis calls a "discovery sign." In the context of the presence of women on MTV, Lewis speaks of this and "access signs." Access signs are those in which women appropriate men's space, "enact an entrance into a male domain of activity and signification. . . . Symbolically . . . [they] execute takeovers of male-space, the erasure of sex-roles, and demand parity with male privilege." In Indian films, access signs would include the streets, colleges, bicycles, highways and the like. Discovery signs, on the other hand,

celebrate distinctly female modes of cultural expression and
experience. Discovery signs attempt to compensate in mediated
form for female cultural marginalization by drawing pictures
of activities in which females tend to engage apart from
males . . . [They] rejoice in female forms of leisure and
cultural expression, and female sources of social bonding, to
which . . . boys have little access. By representing girl[/female]
practices, the videos [here film] set a tone that celebrates
female resourcefulness and cultural distinctiveness.[13]

The loss of "women's space" in the midst of rapid urban modernization has meant a collective forgetting of traditional folk songs and
customs. Self-conscious attempts by the women's movement to recover
traditional celebration modes are didactic, and often disconnected from
the fêted life-stages of marriage, birth, and death—thus failing to substitute the affective affirmation the traditional family and community
provide.[14] The film industry has been more effective in appropriating
the folk culture tradition, with its risqué innuendo and suggestive play
on words and images. The extended sequence in *Hum Aapke* celebrating women's traditional space functions as the "discovery sign," or reverses the "access sign," making men within the diegesis—and the film's
audience—voyeurs, taking pleasure in women's revelry.

On MTV the representation of access signs—women taking over
the streets, pushing men aside, and returning glances in an equal exchange of looks—implies a role reversal. Access signs offer textual solutions to gender inequalities. But combined with discovery signs, they
push "beyond the mere transposition of sex roles and practices," valu-
ing a specific "culturalism" of female adolescence.[15] In Hindi films,
access signs are traceable in the more recent, MTV-influenced chore-
ography. These sequences adapt an earlier narrative convention, where
the city-bred couple met in a bucolic environment and later lead the
village/tribal folk dance.

The 1990s' films extend this stylized spectacle in which a multitude of men and women perform a carefully choreographed mix of aero-
bics, jazz, and modern dance in streets, colleges, and dance halls. The
numbers that narrativize the romantic encounter or depict moods are
filmed almost entirely in long shots. *Dil* and *Qyamat se Qyamat Tak*,
for example, reverse the courtship rituals: the woman pursues the man

rather than wards him off. Traditionally dance numbers are paced much like sexual foreplay in which the climactic moment is when the boy "gets" the girl. Now newer access signs operate with women coming into the domain occupied by men, teasing them, fighting them off, and enticing men in their own coquettish way.

In *Dilwale Dulhaniya Le Jayenge* (The Lover Wins the Bride, Aditya Chopra, 1996), another blockbuster success on the heels of *Hum Aapke*, Baldev Singh (Amrish Puri), a resident in Britain, takes his daughter, Simran (Kajol) back to India to marry her off to his friend's son, Kulwant. The trip is precipitated by Baldev's discovery of Simran's romantic involvement during a trip to Europe. Raj (Sharukh Khan), Simran's lover, follows her to India and infiltrates the family masquerading as a Non-Resident Indian (NRI) scouting for investment prospects in India.[16] When he is discovered, Raj incurs the wrath of Baldev and Kulwant—although Simran's mother supports Raj, even urging him to run away with Simran. Raj refuses this option as "improper" and is resigned to his defeat. At the eleventh hour Baldev relents and Simran and Raj are united. *Pardes* (Foreign Land, Subhash Ghai, 1997) is similar to *Dilwale* except that the female protagonist, the prospective bride, travels to Los Angeles to live with her future in-laws, maintains her chastity against all odds, and is ultimately paired with the hero, her fiancé's foster brother, who both recognizes and protects her chastity despite his own conflicting desires.

According to Purnima Mankekar, *Dilwale* affirms the Indian male's agency by casting him in the figure of the NRI investor and the custodian of the Indian woman's sexual purity—the quintessential trope of Indian identity—thus replaying the classic woman/nation conflation.[17] For Patricia Uberoi the NRI figure at best represents the temporary abeyance of the "Americanization" of Indian identity, under siege in the era of globalization. In this she echoes Arjun Appadurai's prophecy—telescoped from the experience of the Indian diaspora, the class of mobile labor, an internationalized mass media, and Internet communication—that the demise of the nation is nigh. In Hindi cinema the figure of the diasporic Indian is metonymic of this anxiety of the invasion of the west and disappearance of an "Indian identity," which it cleverly manipulates to reimagine the nation in response to changing conditions.

Women's protest is also voiced in this film. Patricia Uberoi argues that "women (especially older women) . . . articulate the injustice of 'tradition' . . . though such misgivings are discounted in the final resolution."[18] The older women's descriptions of their experiences are poignant moments, especially in *Dilwale*, and are strikingly similar to scripts in feminist street plays Indian women's groups produced almost two decades ago.[19] Consider Simran's mother, urging her to give up Raj:

> MOTHER: As a little girl I heard my grandfather say there's no difference between a man and woman. They have the same rights. When I grew up I learnt otherwise. My education was stopped, so that my brothers' could continue; their education was more important than mine. I sacrificed my life as a daughter and then as a daughter-in-law.
>
> But when you were born I vowed you would not make the same sacrifices I did . . . But Simran I was wrong. I forgot that a woman has no right to make such pledges. Women are born to make sacrifices for men . . . I beg you, give up your happiness and forget him. Your father won't ever allow it [marriage of her choosing].

Despite quoting these lines Uberoi discounts them, and points to patriarchal underpinnings that cast the woman as an object transacted between her father and husband in *Dilwale* and *Pardes*. However, romance has always expressed the "modernist project of freedom and emancipation," and, as Eva Illouz argues, romantic "love invokes values and principles that have . . . an emancipatory potential . . . individualism, self-realization, affirmation of the individual's personal qualities and equality between the sexes in the mutual experience of pleasure."[20] Feminist agency is important, and *Dilwale* presents the younger generation as having choice (carefully avoiding its economic basis in contemporary realpolitik). The film represents choice strictly in terms of picking a romantic partner, which contravenes social conventions.

Films such as *Dilwale* (as well as *Pardes*) creatively deploy feminism—bourgeois feminism—using a woman-centered discourse that gained widespread currency in the Indian middle class, thanks in no small part to the women's movement's efforts.[21] In Hindi cinema's romance genre the female protagonist is located firmly within the bourgeois terrain, the rising new middle class or the NRI—emblematic of

26. The morning-after scene in *Dilwale Dulhaniya le Jayenge* (The Lover Wins the Bride), Aditya Chopra, 1996.

the local within the global, of which the nation is increasingly conscious. The bourgeois woman experiences the strain of tradition, community, and family and can most credibly chafe, throw off, or negotiate them.

Mankekar and Uberoi disavow *Dilwale's* subversive message, hinging their argument on the suggestion and then containment of premarital sex which in the narrative regulates female sexuality. Likewise, Dwyer too finds the film conservative, not challenging social "prohibitions."[22] Much is made of the morning in *Dilwale* after Simran and Raj spend a night together—accidentally of course, in an *It Happened One Night* style—and the audience is set up to expect but then assured, despite signs to the contrary, that "nothing happened."[23]

Romance films, recently at least, carefully take up the cause of romantic love—not premarital sex. Also important is that in the discursive framework of the romance genre exploring individual and family politics, the antagonistic, vilified figure is always the patriarch. The romance expresses agency, transgression, and transformation—all directed at challenging the "law of the father."

Romance in Hindi cinema has its lineage in the fictional world of the novel and in Hollywood films that inscribed it as a mandatory subplot along with the hero's action-oriented goal.[24] Using romance to trace the topos of conflict is not new in Hindi cinema, and throughout the

Nehruvian era romance maps and challenges social divisions based on caste and class. As in premodern Europe so in India,

> romantic love was perceived to oppose strategies of reproduction normally safeguarded by the institution of marriage. It stood for such values as disinterestedness, irrationality, and indifference to riches. . . . In proclaiming the supremacy of human relationships governed by the disinterested gift of oneself, love not only celebrates the fusion of individual souls and bodies but also opens up the possibility of an alternative social order. . . . Romantic love has been and continues to be the cornerstone of a powerful utopia because it reenacts symbolically the rituals of opposition to the social order through inversion of social hierarchies and affirms the supremacy of the individual.[25]

Hence romance is *the* trope for transgression, and the romantic couple's bond stands for transforming the status quo. The "romance genre" since the late 1980s reconfigured the elements in Hindi films: the patriarch turns into a villain, treated sympathetically or otherwise, and the romance once limited to a subplot becomes the main plot— the genre's defining feature.

Romantic Love and the Culture of Consumption

Romantic love has been viewed as "accompanying or even facilitating the rise of capitalism. . . . Love became central to the capitalist entrepreneur's 'cultural ideals of privacy and the nuclear family.'"[26] In the American context premodern love moved from the religious to the secular domain, and its most powerful mythology was the new "equation of love—and marriage—with personal happiness. The systemic association between love, marriage and bliss was different from nineteenth-century representations, in which love was more often tragic rather than a happy feeling."[27] This parallels the Indian context, especially Urdu poetry, where *dard* (pain) is the quintessential emotion of true love. But over the twentieth century love became increasingly important in the pursuit of happiness, and was defined hedonistically in "individualistic and private terms." Love is entwined with marriage and conjugal bliss as true happiness, and the happy ending is married life.[28]

Interestingly, the romance genre's eruption coincides with increasing liberalization of the Indian economy, first half-heartedly by Rajiv Gandhi in the mid–1980s and then more aggressively by Narsimha Rao in 1991. While "western" presence maintained itself in India throughout India's post-independence era, it was characterized by the desires of a small middle class (6 percent of the population) which experienced a time lag in products, fashions, and cultural trends arriving from the west. With liberalization the pace of transactions with western-style production and consumerism accelerated in the 1980s, and by the 1990s the time lag was replaced by dramatic simultaneity. The National Council of Applied Economic Research (NCAER) estimates that the "middle class," or more appropriately the "consuming class," doubled in size to 12 percent in the 1980s and to about 18 percent by the end of the 1990s.[29]

The information technology revolution, serviced in no small part by Indian software engineers, abetted the simultaneity in flows of goods, services, information, and cultural products. Thus limits on U.S. cultural imports in the form of novels, films, and television programs gave way to a prolific and instant flow through the media and the Internet— with an eye on promoting consumption. As Arif Dirlik, keen to return postcolonial discourse to its political economic roots, puts it: "Eurocentrism . . . is evident above all in the rendering of EuroAmerica and its many products into objects of desire globally."[30]

If, as Gurcharan Das laments, the Congress officials instituting liberalization policies in 1991 lacked the political vision and will to win legitimacy for them and sell them to the voter, he can be assured that Hindi films stepped in successfully to do this work—ensuring the hegemony of consumer culture. The ascent of a bourgeois lifestyle is unmistakable in the romance genre, and as Rachel Dwyer, making a case for a succession struggle between the old and new middle classes, argues: "It is in the commercial cinema that the new middle classes are establishing their cultural hegemony, their depictions of lifestyle becoming those to which the lower classes aspire."[31] Promoting the market as a site of plenitude and unlimited consumption, the romantic couple's agency and desire entwine commodity culture, new middle-class tastes, and egalitarianism associated with the freedom of choice in intimate relations.

Thus we see in these films a "symbolic and practical penetration of romance by the market."[32] The "romanticization of commodities" intersects with the "commodification of romance" in which "romantic practices [are] . . . interlocked with and . . . defined by the consumption of leisure goods and leisure technologies offered by the nascent market."[33] Using commodities as props "fetishize[s] consumption, . . . transpose[s] erotic desire onto goods, which in turn [become] . . . the very objects of desire."[34] Combining a visual utopia of affluence, glamor, and leisure with romantic fantasy, the films focus on and encourage pleasure, "creating islands of privacy in the midst of the public realm."[35] The occasional telephone or radio used as a prop in the song-and-dance convention in the 1950s Hindi films is replaced in the 1990s with fast cars, water scooters, shopping arcades, luxury farm houses in rural settings, or palatial homes, all prominently displayed in the mise-en-scène. The "romance gives voice to a new language of commodities."[36]

In the romance genre the Non-Resident Indian provides an imaginative terrain in which to explore the "iconography of abundance."[37] It adds a twist to the trajectory of commodity fetishism in the decade of sudden economic changes at the close of the twentieth century in India.[38] The NRI is Hindi cinema's new aristocrat. Iconic of new wealth the NRI replaces the *zamindar* (landed wealth) and Kunwar *sahibs*, scions of the princely states from previous decades, who now stand effaced from popular cinema's social landscape. As new wealth goes, the line between the NRI and the new middle class, spun by ties to an international economy, blurs with their common consumption desires and tastes.

In Hindi cinema's imaginative world the NRI belongs to a uniformly prosperous class of Indians usually residing in Britain or the United States, whose emotional dislocation can be recentered through a sense of national belonging. As Akhil Gupta argues, "representing the nation in an age where the public sphere is thoroughly transnational is a major challenge facing state elites."[39] Hindi cinema imaginatively refigures the nation now penetrated by transnational forces in an accelerated pace of globalization.[40] India, imagined in films over the decades through binary oppositions—the feudal vs. the modern, country vs. city, east vs. west, rural vs. urban—now pits the national against the transnational. The discourse of the national within the transnational serves a dual function: to assert an "Indian" identity in the discursive field of globalization while simultaneously advertising commodity flows, and to whet consumer appetite by conflating bourgeois romantic desire and commodity fetishism.

Opulence in the form of leisure spaces, travel, and tourism are well-established sites in Hindi cinema for the romantic encounter and its progression.[41] In the romance genre it retreated into the home: in some instances it was the home away from home, the lovers' nest established in defiance of patriarchal authority, symbolically rupturing with the family (*Dil* and *Qyamat*); in others, in a reconciliatory move, it relocated in the domestic space of the parental home (*Maine Pyaar Kiya*, *Hum Aapke*, *Dilwale*, and *Pardes*). Despite this "domestication," the couple oscillates between a fantasy land and home with the camera fixing its fetishistic gaze on the "iconography of abundance," be it upscale resorts, exotic locales, or a dazzling array of appliances in fabulous houses.[42]

The wedding scenario, a feature in *Hum Aapke* and in *Dilwale*, intensifies the conflict between the forces encapsulated in these films. The romance, developed amidst a cornucopia of fine food, clothes, and jewelry, provokes the contest between the changing conditions underlying the abundance iconography and the affirmation of family ties that condense around the wedding. A significant ritual connecting the couple, the family, and the community, the wedding is a dramatic site underscoring the difficulty of choosing between competing forces—the "communitas" of the family or the couple.[43]

The End of the Nehruvian Era

While the romantic couple as a symbol of agency is an old ploy, Hindi cinema shifted its target of attack in the late 1980s and 1990s. In these decades the Indian middle class underwent rapid transformation, and thus the romance relocated itself exclusively in the expanded bourgeois terrain. Propelled by new economic conditions and their attendant emphasis on individualism, personal freedom, and choice, the romantic couple made the authoritarian patriarch its nemesis. The resolution of course varied: elliptical devices such as divine intervention in *Hum Aapke*, and a sudden change of heart on the part of the patriarch in

Dilwale, soften the blow against patriarchy.[44] Simultaneously, they overturn sociologist M. S. Gore's description of the Indian extended family, which requires "minimizing the significance of the conjugal bond."[45] Aside from differences between *Hum Aapke's* conservative family ideals (which Rajshree Productions proudly upholds) and Aditya Chopra's *Dilwale* being a tribute to his father Yash Chopra's brand of challenging-moral-values filmmaking, both films at their core negotiate the fraught relationship between the individual/couple's romantic love and family/community interests—and wishfully preserve both, accounting perhaps for their stupendous success.[46]

Some films thus rehabilitate the family and reconcile with patriarchal authority in a genre that as a whole is devoted to negotiating that authority and what it stands for through confrontation—and sometimes reconciliation. In a society where for centuries individuals have played out prescripted roles, *Maine Pyar Kiya* and *Hum Aapke Hain Kaun* rehearse the cultural confusion over the family's place transformed by new ideas about the personal and the private. While the family gracefully makes space for individual freedom and personal choice, it still does not abdicate its centrality.

Women's agency, mobilized to assert the couple's supremacy, strains family bonds and a community-oriented order, as in *Dilwale.* The conflict is genuine and feminist articulations by older women combine with younger women's agency, resonating across the generational divide. However, this occurs at the cost of banishing other minority groups from the films. In *Madhumati* a tribal woman's narrative dominates the screen, but such representations have disappeared altogether from Hindi cinema. At the same time the locus of conflict has shifted to a bourgeois terrain avowing the profusion of goods made available by a liberalized economy, while disavowing its threat to the family by attempting different resolutions to the conflict against the patriarchal family, for long central in social relations. With its bourgeois feminist stance the romance plot lost sight of the class battles it once championed in the Nehruvian era.

Conclusion

I_N THIS BOOK I take some first steps in a relatively uncharted terrain, reading popular Indian cinema as narrating the nation's social history. I trace the lay of cultural politics along the topos of Hindi films. The logic of the colonial Empire produced a nation concretized through political, economic, and legal measures. But it is through cultural productions that the nation is imagined: the sphere of education, history, literary fiction, newspapers, television, and, the most overlooked of all—Hindi cinema, which popularizes that imagination.

The nation is an abstraction, toward which consent and loyalty are constantly being secured. Hence it is that the nation is incessantly remapped in the popular imagination, in response to passing anxieties and threats. From lauding the move from monarchy (read: colonialism) to democracy in the 1950s (*Aan*), to condemning regional separatism in the 1980s (*Karma*), and invoking tradition—that insignia of an imagined community—in representations of country versus city, east versus west, and the national versus the transnational, the nation in Hindi cinema is constantly resecured and reimagined.

Judging by reports of the wild success in 2001 of *Gadar* (Mayhem, Anil Sharma) and *Lagaan* (Tax, Ashutosh Gowariker), yet another innovative ploy for feting the nation may have been found. *Lagaan* celebrates the struggle against the empire: the transnational forces of another moment, that noble moment to which the nation owes its origin and to which Hindi cinema has only made muted references before. The anticolonial struggle might become the latest imprint to imagine the nation—more than a hundred years after the nationalist movement began in earnest and fifty years after the nation's independence. It was an event marred by the trauma of Partition invoked in *Henna* in 1991, and revisited more forcefully in *Gadar*, ten years later. The dramatic appeal of the now-historic anti-imperial victory might make it yet another enduring strategy to glorify the nation racked with internal polarizations, confused about contending with intensifying globalization forces, and willing to repress and displace the trauma of two nations with the self-aggrandizement of becoming a regional superpower.

Powerful nationalist rhetoric dominates everything from the public sphere to individual subjectivities—our very personal identity. Apart from the challenge of writing the "history" of the contemporary, there is the difficulty of understanding "nation" and "nationalism" that thoroughly infuses our consciousness, positioning us within it—with limited possibilities of distancing, much less escaping it. Yet paradoxically, equally inescapable are the nation's tenuousness, its artifice, and its gloss over fault lines.

Popular Hindi films locate these fractures within the nation by projecting a national edifice *and* the rumblings against it. The nation not only subsumes personal identities but also collectivities identified by class, gender, sexuality, community, and caste, although social movements centered around these threaten the hierarchies (feudal, capitalist, and patriarchal) maintained by the nation state. Hindi films explore the tensions these collectivities generate, even openly articulate their conflicts within the nation; they offer a glimmer of change—and then contain it.

Social and economic inequalities that the bourgeois national liberation movement failed to undo mute the nation's jubilance. Worker-capitalist, peasant-landlord, city-country, tribal-"civilized," East-West, tradition-modernity, man-woman—all are divisions with sharp inequalities, not just *difference*. *Aan, Upkaar, Roti Kapada aur Makaan, Shri 420, C.I.D., Bobby,* and numerous other films stage these unresolved tensions, each time assuring amicable conflict resolution. The hero is the agent affecting this resolution, wrestling with danger, tackling the nation's enemy, solving its problems, and defusing that one imminent threat—disintegration. *Pratighaat,* produced towards the end of the Nehruvian era, acknowledges the failure of a whole generation of male heroes and instates the (albeit middle-class) "new Indian woman"—a figure constantly recharged by contemporaneous discourses—as the nation's savior.

Women, or rather the symbolic field of gender, is deployed by the anticolonial impulse, positing the "east" as the binary opposite of the "west"—critical to imagining the new nation. Women are set up as repositories of an "Indian" tradition to establish difference, even superiority, over the west's material affluence. A deflated Indian cultural ego inscribes this ideal woman's image—a blend of Victorian-Brahmin qualities—as its own insignia. This history shapes dominant representations of women in Indian culture, particularly in popular Hindi films. The films disavow gender equality by repeating taming-the-shrew narratives, as in *Purab aur Paschim* and *Mr. and Mrs. 55,* assuaging anxieties caused by the dramatic push toward gender parity. In *Aan* the trope of the woman is even used to allegorize the traumatic transformation from Empire to nation and from feudalism to democracy. In each film the errant westernized Indian woman is brought to heel when she discovers "Indian" tradition under the hero's stern guidance.

If women are portrayed sympathetically, it is by framing them in narratives charged with dilemmas about romantic love, or as abject victims of patriarchy. Reference to troubled gender relations are either oblique, or, as in the tradition of melodrama, the films "resolve" what are really irresolvable conflicts of affect relegated to the family.[1] In these instances we hear the woman's voice in moments of excess, when she speaks out against marriage or the injustices of monogamous heterosexual love—even as the grain of the text strains to resurrect these institutions. "Happy endings" affirming faith in heterosexual love (as in *Gumrah, Sangam,* and *Pyaasa*) are meant to resolve problems in the social text.

In fact, next to the hero's "action" in Hindi films, romantic love is the most potent force that overcomes the nation's ills. The all-powerful force of heterosexual love resolves class conflict, the city-country divide, and communal strife. Asserting bourgeois individualism is still unwelcome in the family's code of sexual conduct, so romantic love becomes a perfect site to stage these conflicts and contradictions that are then overcome by "true" love. The family is a trope for the ideal nation, a site to invoke the nation's problems through the protagonist's relation with his antagonist—his father, brother, or the villain. Metonymically, these represent conflicts between law/outlaw, rich/poor, city/country and other binary oppositions which Hindi films favor. The unprecedented success of recent romance stories in which the villains have shifted from unscrupulous businessmen to tyrannical patriarchs is testimony to the change in focus from class to patriarchy.

The family is under siege in India today, and its centuries-old organizational pattern, which privileges its own interest over the individual's, is disintegrating. With the entry of the women's movement and its assertion of the individual's rights within the family, the bourgeois idea of individual will itself is contested. Heterosexual love battles patriarchal authority and Hindi films, taken as a whole, have been equivocal about resolving this problem. While the films celebrate individualism, they rehabilitate the family on the terms of individual will; the family calls a truce with the transgressing couple and both seek comfort in the idea that they can coexist through negotiation. This resolution of the ongoing family saga in Indian culture denies the inevitable outcome caused by broad social changes encouraging robust individualism that steadily erode community feelings. Films such as *Dil*, *Qyamat se Qyamat tak*, *Maine Pyaar Kiya*, *Hum Aapke Hain Kaun*, and *Dilwale Dulhania Le Jayenge* plot the unfinished business of mediating between the family and individualism.

Such bourgeois individualism enables the women's movement too; it has been traduced as "western" in order to subordinate Indian women. Consequently, representations of women are a war zone in contemporary culture and have been in a state of flux for the last two decades. Hindi films have begun to portray women with agency: they refuse to suffer as victims, fighting back instead in revenge fantasies. Rape is the classic trope for women's oppression in popular films, and the female protagonist heroically avenges this.

Insaaf ka Taraazu is the film that marks the beginning of the film industry's recognition of the women's movement. Though the film attempts to air women's voices and grievances—for long silenced—one cannot overlook its duplicity in deliberately conflating power with desire and reintroducing the blame-the-victim stance it supposedly undermines in its examination of rape. The film gives full reign to the fetishized female body and the voyeuristic male gaze, obfuscating differences between lust, desire, and power; worse, the resolution decries rape by invoking a classic patriarchal fiat—to protect women's "purity" and "honor."

As in the discourse on womanhood, the popular film indexes changing tensions and conflicts within the social text of the nation. The hero tackles social problems manifested in the changing guise of the villain—mapping the topos of the nation's anxieties. Like the hero and heroine, the villain is a fixed feature in Hindi films, a figure registering threats the nation perceives. The hazards change—from the capricious nature of the city, unscrupulous nature of big business, antinational "smugglers," separatist terrorists, and violent communalists who threaten the official rhetoric of a secular nation. The transition from one villainous type to another is fraught with risk—censorship, negative audience reaction, or a collective disavowal of pressing exigencies.

An example of this is the industry's prolonged hesitation to break its silence on the nation's hollow claims to secularism. References to communal strife are oblique, and the films carefully repress its role in searing the nation at birth, during the Partition. When examining communal sentiments, the interrogation is veiled or elaborately allegorized as another conflict (among nations, within communities, or from times past); *Henna, Amar Akbar Anthony*, and *Qyamat se Qyamat tak* are all examples of this sublimation. As expected, the impact of the first articulation of Hindu-Muslim amity—depicted in *Bombay*—was not without tremors. Although the film deploys romantic love, this time to oppose communalism and promote a secular sensibility, the narrative does not end in the success of the transgressive Hindu-Muslim marriage. The problems only begin after the couple marry. The film traces the tribulations of an intercommunity marriage that first faces rejection from the family and is then trapped in the December 1992 communal holocaust. The public conflagration of communal animosities intensifies the suffering in the couple's personal lives.

Popular films are mute about several other conflicts that pervade the public and private spheres. Caste politics is elided in popular Hindi films, and certainly nothing beyond platitudes against *oonch-neech* (high-low) is ever mentioned. Suppressing caste within the subtext of class is

a sign of the extent to which caste and community distinctions are observed covertly. Although I constantly point to how the films dilute
conflicts and contain contradictions, it is articulating the problem—
airing conflicts—that I believe is important. This is what accounts for
the films' resonance with audiences, their popularity. The "containment"
at the end is merely the impulse for resolution, the logic of narrative
closure.

In this project I have presented a nonlinear history, one that es-
chews recounting a chronology of "facts." I have shown that the films
are not unchanging. Rather, they reflect and are informed by social and
historical change. The history of Hindi films can be narrated as the films
themselves narrate the nation's history. Though a variety of elements
within a complex and changing polity have been isolated and discussed
independently, they also exist simultaneously and interact dynamically
within the social text. In films they appear dominant or regressed, in
the foreground or background, at the center, or in the margins of the
frame.

I also wish to reiterate that paying serious attention to Hindi films—
the most vibrant aspect of popular culture in India today—swims against
a strong current of derision. Arjun Appadurai and Carol Beckenridge
map Indian modernity by identifying its key players—the growing
middle class, the state, the booming magazine-music-sports-restaurant
culture, travel, tourism, and televisual media—but excluding Indian
popular cinema. Not only does cinema predate television, dominate its
air time with reruns, and provide more than fashion, glamour, and ce-
lebrity culture glorifying consumption, it cuts across class, urban-rural,
and transnational divisions in a way television does not. Enabled by
video and now DVD technology, Hindi cinema reaches viewers overseas and in small town and village video parlors. The current boom in
television, magazine, video recording, and the audio industry is part of
a world-wide explosion "whose cultural contours are barely understood."[2] Popular films, while part of those contours, also help in mapping them.

The hermeneutic I provide uses broad strokes to present a picture
of contemporary history and culture which is often difficult to account
for while one is in the thick of it. The recent spate of writing on Hindi
popular cinema of the 1990s reflects a welcome growing interest in and

acknowledgement of popular cinema's importance. However, it is skewed by a "recency" effect and lacks historical perspective. Going back further, to the pre-independence period's films, is important in order to contextualize a study of post-independence films. Additionally, we need more "textured accounts" of contemporary culture.[3] For instance, the elements of homoeroticism in Hindi films that I explored in chapter 6, and its latent and explicit manifestation, is certainly a promising area for future research. Alternative sexualities are beginning to appear on the Hindi film screen, not surprisingly coinciding with the emergence of an Indian gay and lesbian movement in the 1990s. Future research must be directed toward this.

Research open to an audience (rather than limited to a text-centered approach) will not only relate films to audiences' changing tastes, but also map Hindi cinema's local and transnational popularity. Also, comparing popular films to their clones that failed at the box office, to see how their textual strategies diverge from or converge with successful films, can add details to the themes I have only begun to explore in this book. We also need intensive genealogical studies of concentrated periods of film history, which will critically examine the usefulness of the taxonomy I present here and test if the axes along which I plot the films yield a homology between text and the context in which films are produced. A critique that challenges the taxonomy I present—even if it dismantles and replaces it with a different framework—can only add to the richness of film history. Alternative ways of conceptualizing film history will enrich that textured account of contemporary culture.

In Wimal Dissanayake's broad taxonomy of Indian cinema he groups films into "the popular, the artistic, and the experimental," assigning the latter two categories only with the function of critiquing and interrogating the "hegemonic project of the nation-state."[4] Although I do not deal with art films or their distinction from the popular, it is a corpus that warrants careful comparative treatment. However, contrary to Dissanayake's judgment, I show that popular films do indeed interrogate the status quo. Given any narrative's demand for conflict, Hindi films use this effectively to challenge and reveal problems within the hegemonic ideal of nation. And although the nation is vigorously reinstated through forceful rhetoric, the films certainly question, or at least spell out, its precarious nature.

While the Hindi film industry as a whole maintains the nation in the interest of a bourgeois hegemony instated since the bourgeois democratic state was established, in passing moments different classes, collectivities, and constituencies have contested that hegemony—which in theory is always unstable and in practice never total. Thus the "old" middle-class, upper-caste male professional ceded ground to the working class briefly in the 1970s, and to the bourgeois woman in the 1980s. While I have explored popular films to point to the changing lay of cultural politics and the dominance of various interests at different moments, less visible strains do persist. For instance, even though romance and contestations in family politics dominated the screen in the 1990s, gangster-action films successful in the 1970s and 1980s continued exploring crime and the underworld of politics with varying degrees of realism in films such as *Parinda* (Pigeons, 1989), *Khalnayak* (Antagonist, 1993), and *Satya* (Truth, 1996).

The cross-section of films chosen for this book do not reveal a monolithic ideology or monological voice, even within a broadly status quoist industry. Admittedly, profit maximization prompts the industry to play it safe by not straying from the dominant ideological current; most films only attempt a circumspect interrogation. My intent here has been to point to the mélange of images and the polyphony of accompanying voices which respond, contradict, or challenge one another in a creative intertextual relay among the films. The combination of contradictory discourses the films draw from make the silver screen a fun-house mirror reflecting society. Taken together, they are palimpsests with traces of Indian culture, ideology, and politics.

It is clear that Hindi cinema privileges certain elements: the family, the villain, the hero, and the heroine. Adjustments between them are managed through rearticulations of gender: masculinity, femininity, and the special relationships Hindi cinema favors such as the heterosexual couple, or the mother and son. The relationships and varied scenarios are unstable tropes or signifiers and are deployed in different ways by films. Heterosexual romance in *Mr. and Mrs. 55*, for instance, upholds conservative ideals compared to the depictions in *Dil* or *Dilwale*; the premarital sex openly suggested in *Aradhana* has punitive consequences, while in *Dilwale* its suggestion, while equivocal, is not punished. In *Aradhana* the nation-state applauds a mother's sacrifice for her son, while in *Mother India* (and *Deewar*) sacrificing the son is itself a daring act, marshaled ultimately to affirm the good citizen's service and subordination to the community/nation.

The task is to identify the culturally favored tropes Hindi cinema uses compared to popular regional or international cinemas, the specific ways it redeploys them, and how shifting discourses about the nation inflect them at different historical moments. Hence heroes, heroines, villains, the family, romance, maternal love, and so on are a fund of unstable signifiers mobilized in varying and conflicting ways by different auteurs to rearticulate, reanchor, and reaffirm the nation while engaging contemporary national discourses. The shifting emphases of tropes in changing contexts demand fresh readings, and this is what makes Hindi cinema a valuable source for mapping Indian cultural politics and social history. It is also this instability of signifiers and the need to creatively redeploy them that leaves filmmakers guessing—hoping that the particular use, twist, and nuance they bring to each new film will succeed with audiences.

Raj Kapoor, a stalwart of the Bombay industry in the Nehruvian era, once called popular films a mix of "commerce with art."[5] The premium "pleasure" and "desire" enjoy in cultural studies has opened our minds to the liberatory aspects of popular culture and the polysemic nature of texts. Yet we are well-served by the cautionary reminder that the force of an unchallenged market ideology drives that pleasure principle. So far we can only conclude that popular films reveal a complex play between hegemony and the challenges to it within the framework of the marketplace.

Appealing to "the masses," the only guarantee to that elusive success at the box office, is of utmost importance to the moguls in the film industry. Unlike politicians, who turn their backs on this constituency once elected, the industry never neglects the desires of its audience, drawn predominantly from the underprivileged, the working-class, the subaltern. What might offend, insult, or please them is taken very seriously. Yet gauging the audience—tracking their desires and what will please them—is tricky business, unpredictable and contradictory, and this is worth noting with a brief anecdote. When I interviewed the commercially successful don of Rajshree Productions, Raj Barjatya, I gleaned a sense of the intense anxiety experienced on the day of a film's release.

When *Maine Pyaar Kiya* was released in 1989, after the usual hectic publicity campaign, the Barjatyas' chauffeur saw the first show. After seeing the film he reportedly told Barjatya, "*Saheb*, this film will be a success." And it was. Raj Barjatya maintains he has deep faith in his domestic staff's counsel.

This ironical inversion of class attitudes—the reverence toward the "Fourth Estate," echoed by several rich and successful film entrepreneurs—is unparalleled elsewhere in Indian public life. The anecdote points to the singular importance, the near reverence the industry magnates have for the commoner, the plebeian, the woman or man on the street. Succeeding or failing at tracking their tastes and desires makes or breaks the producer—a striking inversion of social hierarchy in the Indian public sphere and a tribute to the power of the popular film.

Notes

Preface

1. "Film and Media Theory," paper presented by Teresa de Lauretis at the Society for Cinema Studies conference, Palm Beach, Florida, 1999.
2. Ella Shohat and Robert Stam, *Unthinking Eurocentricism: Multiculturalism and the Media* (New York: Routledge, 1994), and Paul Willemen, *Looks and Frictions: Essays on Cultural Studies and Film Theory* (Bloomington: Indiana University Press, 1994), 207.
3. J. Martín-Barbero, "Communication from Culture: The Crisis of the National and the Emergence of the Popular," *Media, Culture and Society* 10 (4): 447–465, cited in Ien Ang's *Living Room Wars: Rethinking Media Audiences for a Postmodern World* (New York: Routledge, 1996), 141.
4. Mary Louise Pratt suggests that "hybrid" may be better described as "transculturation—where members of subordinated and marginalized groups "select and invent from material transmitted by a dominant or metropolitan culture." See her "Transculturation and autoethnography," *Colonial discourse/postcolonial theory*, eds. Francis Baker, Peter Hulme, and Margaret Iversen (New York: Manchester University Press, 1994), 31.
5. *Granta* 57 Spring (1997) special issue, "India! The Golden Jubilee"; Salman Rushdie, "Damn, This is the Oriental Scene for You! An introduction to Indian fiction," *New Yorker* June 30 (1997): 50. Also see Pankaj Mishra's "A Spirit of Their Own," *New York Review of Books* May 20 (1999): 47–53.
6. Edward Said, *Culture and Imperialism* (New York: Vintage, 1994), 316–324.
7. Edward Said, *Orientalism* (New York: Vintage Books, 1978).
8. Bill Ashcroft, Gareth Griffiths, and Helen Tiffin, among others, point to the fuzziness of the term that collapses disparate colonization experiences of time (the eighteenth and nineteenth centuries) and space (countries in Asia, Latin America, North America and Australia). See their *The Empire Writes Back: Theory and Practice in Post-Colonial Literature* (New York: Routledge, 1989), 2.
9. See Ien Ang, *Living Room Wars*, 138–149. If the Frankfurt School treated ideology as the unproblematized epiphenomenon of the capitalist production mode,

ethnographic/audience studies in our current era of unprecedented capitalist consolidation declare "the audiences' independence in the cultural struggle over meaning and pleasure. . . . The euphoria over the vitality of popular culture has tended to make the question of hegemony rather unfashionable" (139–140).

10. Film historian Erik Barnouw's *Indian Films* (New Delhi: Oxford University Press, 1980) is an expansive overview of its history; Kishore Valicha's *The Moving Image: A Study of Indian Cinema* (Bombay: Orient Longman, 1988), Sumita Chakravarty's *National Identity in Indian Popular Cinema, 1947–87* (Austin: Texas University Press, 1993), and Madhava Prasad's *Ideology of the Hindi Film: A Historical Construction* (New Delhi: Oxford University Press, 1998) document and analyze film history; the *Encyclopaedia of Indian Cinema* commissioned by the British Film Institute, compiled by Ashish Rajadhyaksha and Paul Willemen (New Delhi: Oxford University Press, 1995) provides an extensive filmography; Ashis Nandy, ed., *The Secret Politics of Our Desires: Innocence, Culpability, and Indian Popular Cinema* (New Delhi: Oxford University Press, 1998) and Ravi Vasudevan, ed., *Making Meaning in Indian Cinema* (New Delhi: Oxford University Press, 2000) are anthologies; Rachel Dwyer's *All You Want is Money, All You Need is Love: Sex and Romance in Modern India* (London: Cassell, 2000) selectively analyzes films and pulp fiction; and Vijay Mishra's *Bollywood Cinema: Temples of Desire* (London: Routledge, 2002) presents a semiotic analysis of Hindi films. In addition, occasional essays in *Screen*, *Quarterly Review of Film and Video*, and a few other anthologies (in India, Britain, and the United States) constitute most of the literature on popular Hindi cinema.

11. Prasad, *Ideology of the Hindi Film*, 42–49, and Mishra, *Bollywood Cinema*, 13. The term "dharma" in this context refers to a Hindu code of conduct.

12. Barbara Christian's caution against the "race for theory" in the context of black women's literature is worth heeding, because, she argues, it tends to force a prescriptive reading rather than opening multiple ways of seeing how class, race, and gender intersect. Recalling the Black Arts Movement that sprang from black nationalist separatism in the 1960s, she reminds us of the dangers of aggregation and the threat of repression and censorship accompanying a monolithic canon that denies life's variety and complexity. See her "Race for Theory," *Feminist Studies* 14.1 (1987): 68–79.

13. Chakravarty, *National Identity*, 4–5.

14. Said, *Culture and Imperialism*, 316.

15. Nehru's *Discovery of India* was first published by Oxford University Press in 1946. It is a collection of letters from Nehru to his daughter, Indira Gandhi, written during his incarceration by British colonial authorities.

16. Rajadhyaksha and Willemen, *Encyclopaedia*, 8, 9, and 11.

Introduction

1. See Preface, note 10.

2. In contrast is the "art cinema" that the literati love. A relatively small film corpus, its form, aesthetic, and content is fashioned after internationally acclaimed filmmaker Satyajit Ray's films, made from the 1950s on. Art cinema gained popularity around the 1970s and has monopolized critical attention.

3. Film critics Iqbal Masud and Kishore Valicha, proponents of this approach, have taken popular male stars—Dilip Kumar, Raj Kapoor, Dev Anand, Shammi Kapoor and Amitabh Bachchan—as romantic heroes with particularities that resonate with the mood of different generations.

4. Vijay Mishra, "Towards a Theoretical Critique of Bombay Cinema," *Screen* 26.3–4 (1985): 133–146; "Decentering History: Some Versions of Bombay Cinema," *East-West Film Journal* 6.1 (1992): 111–155; and *Bollywood Cinema*.

5. Ashis Nandy is this strategy's most vocal proponent. See his *The Intimate Enemy: Loss and Recovery of Self Under Colonialism* (New Delhi: Oxford University Press, 1988), *At Edge of Psychology: Essays in Politics and Culture* (New Delhi: Oxford University Press, 1990), and *The Savage Freud: and Other Essays on Possible and Retrievable Selves* (New Delhi: Oxford University Press, 1995).

6. Kumkum Sangari, "Introduction: Representations in History," *Journal of Arts and Ideas* 17–18 (1989): 4. Sangari speaks of the need to get beyond "reactive indigenism," which dominates the space of resistance ideologies, ever since Marxism was evicted along with other "linear master-narratives" by the post-structuralist Enlightenment "bogey."

7. Mary E. John and Janaki Nair argue that the desire to avoid the west as if it were "an act of violation . . . is itself a western legacy." See their "Introduction," *A Question of Silence: The Sexual Economies of Modern India*, eds. Mary E. John and Janaki Nair (New Delhi: Kali for Women, 1998), 6.

8. Frederic Jameson, "On 'Cultural Studies,'" *Social Text* 34 (1993): 17. Also see Chandra Mukerji and Michael Schudson, *Rethinking Popular Culture: Contemporary Perspectives in Cultural Studies* (Berkeley: University of California Press, 1990), 1–61.

9. Theater, for instance, drew upon the tradition of Sanskrit drama, but it was also influenced by the nineteenth-century European novel. Hindi cinema drew from both these traditions, as well as from Indian painting influenced by photography.

10. Ashis Nandy argues that "Marginalized categories still make sense to Indians not fully socialized . . . [by] modern political institutions. . . . They are categories which confuse and exasperate metropolitan Indians who consider themselves the sane, rational, tough-minded political analysts of Indian culture" (*The Savage Freud*, ix).

11. I locate my project at this intersection cautiously, aware that the term "postcolonial" is imprecise and contradictory. The continuity with colonialism, for example, legitimizes skepticism about the very suffix "post." See Ella Shohat, "Notes on Post-Colonial," *Social Text* 31/32 (1992): 99–113. She speaks of a range of ambiguities swept under the term and favors the older, more accurate term "neo-colonial."

12. Although the state continues to control radio and television, programming in the latter was revolutionized during the 1990s because of competition from new channels (Zee TV, MTV beamed from Singapore, and CNN) and international broadcasting companies keen to invest. See Amit Aggarwal, "A Galaxy of Choices," *India Today* 28 Feb. 1995: 96–99, and "Battling for the Big Bucks," *India Today* 31 Mar. 1995: 120–122.

13. Apart from the fact that films are common to both TV and film industries, there is constant crossover of capital and talent (directors, actors, and producers). See Ruben Bannerjee, "Legends of the Fall," *India Today* 31 Dec. 1995: 130–133.

14. Ann McClintock, in her book *Imperial Leather: Race, Gender and Sexuality in the Colonial Conquest* (New York: Routledge, 1995), speaks of the "dazzling marketing success of the term postmodernism (392)" and offers a thorough critique of the imprecision embodied in the use and understanding of the term, suggesting, for instance, it should mark not "everything that has happened since

European colonialism but rather everything that has happened from the very beginning of colonialism (12)." For more details about her critique, see pages 9–17 and 391–396. For an engagement with McClintock's and Shohat's critiques, see Stuart Hall, "When was 'the post-colonial'? Thinking at the Limit," *The Post-Colonial Question: Common Skies, Divided Horizons*, eds. Iain Chambers and Lidia Curti (London: Routledge, 1996), 242–260.

15. Fredric Jameson, "Third-World Literature in the Era of Multinational Capitalism," *Social Text* 15 (1986): 65–86.

16. Aijaz Ahmad, "Jameson's Rhetoric of Otherness and the 'National Allegory,'" *Social Text* 17 (1987): 3–25; Madhava Prasad, "On the Question of a (Third World) Literature," *Social Text* 31/32 (1992): 57–83.

17. Ahmad, "Jameson's Rhetoric," 3, 21.

18. You-me Park's "Introduction" to "Bodies Against Metaphors: Decolonization and the Discourse of Body in Korean Nationalist Literature" (Ph.D. diss., George Washington University, 1995), 28–29. She provides an excellent shorthand to key issues of gender, nation, class, community, and sexuality (which I deal with in Indian cinema's context).

19. Park argues that Edward Said's *Culture and Imperialism* and Homi Bhabha's attempt to theorize domesticity in the extra-territorial space beyond the national boundaries of "home," and the recognition of women as "figures," "allegories," or "tropes," sorely lacks an appreciation of tensions between "imperial practice and domestic reality" and real women's victimization in the material, economic, and cultural domain. Ibid., 34.

20. Andrew Higson, *Waving the Flag: Constructing a National Cinema in Britain* (Oxford: Clarendon Press, 1995), 6, citing James Donald's "How English is it? National Culture and Popular Literature," *New Formation* 6 (1988): 32.

21. Benedict Anderson, *Imagined Communities: Reflections on the Origin and Spread of Nationalism* (London: Verso, 1990); Ernest Gellner, *Nation and Nationalism* (Ithaca: Cornell University Press, 1983); E. J. Hobsbawm, *Nations and Nationalism Since 1780* 2nd ed. (New York: Cambridge University Press, 1992); Tom Nairn, *The Break-up of Britain: Crisis and Neo-Nationalism* (London: New Left Books, 1977); Hugh Seton-Watson, *Nations and States: An Inquiry into the Origins of Nations and the Politics of Nationalism* (Boulder, Colorado: Westview Press, 1977); and David Lloyd, "Nationalism against the State," *The Politics of Culture in the Shadow of Capital*, eds. Lisa Lowe and David Lloyd (Durham: Duke University Press, 1997), 174–175.

22. *Faces of Nationalism: Janus Revisited* (London: Verso, 1997).

23. Invoking Anderson's image of a nation reading newspapers at the same time, Rick Altman talks of the movie screen marshaling peoples' attention at the same time and in one direction. See his "What can genres teach us about nations," *Film/Genre* (London: BFI, 1999), 205.

24. For Robert Burgoyne nationalism is alive and well even in the era of globalization. The nation is "not . . . the repository of a unitary, immutable, and essentialized identity, but rather . . . the basis . . . for interrogating and exposing the relations of power that lie at the heart of the idea of nation." See his *Film Nation: Hollywood Looks at U.S. History* (University of Minnesota Press, 1997), 11.

25. Andrew Higson, "The Concept of National Cinema," *Screen* 30.4 (1989): 36–47 and *Waving the Flag*; Pierre Sorlin, *Italian National Cinema 1896–1966* (New York: Routledge, 1996), 5 and *European Cinemas, European Societies 1939–1990* (New York; Routledge, 1991), 1–23; Sara Street, *British National Cinema* (New York: Routledge, 1997), 1–8; and Michael T. Martin, ed., *New Latin American Cinema* (Detroit: Wayne State University Press, 1997).

26. Invoking Michael Ignatieff, Burgoyne distinguishes between ethnic and civic nationalism: the former he associates with a "tribal" appeal to language, religious, and regional ties, and the latter to secular consciousness and claims to "liberal virtues—tolerance, compromise, reason." See Michael Ignatieff, *Blood and Belonging: Journeys into the New Nationalism* (New York: Farrar, Straus and Giroux, 1993), 6, cited in Burgoyne, *Film Nation*, 9.

27. Lloyd, "Nationalism against the State," 183. Also see 188–189. He elaborates: "the desire of nationalism is to saturate the field of subject formation so that, for every individual, the idea of nationality, of political citizenship, becomes the central organizing term in relation to which other possible modes of subjectification—class or gender, to cite only the most evident instances—are differentiated and subordinated. . . . The challenge both feminism and class politics present to nationalism is commensurate with the resistance that they must ultimately pose, ideologically and practically, to the state (182)."

28. See Iain Chambers, *Border Dialogues: Journeys in Postmodernism* (London: Routledge, 1990), 47 and Graeme Turner, "The End of the National Project? Australian Cinema in the 1990s," *Colonialism and Nationalism in the Asian Cinema*, ed. Wimal Dissanayake (Bloomington: Indiana University Press, 1994), 214. Also, Rick Altman points out that "[Benedict] Anderson concentrates on the moment when the nation was formed and stops there, failing to acknowledge the ongoing nature of the process he has described," in "What can genres teach us," 198.

29. Nehru's development model adopted by the new nation entailed extensive government intervention in the economy. Economic "liberalization" in the 1990s (discussed in chapter 6) displaced "Nehruvian socialism" with a more free market orientation.

30. Trade journals categorize films according to their success, without ever offering exact figures. Film ratings fall in three classes, "A," "B," and "C," and are accompanied by a number. A higher number indicates greater success. Thus, an AII film is at the apex, while a CI falls far below. The ratings are based on profits the film makes, although these are never reported. The reports only indicate if the film broke even or grossed once, twice, or several times its initial cost.

31. The selection of popular films neither exhausts *all* popular films nor the textual exegesis of each of these films. Different readers will recall one or another film that has not been included. *Sholay* (Flames, 1975) and *Coolie* (Porter, 1983) are glaring examples of popular films not included. These films are dense enough to warrant independent attention (although some of the themes they touch upon, such as class war and threatened community, are discussed in this book as well).

32. Raymond Williams, *Keywords: A Vocabulary of Culture and Society* (New York: Oxford University Press, 1983), 237.

33. Mukerji and Schudson, *Rethinking Popular Culture*, 36–37.

34. David Forgacs, "National Popular: Genealogy of a Concept," *The Cultural Studies Reader*, ed. Simon During (New York: Routledge, 1993), 177–190. The essay surveys Antonio Gramsci's writings: *Selections from the Prison Notebooks*, ed. and trans. Quintin Hoare and Geoffrey Nowell-Smith (London: Lawrence and Wishart, 1971), *Selections from the Political Writings*, ed. and trans. Quintin Hoare (London: Lawrence and Wishart, 1978), and *Selections from Cultural Writings*, ed. David Forgacs and Geoffrey Nowell-Smith (London: Lawrence and Wishart, 1985).

35. Ibid., 187.

36. Rachel Dwyer views Hindi cinema as the ground on which the old and new middle class contest their leadership. See her *All You Want is Money, All You Need is Love: Sex and Romance in Modern India* (London: Cassell, 2000), 4–5.

37. Forgacs, "National Popular," 186.

38. McClintock, *Imperial Leather*, 357.

39. Mahatma Gandhi is called *bapu*, the "father of the nation," and children call Nehru, the first Prime Minister, *chaacha* (uncle) Nehru because of his professed fondness for them. (*Chaacha* refers to the father's younger brother in north India.)

40. In Bhaskar Sarkar's view these are sublimated tales of upheaval that Indian families suffered during the 1947 Partition. "Runes of Laceration: National Partition in Popular Indian Cinema," paper presented at the Society for Cinema Studies Conference at Chicago, Illinois, March 2000.

41. McClintock, *Imperial Leather*, 5.

42. Cynthia Enloe, *Bananas, Beaches and Bases: Making Feminine Sense of International Politics* (Berkeley: University of California Press, 1989); Nira Yuval-Davis and Floya Anthias, eds., *Women-Nation-State* (London: MacMillan, 1989); Andrew Parker, Mary Russo, Doris Summer, and Patricia Yaeger, eds., *Nationalisms and Sexualities* (New York: Routledge, 1992).

43. Sumita Chakravarty reads the poverty-wealth divide, a popular binary in Hindi films, as an aspect of "Indian" philosophical preoccupation with ascetic ideals: to eschew wealth because it belongs to the ephemeral material world and favor renunciation to achieve salvation. See *National Identity in Indian Popular Cinema, 1947–87* (Austin: Texas University Press, 1993) 107–108. This interpretation makes a procrustean fit between Indian spiritualist material renunciation and Hindi films' rich-poor divide. It essentializes "Indian" as spiritual and falls into an Orientalist trap.

44. McClintock, *Imperial Leather*, 353.

45. This affirmative action policy is called "reservation"—of seats or quotas in professional schools and government jobs in India.

46. On rare occasions popular Hindi films represent caste politics. *Achhut Kanya* (Untouchable Girl, 1936) and *Sujata* (1959), technically speaking, are beyond this project's film sample: the former falls outside the period under study, the latter is not a major box office success. These films use heterosexual love as a symbolic bond uniting upper and lower castes. In *Achhut Kanya*, a pre-independence film, an inter-caste marriage is subverted by the female protagonist's accidental death. As such, this denouement is more honest and representative of the social text, the impossibility of crossing caste and community boundaries.

47. Ravi Vasudevan reads the city-country divide popular in the 1950s as a trope for the Partition. See "Dislocations: The Cinematic Imagining of a New Society in 1950s India," *Oxford Literary Review* 16.1–2 (1994): 93–124.

48. Historical events may affect "conventions and cultural perceptions, attitudes to love and marriage, kinship and patrimony, locality and nation, tradition and modernity . . . [that are] governed not by commonsensical laws of cause and effect, as wars or economic changes are often explained, but by a network of influences and reactions" in ordinary peoples' lives. See Pierre Sorlin, "Television and our Understanding of History: A Distant Conversation," *Screening the Past: Film and the Representation of History*, ed. Tony Barta (Westport, Connecticut: Praeger, 1998), 217–218.

49. Recent works such as Tony Barta, ed., *Screening the Past*, Robert Burgoyne's *Film*

Nation, and edited anthologies by Vivian Sobchack, *The Persistence of History: Cinema Television and the Modern Event* (New York: Routledge, 1996) and Marcia Landy, *The Historical Film: History and Memory in Media* (New Brunswick, New Jersey: Rutgers University Press, 2001), for example, explore the relation between nation/film and history/film.

50. Paul A. Ricouer, *Time and Narrative* (Chicago: University of Chicago Press, 1988), 351, cited in Prasenjit Duara's "Bifurcating Linear History," *Positions* Special Issue on the nationalism question 1: 3 Winter (1993): 793.

51. For example, Dipesh Chakrabarty, chafing against the bounds of imagining social justice strictly through modern institutions and the language of social science, points to the impossibility of documenting worker insurrections inspired by gods and spirits in conventional history. See his "The Time of History and the Time of Gods," in *The Politics of Culture in the Shadow of Capital*, ed. Lowe and Lloyd, 55–56.

52. Aditya Sinha, "RSS Targets History Textbooks," *Hindustan Times*, June 16 1998. The bid by the Hindu fundamentalist organization, the RSS (*Rashtriya Swayamsevak Sangh*, trans. National Service Corps), to reconstitute the ICHR shocked Indian academics concerned about a "cultural nationalist" revision of Indian history.

53. Sorlin, "Television and Our Understanding," 218–219.

54. Tony Barta, "Screening the Past: History Since the Cinema," in Barta, *Screening the Past*, 2.

55. In some states (Uttar Pradesh [U.P.] and Bihar) Urdu declined due to active discrimination against it. It finally gained official recognition in districts of Andhra Pradesh, Bihar, and U.P. For more details see Paul Brass, "Language Problems," *The New Cambridge History of India: The politics of India since independence* IV.1 (New York: Cambridge University Press, 1990), 135–168; Christopher King, "Introduction," *One Language Two Scripts: The Hindi Movement in Nineteenth Century North India* (Bombay: Oxford University Press, 1994), 3–22; and Sumathi Ramaswamy, "The Demoness, the Maid, the Whore, and the Good Mother: Contesting the National Language in India," *The International Journal of the Sociology of Language* No. 140 (1999), 1–28, and *Passions of the Tongue: Language Devotion in Tamil Nadu, 1891–1970* (Berkeley: University of California Press, 1997).

56. Hobsbawm, *Nations and Nationalism*, 111–112.

57. Meenakshi Mukherjee, *Realism and Reality: The Novel and Society in India* (New Delhi: Oxford University Press, 1985), 59–60, 64.

58. This gives credence to Hobsbawm's argument that language is contentious only among the educated—the potential candidates of the bureaucracy—for whom linguistic proficiency has high stakes in matters of recruitment and job prospects.

59. Mukul Kesavan, "Urdu, Awadh and the Tawaif," *Forging Identities: Gender Communities and the State*, ed. Zoya Hasan (New Delhi: Kali for Women, 1994), 249–250 (also see note 55 above).

60. Ibid., 246–247.

61. Ibid., 247. In Vijay Mishra's view, "the discourse of Hindi cinema remains to this day markedly Urdu." *Bollywood Cinema*, 63.

62. On Hollywood-style elements see Stephen Crofts, "Reconceptualizing National Cinemas," *Quarterly Review of Film and Video* 14.3 (1993): 50. Andrew Higson perceives a growing difficulty in establishing difference in the case of cinema, given the increasing internationalization of "standards and values of cinema,"

audience expectations, and film production, distribution, and exhibition practices that reproduce these standards. Hollywood, internationally the most powerful cinema, has for many years been an integral and "naturalized part of the national culture, or the popular imagination, of most countries in which cinema is an established entertainment form. . . . Hollywood has become one of those cultural traditions which feed into the so-called national cinemas." See "The Concept of National Cinema," *Screen* 30.4 (1989): 36–39. Stephen Crofts reinforces this position but presents a far more nuanced picture of the state of national cinemas in an international frame. Hollywood's overwhelming importance—its transnational reach—often dictates a national cinema's agenda. Yet he concedes weakness in Hollywood's stranglehold, especially on Asian cinema, which maintains its own "terrain." In his taxonomy films are marked by their distance from Hollywood. Despite Hollywood's narrative and stylistic influence, Crofts admits the existence of cinemas that differ from Hollywood, and do not compete with it (even ignore it), targeting a different audience.

While Hollywood's economic and cultural power may be difficult to contest, it is not altogether ubiquitous. Both Higson and Crofts point to the availability of large domestic markets, as in the case of the Bombay film industry, which give national cinemas a chance to compete against Hollywood. In addition, Crofts mentions active protectionist trade policies employed by a nation-state, within which cinema may "arise and flourish." See "Reconceptualizing National Cinemas," 50, 55.

These authors take important factors into account while discussing national cinemas in a global context. In the case of Hindi cinema (which both only cursorily acknowledge), a large domestic market is however an insufficient explanation for its success.

63. Ajit Pillai and Sudha G. Tilak, "Bettering Bollywood," *India Today* 15 Mar. 1995: 106–109; Kavita Shetty, "A Shooting Success," *India Today* 15 Feb. 1994: 76–77. Mani Ratnam's success with *Roja* (1992) and *Bombay* (1995), originally made in Tamil, are successful regional language films that claim a national audience.

64. Other sites are art and history writing.

65. *Communalism Combat* 6 (49) 1998: 7–18. The Indian state asserts its authority through censorship, assuming unusual moral, cultural, and regulatory power.

66. During Prime Minister Indira Ghandhi's national Emergency, rumor has it that Sanjay Gandhi, her son, ordered *Kissa Kursi Ka*'s destruction. *Border* anticipated the summer of 1999, when India and Pakistan fought a small-scale war in Kargil, situated in the disputed Kashmir region.

67. See *India Today*, June 7 1999: 12 and July 26 1999: 12–19.

68. The film adapts Mala Sen's biography of Phoolan Devi, *India's Bandit Queen: The True Story of Phoolan Devi*, revised and updated edition (San Francisco: Pandora, 1993), and is based on interviews conducted while Phoolan Devi was in prison. (Also see chapter 5.)

69. *Dalit* (oppressed) is a term claimed by lower castes designated "untouchable" in the traditional caste system and *harijan* (God's people) in Gandhi's sympathetic but patronizing neologism. The *dalit* social movement poses a credible challenge to fundamentalist Hindu orthodoxy because they undermine the legitimacy of Pan-Hindu nationalism by pointing to its hierarchical structure.

70. The films reflect changes in social deep structures. For too long the connection between politics and film has been limited to pointing to reality in fiction suggested by the actor-turned-politician phenomenon, or films' imitation of life; public outbursts, protest, social action, or unrest get far less attention.

Chapter 1 **Nation and Its Discontents**

1. E. J. Hobsbawm, *Nation and Nationalism Since 1780: Programme, Myth, Reality.* 2nd ed. (Cambridge: Cambridge University Press, 1992), 5.
2. José Carlos Mariátegui's *Seven Interpretive Essays on Peruvian Reality*, trans. Marjory Urquidi (Austin: University of Texas Press, 1971), 187–188, qtd. in Timothy Brennan, *Salman Rushdie and the Third World* (New York: St. Martin's Press, 1989), 7.
3. Benedict Anderson, *Imagined Communities: Reflections on the Origin and Spread of Nationalism* (London: Verso, 1990), 15.
4. Ibid., 19.
5. In an appraisal of several master-codes Fredric Jameson favors Northrop Frye's reading of religion—a mode through which a community thinks of and celebrates its unity. Jameson takes Frye a step further, arguing that literature is a "weaker form of myth or a later stage of ritual," informed by a political unconscious: "All literature must be read as a symbolic mediation on the destiny of the community." *The Political Unconscious* (Ithaca: Cornell University Press, 1981), 69–70.
6. In India the formation of the nation did not displace religion in the same way (see chapter 2). Instead, it came to reside beside it, and religious identity gets called upon to seek the subject-citizens' allegiance in support of or against the nation.
7. Hobsbawm, *Nation and Nationalism*, 25, 28–29.
8. Ernest Gellner, *Nations and Nationalism* (Ithaca: Cornell University Press, 1983), 140.
9. Partha Chatterjee, *Nationalist Thought and the Colonial World: A Derivative Discourse* (Minneapolis: University of Minnesota Press, 1993).
10. Anderson, *Imagined Communities*, 15.
11. Brennan, *Salman Rushdie*, 4, 7.
12. Victoria Glendinning's "A Novelist in the Country of the Mind," *The Sunday Times* 23 Oct. 1981: 38, qtd. in Brennan, *Salman Rushdie*, 123.
13. Brennan, *Salman Rushdie*, 10–11.
14. Gellner offers his own answer to the question, "What is a nation?" Will and culture, he says, are two ways of theorizing a nation—but "neither is remotely adequate." In all group formations "will," "identification," "loyalty," and "solidarity" work as catalysts. But "will" and "identification" are too wide a category. So is culture for that matter, as its boundary can be "sharp" or "fuzzy." Standardization, literacy, and communication create the impression that nationality is based on shared culture. When an educated and elite notion of culture spreads among the majority, it evokes identification and cultures become "the natural repositories of political legitimacy. . . . Polities then will extend their boundaries to the limits of their cultures, and to protect and impose their culture within the boundaries of their power. The fusion of will, culture and polity becomes the norm, and one not easily or frequently defied" (Gellner, *Nations and Nationalism*, 55).
15. Hugh Seton-Watson, *Nation and States: An Inquiry into Nations and the Politics of Nationalism* (Boulder: Westview Press, 1977), 5, qtd. in Brennan, *Salman Rushdie*, 5.
16. Hans Kohn, *Nationalism: Its Meaning and History* (Cincinnati: D. Van Norstrand, 1965), 11, qtd. in Brennan, *Salman Rushdie*, 21.
17. Kaviraj compares thinkers, writers, and intellectuals with a political consciousness in the early nineteenth century in the entity now called India to those in

the later part of the same century. The former, even if they were anti-imperialist, could never imagine independence, autonomy, or a separate nation in the manner fashioned by the conscious nationalist movement produced by the contingencies of the late nineteenth and early twentieth centuries. Yet history today is written as a linear account in which the early period is presented quite simply as a paler version of its later development. Kaviraj maps the transformation between these two periods—from a negative reaction to colonialism, to a positive consciousness of a new identity, a "we" forged from fragmented identities, enunciated by a collective. Sudipta Kaviraj, "Imaginary Institution of India," *Subaltern Studies* 7 (1992): 1–49.

18. Antonio Gramsci, *Selections from Cultural Writings* (London: Lawrence and Wishart, 1985), 253, qtd. in Kaviraj, "Imaginary Institution," 9.
19. Kaviraj, "Imaginary Institution," 16.
20. Brennan, *Salman Rushdie*, 11–12.
21. Andrew Higson, "The Concept of National Cinema," *Screen* 30.4 (1989): 36–37.
22. In fact, Higson suggests two methods of establishing this coherence. One, to compare one nation's cinema to another. The second is to compare cinema to other cultural forms within the nation state. "The Concept of National Cinema," 38.
23. On song and dance see Erik Barnouw and S. Krishnaswamy, *Indian Film* (New York: Oxford University Press, 1980). On time and space see Mukul Kesavan, "Urdu, Awadh and the Tawaif: the Islamicate Roots of Hindi Cinema," *Forging Identities: Gender, Communities and the State*, ed. Zoya Hasan (New Delhi: Kali for Women, 1994), 244–257. And there are many sources on frontality, among them Ratnabali Chattopadhyay, "Nationalism and Form in Indian Painting: A Study of the Bengal School," *Journal of Arts and Ideas* 14–15 (1987): 5–46; Geeta Kapur, "Mythic Material in Indian Cinema," *Journal of Arts and Ideas* 14–15 (1987): 79–108, Gulam Mohammed Sheikh, "Viewer's View: Looking at Pictures," *Journal of Arts and Ideas* 3 (1983): 5–20; Tapati Guha-Thakurta, "Recovering the Nation's Art," *Texts of Power: Emerging Disciplines in Colonial Bengal*, ed. Partha Chatterjee (Minneapolis: University of Minnesota Press, 1995), 63–92 and "The ideology of the 'aesthetic': the purging of visual tastes and the campaign for a new Indian art in late nineteenth/early twentieth century Bengal," *Studies in History* 8, 2, n.s. (1992): 237–281. On photography see Judith Mara Gutman, *Through Indian Eyes: Nineteenth and Twentieth Century Still Photography in India* (New York: Oxford University Press, 1982) and Christopher Pinney, *Camera Indica: The Social Life of Indian Photographs* (Chicago: University of Chicago Press, 1997).
24. Meenakshi Mukherjee, *Realism and Reality: The Novel and Society in India* (New Delhi: Oxford University Press, 1985), 3.
25. Brennan, *Salman Rushdie*, 18.
26. Distinctions of taste stratify Hindi films in general. "Art," "parallel," and "middle" cinema are identified with "high" culture, while popular cinema is the lowest denominator.
27. Mukherjee, *Realism and Reality*, 4.
28. Ibid., 10.
29. Higson, "The Concept of National Cinema," 43–44.
30. Brennan, *Salman Rushdie*, 19–20.
31. Gellner defends nationalism as that which does not impose cultural homogeneity. Rather, he argues, there is an "objective need for homogeneity which is

reflected in nationalism. If . . . a modern industrial state can only function with a mobile, literate, culturally standardized, interchangeable population, . . . then the illiterate, half-starved population sucked from the erstwhile rural cultural ghettoes into the melting-pot of shanty-towns yearns for incorporation into some one of those cultural pools which already has, or looks as if it might acquire, a state of its own, with the subsequent promise of full cultural citizenship, access to primary school, employment and all. Often, these alienated, uprooted, wandering populations may vacillate between diverse options, and they may often come to a provisional rest at one or another temporary and transitional cultural resting place." Gellner, *Nations and Nationalism*, 46.

32. I thank Gina Marchetti for this succinct formulation.

33. Back in 1992 in an interview with Yash Chopra, a leading Bombay industry filmmaker, I asked why Hindi films, otherwise presumed to have a secular sensibility, had never represented Hindu-Muslim romance stories. Slightly alarmed by the question, Chopra speculated such a representation would provoke riots. Ironically, *Bombay*, the first film to transgress the rigid Hindu-Muslim divide, was made on the heels of the worst riots since Partition, in the aftermath of the desecration of the fifteenth-century Muslim mosque, the Babri Masjid, in Ayodhya.

34. The farmers' movement gathered momentum in several states beginning in the late 1970s (despite differences among them). Maharashtra's Sharad Joshi articulates its views most clearly: the acutely uneven development of urban and rural areas is built into national plans, siphoning off resources from the countryside, concentrating wealth in urban centers, and impoverishing the majority in the countryside. This sentiment is echoed by the anti-Narmada dam movement that gained international attention in the 1990s.

35. Mukherjee, *Realism and Reality*, 4.

36. Ibid., 69.

37. Ibid., 68–70, on Indian novels.

38. Sumita Chakravarty, *National Identity in Indian Popular Cinema, 1947–87* (Austin: University of Texas Press, 1993), 141.

39. Colonial history began to be used as the central narrative only in the 1990s. *1942 A Love Story* (Vinod Vidhu Chopra, 1994) is a significant example. Covertly, of course, anything western, perhaps due to the colonial past, is constantly vilified through portrayals of hedonism and decadence. This is consistent with Hindi cinema's elliptical references to the political sphere.

40. Akbar S. Ahmed points out that Nadira's performance in *Aan* is fashioned after Marlene Dietrich's in *Kismet* (1944). See his "Bombay Films: The Cinema as Metaphor for Indian Society and Politics," *Modern Asian Studies* 26, 2 (1992): 291.

41. Tribal dispossession in India begun during colonial rule and continued by the Indian state is not different from the trajectory of Native Americans in North America, the original inhabitants placed in reservations, enclosures in their own land.

42. Aijaz Ahmad, "Jameson's Rhetoric of Otherness and the 'National Allegory,'" *Social Text* 17 (1987): 22. Additionally, in the context of *Madhumati* and *Mahal* (The Mansion, Kamal Amrohi, 1949), according to Vijay Mishra, theories of Indian karma and western reincarnation were creatively absorbed by Indian gothic and manifested in Bombay cinema's sentimental melodrama. *Bollywood Cinema*, 49–59.

43. *Hafta* is money extorted by gangsters from their constituency marking their territory and sphere of influence.

44. Rameshwari and Angela Koreth, "The Mother Image and the National Ethos in Four Recent Mainstream Hindi Films: *Pratighaat* (Retribution, 1987), *Haq* (Rights, 1990), *Amba* (1990) and *Prahaar* (Attack, 1991)." Paper presented at the Miranda House College Seminar, University of Delhi, April 1992.

45. In the short story "Toba Tek Singh," set in the days leading to the Partition, the eponymous protagonist is located in a Pakistani asylum, which ironically appears saner than the rest of the subcontinent. The two states decide to transfer asylum inmates to the country of their relatives' choosing. Toba Tek Singh resists the transfer to an asylum in India but dies in a no-man's-land between the two borders that is neither India nor Pakistan.

46. Women who are sexually harassed by men on the streets often succeed in chastising them by invoking men's relationships with their mothers and sisters.

47. As Rameshwari and Angela Koreth argue, "What seems enabling in *Pratighaat* could also be disturbing . . . the overvaluation which arises from deification . . . the mythic substructure which ensures the success and glorification of an action or individual, also sets it apart as . . . special, as something that only the unique individual marked by divinity is capable of. It could signal passivity and meek compliance for the rest who are not marked by divine charisma." Paper presented at the Miranda House College Seminar, University of Delhi, April 1992.

48. It is perhaps this urban middle-class bias in the women's movement that prompts women politically active in rural areas to begrudge the disproportionate attention paid to domestic violence—dowry and dowry deaths, rather than land and property rights.

Chapter 2   The Idealized Woman

1. Kumkum Sangari, "Figures of the Unconscious," *Journal of Arts and Ideas* 20–21 (1991): 67.

2. Partha Chatterjee, "Women and the Nation," *The Nation and its Fragments: Colonial and Postcolonial Histories* (Princeton: Princeton University Press, 1993), 137–140.

3. Susie Tharu and K. Lalitha, ed., "Introduction," *Women Writing in India 600 B.C. to the Present Volume ll: The Twentieth Century* (New Delhi: Oxford University Press, 1993), 39–40.

4. Ibid., xx, xxii.

5. Communities refers to religious groups, and communalism connotes strife among them.

6. Partha Chatterjee, "The Nationalist Resolution of the Women's Question," in *Recasting Women: Essays in Colonial History*, ed. Kumkum Sangari and Sudesh Vaid (New Delhi: Kali for Women, 1989), 233–253.

7. Sumanta Bannerjee, "Marginalization of Women's Popular Culture in Nineteenth Century Bengal," in *Recasting Women: Essays in Colonial History*, ed. Sangari and Vaid, 127–179.

8. Uma Chakravarti, "Whatever Happened to the Vedic Dasi? Orientalism, Nationalism and a Script from the Past," in *Recasting Women: Essays in Colonial History*, ed. Sangari and Vaid, 27–87; quoted material on 79.

9. Susie Tharu, "Reform and the Nationalist Movements," *Women's Writing in India: 600 B.C. to the Present: Volume I 600 B.C. to the Early 20th Century*, eds. Susie Tharu and K. Lalitha (New Delhi: Oxford University Press, 1991), 172.

10. Indira Chowdhury-Sengupta, "Mother India and Mother Victoria: Motherland and Nationalism in Nineteenth Century Bengal," *South Asia Research* 12.1 (1992): 25–26.

11. Rajkrishna Ray's *"Bharat Gan: Bharater Prachin O Bartaman Sambandhiya ebang Swadeshanuraguddipak ek sata Git"* (One Hundred Inspirational Songs about the Past and Present State of India, Calcutta, 1879), 28, 7, qtd. in Chowdhury-Sengupta, "Mother India," 28.

12. Meenakshi Mukherjee, *Realism and Reality* (New Delhi: Oxford University Press, 1985), 49.

13. Jashodra Bagchi, "Representing Nationalism: Ideology of Motherhood in Colonial Bengal," *Economic and Political Weekly* 20 Oct. 1990: WS 66–68; Tanika Sarkar, "Nationalist Iconography: Image of Women in 19th Century Literature," *Economic and Political Weekly* 21 Nov. 1987: 2011–2015.

14. Chowdhury-Sengupta, "Mother India," 20–22.

15. For an update on the complexities of this resurfaced debate in the 1990s, see Rajeswari Sunder Rajan, "Women between Community and State: Some Implications of the Uniform Civil Code Debate in India," *Social Text* 65, Vol. 18, no. 4 Winter (2000): 55–82.

16. D.A. Washbrook, "Law State and Agrarian Society in Colonial India," *Modern Asian Studies* 15.3 (1981): 652–653.

17. Jana Matson Everett, *Women and Social Change in India* (New York: St. Martin's Press, 1979), 142–143.

18. Ibid., 166–169 and 176.

19. Lotika Sarkar, "Jawaharlal Nehru and the Hindu Code Bill," *Indian Women From Purdah to Modernity*, ed., B. R. Nanda (New Delhi: Vikas, 1976), 87, 92.

20. Everett, *Women and Social Change*, 162.

21. Ibid., 156.

22. Ibid., 170.

23. Ibid., 187–188.

24. Archana Parashar, *Women and Family Law Reform in India* (New Delhi: Sage Press, 1992), 230–231.

25. Ibid., 226, and 159–160..

26. Kumkum Sangari, "Politics of Diversity: Religious Communities and Multiple Patriarchies," *Economic and Political Weekly*, December 23 (1995): 3290.

27. Parashar, *Women and Family Law*, 233.

28. Ibid., 173–176.

29. Ibid., 182–183.

30. In 1987 Roop Kanwar immolated herself on her husband's pyre in Deorala, a small town in northwest India. The act polarized the nation: one segment hailed her as a goddess and the other decried the act for resurrecting the *sati* ritual outlawed in the nineteenth century. Women's groups' protests were drowned out by the fervor whipped up by fanatical Hindus and the weak-kneed charade put on by the government.

31. Prem Chowdrey points to the historical film portraying Mughal tolerance and syncretism, a trend in the colonial period that continued after independence in popular films like *Baiju Bawra* (Vijay Bhatt, 1952), *Anarkali* (Nandlal Jaswantlal, 1953), and *Mirza Ghalib* (Sohrab Modi, 1954). See *Colonial India and the Making of Empire Cinema: Image, Ideology and Identity* (Manchester: Manchester University Press, 2000), 256–257.

32. Ratnam's film seems to have opened the floodgates on the long repressed issue of communalism. In the 1996 International Film Festival a slew of films appeared dealing with this theme, notably Saeed Mirza's *Naseem* (1996) and Shyam Benegal's *Mammo* (1996). See *India Today* 16 Jan. 1996: 122–124. Contrary to traditional expectations, this time "art" film directors are taking their cue from a "commercial" filmmaker.

33. Usha Zacharias, "Cultural Crisis and Female Sexuality: A Study of *Bombay*," Paper presented at the Annual Film Conference at the University of Athens, Athens, Ohio, November, 1995.

34. *Roja* (1992), an earlier Ratnam film in Tamil was a nationalist plea against Kashmiri separatism that unleashed controversy.

35. Mary E. John, "Globalisation, Sexuality and the Visual Field: Issues and non-issues for cultural critique," *A Question of Silence? The Sexual Economies of Modern India*, eds. Mary E. John and Janaki Nair (New Delhi: Kali for Women, 1998), 383–386. Also see Tejaswini Niranjana, "Banning *Bombay*: Nationalism, Communalism and Gender," *Economic and Political Weekly* June 3 (1995):1291–1292.

36. Kathleen Rowe, "Comedy and Gender: Theorizing the Genre of Laughter," *Classical Hollywood Comedy*, eds. Kristine Brunovska Karnick and Henry Jenkins (New York: Routledge, 1995), 41.

37. Everett, *Women and Social Change*, 165.

38. Ibid., 159.

39. The Constituent Assembly *Debates* 11, p 996, qtd. in Everett, *Women and Social Change*, 175.

40. *Roshni* June 1949: 9–13, qtd. in Everett, *Women and Social Change*, 183.

41. The lower class also expresses its antagonism toward the upper class by referring to English-speaking people as *angrez* (British). In this instance the rebuke expresses animosity over differential privilege.

42. Everett, *Women and Social Change*, 185.

43. Steve Neale and Frank Krutnik, *Popular Film and Television Comedy* (New York: Routledge, 1990), 142.

44. Ibid., 144, 147, 151

45. Ibid., 145.

46. Rowe, "Comedy and Gender," 50–51.

47. Ibid., 44, 46.

48. Neale and Krutnik, *Popular Film*, 152.

Chapter 3   *Heroes and Villains*

1. Marcia Landy, "The Family Melodrama in the Italian Cinema, 1929–43," *Imitations of Life: A Reader on Film and Television Melodrama*, ed. Marcia Landy (Detroit: Wayne State University Press, 1991), 571; and Landy, "Introduction," *same volume*, 21.

2. Kishore Valicha, *The Moving Image: A Study of Indian Cinema* (Bombay: Orient Longman, 1988) and Ravi Vasudevan, "Dislocations: The Cinematic Imagining of a New Society in 1980s India," *Oxford Literary Review* 16.1–2 (1994): 93–124.

3. In *Motherhood and Representation: The Mother in Popular Culture and Melodrama* (New York: Routledge, 1992), Ann E. Kaplan discusses specific Hollywood films and uses the concept of the "psychoanalytic" as distinct from the "conscious rational" to distinguish between narratives within texts. These she identifies as "complicit" or "resisting," an "ideological" category she uses to denote the "maternal melodrama" and the "maternal woman's film" respectively. "The former comply passively with the dominant patriarchal mother-discourse (labeled . . . the 'Master' Mother Discourse), while the latter question or expose this discourse(12)." I am particularly interested in how she identifies these categories. Complicit and resisting, she elucidates, refer to whether the narra-

tive positions the mother as controlled by "unconscious mythic processes beyond her control, or . . . historically by social institutions (theoretically open to change). The term 'conscious/rational' connotes conscious psychological processes of knowing and understanding the world, including how institutions function to constrain or define historical subjects; while the term 'psychoanalytic' . . . connotes the unconscious level of the subject's relations and modes of functioning—the level of the Imaginary—that moves the subject without his/her conscious knowledge. The terms reflect ideal-types rarely achieved in practice: most actions, texts and representations include both cognitive/constructive and psychoanalytic elements, but one mode is usually primary.(12)"

I refer to Kaplan's descriptions at some length here, to clarify my own eclectic methodology in this chapter that relies both on institutional and discursive analysis of conscious/rational processes, as well unconscious processes explicated by the psychoanalytic method. I read the two in conjunction with each other, although most readers will discern my own exegesis favors institutional processes.

4. Ibid., esp. 27–56; Frank Krutnik, *In a Lonely Street: Film Noir, Genre and Masculinity* (New York, Routledge, 1991).
5. Frantz Fanon, *Black Skins, White Masks* (New York: Grove Weidenfeld, 1967), 97.
6. Pierre Naville, *Psychologie, Marxisme, Matérialisme*, 2nd ed. (Paris: Marcel Rivière, 1948), 151, cited in Fanon, *Black Skin*, note 33, p. 106.
7. Tying the individual to the social using the Nature to Culture metaphor Bhabha argues the civil state represents the "rational bent of the human mind," and "social instinct is the progressive destiny of human nature. . . . The direct access from individual interests to social authority is objectified in the representative structure of a General Will—Law or Culture. . ." Homi Bhabha, "Remembering Fanon," *Colonial Discourse and Post-Colonial Theory: A Reader*, eds. Patrick Williams and Laura Chrisman (New York: Columbia University Press, 1994), 115–116.
8. Fanon, *Black Skin*, 141–143.
9. Sudhir Kakar, *Intimate Relations: Exploring Indian Sexuality* (New Delhi: Viking, 1989), 131–132.
10. Ibid., 125, 127.
11. Ibid., 136–137.
12. Dr. Girindrasekhar Bose, Kakar says, wrote to Freud in 1929, reporting a difference he observed between his European and Indian patients. Indian males did not suffer the threat of castration to the extent that his European patients did. Freud was "courteous but diplomatic," in his reply, saying the phenomenon (castration) was too important to be hastily dismissed. See T. C. Sinha, "Psychoanalysis in India," *Lumbini Park Silver Jubilee Souvenir* (Calcutta: 1966), 66, qtd. in Kakar, *Intimate Relations*, 129–130.
13. Kakar, *Intimate Relations*, 129.
14. Ibid., 139.
15. Barbara Ehrenreich, *The Hearts of Men: American Dreams and the Flight from Commitment* (New York: Doubleday, 1983).
16. Sudhir Kakar speaks of caring for the young, the old, for ancestors and gods as the "chief quality" prescribed for householders. In fact, marital intimacy is simply a step toward the "development of adult care and generativity." See his *Identity and Adulthood* (New Delhi: Oxford University Press, 1979), 123.
17. I borrow this term from Krutnik, *In a Lonely Street*, 75.

18. Sumita S. Chakravarty, *National Identity in Indian Popular Cinema 1947–87* (Austin: University of Texas Press, 1993), 107–108, qtd. from Vijay Mishra, "Towards a Theoretical Critique of Bombay Cinema," *Screen* 26.3–4 (1985): 139. Chakravarty cities Mishra to point to the semiotic chain between images and ideology that connect wealth/money to worldliness (*nivritti*), pitting it against its opposite, poverty/renunciation (*pravritti*), upheld by Hindu tradition.

19. Aijaz Ahmad, "Jameson's Rhetoric of Otherness and the 'National Allegory,'" *Social Text* 17 (1987): 22. Ahmad discusses the "inward looking" tradition of critically examining the national self in 1950s and 60s fictional writings by Saadat Hasan Manto, Rajinder Singh Bedi, Intezar Hussein, Qurrat ul Ain, Khadija Mastoor, and Abdullah Hussein. This self-appraisal was done without giving "any quarter" to the colonialists.

20. Chakravarty, *National Identity*, 102–105.

21. Ibid., 203–204.

22. Barry Taylor, Review of Joan Copjec's, ed. *Shades of Noir: A Reader* (London and New York: Verso) 1993, and Krutnik's, *In a Lonely Street* in *Screen* 36:2 (1995): 173.

23. Vijay Mishra, "Actor as Parallel Text: Amitabh Bachchan," in *Bollywood Cinema*, 125–156; Ashwini Sharma, "Blood Sweat and Tears: Amitabh Bachchan, urban demi-god," in *You Tarzan: Masculinity, Movies and Men*, ed. P. Kirkham and J. Thumin (London: Lawrence and Wishart, 1993), 167–180; Lalit Vichani, "Bachchan-alias: The Many Faces of a Film Icon," in *Image Journeys: audiovisual media & cultural change in India*, ed. Christiane Brosius and Melissa Butcher (New Delhi: Sage, 1999), 199–230. Jyotika Virdi, "The 'Fiction' of Film and 'Fact' of Politics: *Deewar* (Wall, 1976)," *Jump Cut* 38 (1993): 26–32. In addition, Amitabh Bachchan's indomitable presence between the 1970s and early 1990s is canonized in several Master's and Ph.D. dissertations.

24. N. K. Singh and Farzand Ahmed, "Crime and Politics: The Nexus," *India Today* 31 Aug. 1995: 26–33. The debate was triggered by the murder of Naina Sahini, a Congress-I party worker, allegedly by her husband Satish Sharma, a Congress-I office-bearer. The public outcry was paralleled to the O.J. Simpson trial happening simultaneously in the United States.

25. Madhava Prasad, "Cinema and the Desire for Modernity," *Journal of Arts and Ideas* 25–26 (1994): 77. Prasad reads the police's late arrival at the end, after the hero makes short shrift of the enemy as the modern state's endorsement of a feudal system. I think this could as well read as indicting the state and the citizen-subject's loss of faith—no different from how Hollywood films mock the FBI. At any rate, it betrays a leak in Hindi cinema's official nationalist rhetoric.

26. In *Shri 420* Raj recants; in *Vidhaata* Sher Singh dies, as does Vijay in *Deewar*.

27. The fictitious name chosen for this group resonates in an odd way with recent history: Operation Blue Star was the Central government's June 1984 attempt to flush out terrorists from the Golden Temple in Amritsar. In a reprisal for this action, the Prime Minister, Indira Gandhi, was assassinated in October 1984.

28. Again, this resonates with the hype about cross-border terrorism instigated in neighboring Pakistan.

29. *Sarfarosh* (1997) and *Fizaa* (2000) exemplify a departure from this practice, making candid reference to location—naming Pakistan the enemy state and the border with it a troubled region.

30. Salman Rushdie, *The Moor's Last Sigh* (London: Cape, 1995), 137. For an ex-

tended discussion of the film and Rushdie's caricature of the text, extra-text, and star text, see Rachel Dwyer, *All You Want is Money, All You Need is Love: Sex and Romance in Modern India* (London: Cassell, 2000), 129–137. Also see note 42 below.

31. Kaplan, *Motherhood and Representation*, 15.
32. Ibid., 29, 44–45.
33. Krutnik, *In a Lonely Street*, 82; Peter Matthews, "Garbo and Phallic Motherhood: A Homosexual Visual Economy," *Screen* 29.3 (1988): 22.
34. Krutnik, *In a Lonely Street*, 85.
35. Kaplan, *Motherhood and Representation*, 79; Matthews, "Garbo and Phallic Motherhood," 22; and Kakar, *Intimate Relations*, 135.
36. Kaplan, *Motherhood and Representation*, 65.
37. Rosie Thomas, "Sanctity and Scandal: The Mythologization of Mother India," *Quarterly Review of Film and Video* 11 (1989): 11–30.
38. Kaplan, *Motherhood and Representation*, 12.
39. Bracelets (*kangan*) worn by women, gifts from their husbands, signify their marital vows. As Rosie Thomas and Sumita Chakravarty point out, reclaiming his mother's bracelets is a sign of winning back his mother's honor.
40. Kaplan, *Motherhood and Representation*, 77.
41. Matthews, "Garbo and Phallic Motherhood,' 22.
42. Thomas, "Sanctity and Scandal," 16. Dwyer too underscores the punishing aspect of Radha. In her lively reading of *Mother India*, among other things, she views the woman as upholding "the community (read nation) over her family. . . . dangerous whether as consort or as mother," and balancing public and private duty. She also points out its commonalities with *Deewar*—a mother subordinating her personal love for the state. Dwyer, *All You Want Is Money*, 131, 133–134. And Vijay Mishra points to heterogeneous texts within *Mother India*, including a "postcolonial response" to Katherine Mayo's rabidly colonialist text by the same title. He concludes that the text is "outrageously 'conforming,' yet defiantly subversive." *Bollywood Cinema*, 68 and 87.
43. John Fletcher, Review of Kaja Silverman's *Masculinity in the Margins*, *Screen* 36.1 (1995). Fletcher speaks of how amputation is most generally a sign of male impotence; also see Thomas, "Sanctity and Scandal," 15; and Chakravarty, *National Identity*, 154.

Chapter 4   *Heroines, Romance, and Social History*

1. I use the term "knowledge/power" in its Foucauldian sense: institutional and textual filmmaking practices are constituted by a network of power.
2. In the context of hard-core pornography, Linda Williams discusses how cinema technology implanted "perversion" from its moment of inception. This is exemplified by Eadweard Muybridge's first experiments which capture bodies in motion—"instantaneous photography"—for which he chose animals, men, and women as subjects. (Recorded in eleven volumes of *Animal Locomotion*, published in 1887, and reprinted in three volumes in Mozley's *Complete Animal and Human Locomotion*). In a detailed description of the treatment of men's and women's bodies, Williams contrasts the treatment of each: men perform activities in a matter-of-fact fashion, while women's movements are embellished with "gratuitous" gestures such as holding their breasts or placing a hand on the mouth; the men appear nude, in a pelvis cloth or draped, while women are presented nude or dressed in diaphanous clothing that does not serve the

same purpose as the pelvis cloth concealing men's genitals; likewise, women are provided with elaborate props in place of simple ones supporting men's action. This, Williams suggests, further sexualizes women's bodies.

The fetishization of the woman's body, apparent from the additional props and gestures, is part of the same "social existence" in which, as John Berger puts it, "*men act and women appear.*" See his John Berger, *Ways of Seeing* (New York: Penguin, 1977), 47. Williams concludes rather persuasively that "at the origin of cinema . . . is . . . a psychic apparatus with a 'passion for perceiving' and a technological apparatus that makes this perception possible . . . [and] also . . . a social apparatus . . . [that] ultimately . . . constructs women as objects rather than the subject of vision—for it places women in front of rather than behind the camera." See Linda Williams, *Hard-Core: Power Pleasure and the Frenzy of the Visible* (Berkeley: University of California Press, 1988), 83–89, 96. Others who have discussed the construction of women as objects in cinema are E. Ann Kaplan, *Women and Film: Both Sides of the Camera* (New York: Methuen, 1983), Annete Kuhn, *Women's Pictures, Feminism and Cinema* (London: Routledge and Kegan Paul, 1982), and Teresa de Lauretis, *Technologies of Gender* (Bloomington: Indiana University Press, 1987), 13. De Lauretis points to other work, contemporaneous to Foucault's, on the implantation of gender within filmic representation. These are Laura Mulvey, "Visual Pleasure and Narrative Cinema," *Screen* 16.3 (1975): 6–18 and Stephen Heath, "Narrative Space," *Questions of Cinema* (Bloomington: Indiana University Press, 1981), 19–75.

3. Film theory on melodrama insists that texts are not monolithic. Marcia Landy says, "Such a view raises the possibility of examining texts for their lapses, illogicalities and contradictions" that melodrama makes apparent by exacerbating conflicts rooted in social hierarchies. See her "Introduction," *Imitations of Life: A Reader on Film and Television Melodrama*, ed. Marcia Landy (Michigan: Wayne State University Press, 1991), 19. And Laura Mulvey echoes the same idea: "No idea can ever pretend totality: it must provide an outlet for its own inconsistencies." See her "Notes on Sirk and Melodrama," *Home is Where the Heart Is: Studies in Melodrama and the Woman's Film*, ed. Christine Glendhill (London: BFI, 1987), 75.

4. De Lauretis, *Technologies of Gender*, 10.

5. I draw on Sunder Rajan's arguments about the pivotal nature of "representation" in understanding culture. She finds it useful precisely because it neither privileges foundationalist/materialist theories nor superstructural/cultural ones. See Rajeswari Sunder Rajan, *Real and Imagined Women* (New York: Routledge, 1993), 9. Although this is a highly contentious matter for proponents of each of these camps, who argue for a causal/originary position of either materialism or culture, we have considerable evidence to suggest a highly contradictory and complex relationship between the two, which is particularly apparent in the field of representation. Citing Jacqueline Rose, Sunder Rajan says that representation is a productive domain to engage in since it has "its own substantial political reality and effects." See Jacqueline Rose, "The State of the Subject (II): The Institution of Feminism," *Critical Quarterly* 29.4 (1987): 9–15; esp. 12, qtd. in Sunder Rajan, *Real and Imagined Women*, 10. Sunder Rajan points out how the problems of "real" and imagined women transact with each other and that it is "in and through" the discursive practices of the latter, that "'women' emerge as subjects." Negotiating these, she says, will reveal the stakes involved.

6. Patricia Jeffrey and Roger Jeffrey, "Killing My Heart's Desire: Education and

Female Autonomy in Rural North India," in *Women as Subjects: South Asian Histories*, ed. Nita Kumar (Charlottesville: University Press of Virginia, 1994), 160.

7. De Lauretis, in *Technologies of Gender*, refers to self-representation in the construction of gender as effects of "micropolitical practices" and "local" resistance that emerge in the margins of hegemonic discourse created by technologies (like cinema) functioning to "implant" a representation of gender (18). Feminist (self) representation appears in the "chinks and cracks of the power knowledge apparatii (25)." But, she clarifies, the movement is not from a space outside representation and in the real, rather, she is suggesting "a movement from the space by/in representation, by/in a discourse . . . to the space not represented yet implied (unseen) in them (26)." Within the dominant male-centered forms of representation those other discursive social spaces that exist are "(re)-constructed . . . in the margins" by feminists reading "between the lines" or "against the grain." The dominant and the oppositional do not exist on a signification continuum; "they coexist concurrently and in contradiction (26)."

8. Sunder Rajan, *Real and Imagined Women*, 3.

9. Consider arguments made by Laura E. Donaldson in her essay "The Miranda Complex: Colonialism and the Question of Feminist Reading," *Diacritics* 18.3 (1988): 65–77. In reviewing Sandra M. Gilbert's and Susan Gubar's *The Madwoman in the Attic: The Women Writer and the Nineteenth Century Imagination*, and Gayatri Chakravorty Spivak's "Three Women's Texts and a Critique of Imperialism," *Critical Inquiry* 12 (1985): 243–261, Donaldson makes the case for reading Bertha Mason's suicide in *Jane Eyre* as asserting "resistance rather than defeat." She takes this position on two counts. First, she invokes Phyllis Chesler's account of women's self-destructive behavior in *Women and Madness* (New York: Doubleday, 1972), 49, that tends to be "more toward psychic and emotional self-destruction," while suicide by women "signals . . . ritual readiness for self sacrifice." This "powerlessness" and "psychological martyrdom" Chesler refers to, Donaldson argues, is similar to the analogy Spivak draws between Bertha's death and the ritual self-sacrifice of *sati*. Second, she refers to Hussein Abdilahi Bulhan's argument in *Frantz Fanon and the Psychology of Oppression* (London: Plenum, 1985), 122, along the following lines. The colonizer depends on fear of "biological death" among the colonized. Submitting to oppression may permit a continuation to live and breathe, but exchanges it for a "psychological" and "social" death. Donaldson paraphrases this as, "the more the oppressed seek physical survival, the more their oppression deepens (76)." A position such as this, that hails the woman, the oppressed, and the subaltern, for their self-erasure has dangerous implications. Instead, as Kumkum Sangari argues, a discussion of women's agency, her "transformative capacity" must keep operations of class and patriarchy in sight "because women are simultaneously class differentiated and subject to frequent cross-class expansion." See Sangari's excellent essay "Consent, Agency and Rhetorics of Incitement," *Economic and Political Weekly*, May 1 1993: 867–882.

10. Sunder Rajan homes in on the issue of a woman's agency/resistance versus her acquiescence/will to die in the context of the debate triggered among the Indian intelligentsia in 1987, after Roop Kanwar's *sati* in Deorala, a small but expanding town in Rajasthan. This is the ultimate sticking point between what she perceives as two oppositional camps. Reframing the discourse around Roop Kanwar's *sati*, Sunder Rajan cautions against facile readings of "resistance" (the *sati's* lack of acquiescence in her burning) and insists on the importance of

keeping women's "intention" and "action" associated with "agency" in the picture. This is important, otherwise one falls into the trap of "romantic fiction" that a loose reading of resistance engenders, notwithstanding the well intentioned feminist agenda inspiring it. See Sunder Rajan, *Real and Imagined Women*, 4–5.

11. Ibid., 5. Also see Susie Tharu, "Women Writing in India," *Journal of Arts and Ideas* 20–1 (1991): 49–66.

12. Kumar, "Introduction," in *Women as Subjects*, ed. Kumar, 1–25.

13. Rosi Braidotti's "Or with your brains and my looks," *Men in Feminism*, eds. Alice Jardine and Paul Smith (New York: Methuen, 1987), 231–241, qtd. in Kumar, *Women as Subjects*, 8–9.

14. Kumar, *Women as Subjects*, 5–9.

15. It is all these forms of discourse that Teresa de Lauretis, using a Foucauldian paradigm, calls the "technologies" that "implant" the representation of gender.

16. Kumar, *Women as Subjects*, 20–21.

17. Sumita Chakravarty, *National Identity in Popular Hindi Cinema 1947–87* (Austin: Texas University Press, 1993), 216–218. Chakravarty provides an excellent reading of Sunder's personality. In my own tentative psychoanalytic reading, Radha and Gopal are, figuratively speaking, Sunder's father and mother. Gopal is the absent father, and Radha is the mother figure whom he cannot bear knowing once "belonged" to the father. In the end, the father is killed to complete the union.

18. This resonates with Kakar's findings in *Intimate Relations* about lovelessness and the lack of companionship many Indian couples experience in marriage—echoed in the candid 1992 television series called *Hello Zindagi!*, which examined middle-class lives. In one episode, the couples interviewed declare their disappointment with and the impossibility of finding love and partnership in marriage.

19. Ravi Vasudevan argues this persuasively in his essay "Dislocation: The Cinematic Imagining of a New Society in 1950s India," *Oxford Literary Review* 16.1–2 (1994): 93–124. Renunciation and spirituality in the last phase of a Brahmin's life, the *sanyasa* stage, are integral to Hindu *dharma*.

20. Parvati in *Devdas* is another example of a woman marrying a man she does not love, and the film demonstrates how she sustains her marriage through a powerful sense of duty. In the last scene, when she hears of her ex-lover Devdas's death in the streets of her town, Parvati, defying the decorum of her upperclass stature, lunges out of the inner recesses of the *haveli* (mansion) past the servants, children, and her husband toward the giant gates enclosing this ordered social structure, all the time screaming Devdas's name out loud. As her step-son, husband, and servants stand shocked by the transformation of this apotheosis of motherhood, her husband orders the front gates to be closed to hold Parvati in forever.

21. Raj Kapoor's *Awaara* (The Vagabond, 1951) and *Shri 420* (Mr. 420, 1955) are other examples that suggest the impossibility of imagining a future the protagonists walk toward (see chapter 3).

22. Chakravarty, *National Identity*, devotes an entire chapter to this genre in the book.

23. Ibid., 272.

24. Fareed Kazmi, "Muslim Socials and the Female Protagonist: seeing a dominant discourse at work," in *Forging Identities: Gender, Communities and the State*, ed.

Zoya Hasan (New Delhi: Kali for Women, 1994), 226–243. Kazmi quotes from Lesage's essay "Artful Racism, Artful Rape: Griffith's *Broken Blossoms*," in *Home is Where the Heart Is*, ed. Glendhill, 235–254.

25. Pam Cook, "Border Crossings: Women and Film in Context," *Women and Film: A Sight and Sound Reader*, Pam Cook and Philip Dodd (Philadelphia: Temple University Press, 1993), xiv–xv.

26. Patricia Uberoi's essay "Dharma and Desire, Freedom and Destiny: Rescripting the Man-Woman Relationship in Popular Hindi Cinema," *Embodiment: Essays on Gender and Identity*, ed. Meenakshi Thapan (New Delhi: Oxford University Press, 1997), 145–171 highlights the containment and punitive consequence of a wife's excessive and transgressive sexuality in *Sahib Bibi aur Ghulam*.

27. Cook, "Border Crossings," xv.

28. See Rosie Thomas, "Sanctity and Scandal." *Quarterly Review of Film and Video* 11 (1989): 11–30. Thomas opens tremendous possibilities for reading films and the social text by interposing extra-textual material about the star's life along with the film text. For a similar example of such work see Parama Roy, *Indian traffic: identities in question in colonial and postcolonial India* (Berkeley: University of California Press, 1998), and Jyotika Virdi, "The 'Fiction' of Film and 'Fact' of Politics: *Deewar* (Wall, 1976)," *Jump Cut* 38 (1993): 26–32.

29. Ien Ang, *Watching Dallas: Soap Opera and the Melodramatic Imagination* (London: Routledge, 1985) and Richard Dyer, *Heavenly Bodies: Film Stars and Society* (London: BFI, 1986), cited in Rachel Dwyer's *All You Want is Money, All You Need is Love* (London: Cassell, 2000), 196.

30. In Behroze Gandhy's and Rosie Thomas's essay "Three Indian film stars," *Stardom: Industry of Desire*, ed. Christine Glendhill (London: Routledge, 1991), 107–131, they trace the on–off screen careers of female stars to foreground changing gender politics between the 1930s and 80s.

31. "Meena Kumari," *Sunday World* 16 Apr. 1972.

32. *Ibid.*

33. Anirudha Bhattacharjee, "Lonely Lady," *The Illustrated Weekly of India*, 15 Apr. 1987: 42–43. He attributes the film to Sukhdev Sandhu, which is a source different from that noted in Ashish Rajadhyaksha's and Paul Willemen's *Encylopaedia of Indian Cinema* (New Delhi: Oxford University Press, 1995).

34. Dwyer, *All You Want Is Money*, 190. Her remarks are, however, directed at the one magazine, *Stardust*, whose stance she finds more odd since it is staffed mainly by women. Further, although she examines the magazine's production values since its inception in 1971, the content she analyzes is gleaned from the 1990s.

35. Interview with screenwriter Javed Akhtar, Bombay, July 1992.

Chapter 5   *The Sexed Body*

1. Successful outdoor shooting in *Junglee* (Uncouth, 1960), *Kashmir ki Kali* (Flower of Kashmir, 1963), *Sangam* (Confluence, 1964), and *Evening in Paris* (1967) established this convention.

2. When the couple visit European locales, as in *Sangam* (1964), *Love in Tokyo* (1966), *Evening in Paris* (1967), or *Around the World* (1967), national identity is established in an international order (see chapter 6).

3. *Achhut Kanya* (Untouchable Girl, 1936), *Sujata* (1959), and *Bombay* (1995) are exceptions rather than the rule. They tackle social issues with popular cinema's secular fervor, using heterosexual romance to transgress social boundaries (see note 46 in the introduction and chapter 2).

4. This parallels descriptions of unseen places that appeared in early nineteenth-century novels. Meenakshi Mukherjee discusses one such example, O Chandu Menon's novel *Indulekha* (1888), in *Realism and Reality: The Novel and Society in India* (New Delhi: Oxford University Press, 1985), 83.

5. In "Cinema and the Desire for Modernity," Madhava Prasad speculating about the "unwritten prohibition" on sex and intimacy, suggests it asserts patriarchal authority, which reserves scopophilia associated with intimate sexual relations for itself. On the other hand, the eroticized song-and-dance, the "cabaret" numbers, which Prasad glosses over rather hastily while searching for reasons for the prohibition on sex, arguably stand in for the "real thing." *Journal of Arts and Ideas* 25–26 (1994): 71–86.

6. Personal interview with Hindi film fan, Anju Moccha, a thirty-six-year-old middle-school teacher, living in Lajpat Nagar, New Delhi. This nostalgia for emphasizing eroticism in films through the exchange of glances is also noted by Patricia Uberoi, "Dharma and Desire, Freedom and Destiny: Rescripting the Man-Woman Relationship in Popular Hindi Cinema," *Embodiment: Essays on Gender and Identity*, ed. Meenakshi Thapan (New Delhi: Oxford University Press, 1997), 150 and Akbar Ahmad, "Bombay Films: The Cinema as Metaphor for Indian Society and Politics," *Modern Asian Studies* 26, 2 (1992): 308.

7. In this and the general plot line, the film bears remarkable resemblance to the eroticization of the mother-son relation Mary Ann Doane notes in *To Each His Own*. Doane reads maternal melodramas' relentless thwarting of the love story in Freudian terms, as a "flaw" in women's constantly "misdirected desire—their insistence on struggling for the 'wrong' object." Mary Ann Doane, "The Moving Image: Pathos and the Maternal," in *Imitations of Life: A Reader on Film and Television Melodrama*, ed. Marcia Landy (Detroit: Wayne State University Press, 1991), 301.

8. Susie Tharu, "Tracing Savitri's Pedigree," *Recasting Women: Essays in Colonial History*, eds. Kumkum Sangari and Sudesh Vaid (New Delhi: Kali for Women, 1989), 255–256, 260, 265.

9. Yash Chopra's earlier *Dhool ka Phool* (Blossom of Dust, 1959) narrates the terrible consequences of premarital sex, which occurs off-screen.

10. Christian Viviani, "Who Is Without Sin: The Maternal Melodrama in American Film, 1930–1939," in *Imitations of Life*, ed. Landy, 178.

11. Viviani points out that the maternal melodrama, *Madam X*–style, repeatedly traces the mother's separation from the child. The mother watches the child "from afar; she cannot risk jeopardizing his fortunes by contamination with her own bad repute." Viviani, "Who Is Without Sin,' 171.

12. Marcia Landy, "Introduction," in *Imitations of Life*, ed. Landy, 14.

13. See chapters 2 and 3 for a discussion of the mother-son-state relationship.

14. Viviani, "Who Is Without Sin," 173.

15. Ann Kaplan and Nick Browne take opposing stands on reading melodrama in China as family and political melodrama respectively. Including a "non-western" (Chinese) reading, distinct from her own, Kaplan cites director Hu Mei's exegesis of her film, *Army Nurse* (1986). For Mei a female protagonist is only incidental to her message of party repression that affects women and men and is therefore not a mark of sexual difference. See Ann Kaplan, "Problematising Cross-Cultural Analysis: The Case of Women in Recent Chinese Cinema," *Perspectives on Chinese Cinema*, ed. Chris Berry (London: BFI, 1991), 141–154; Nick Browne, "Society and Subjectivity: On the Political Economy of Chinese Melodrama," *New Chinese Cinemas: Forms, Identities, Politics*, eds. Nick Browne, Paul

G. Pickowicz, Vivian Sobchack, Esther Yau (New York: Cambridge University Press, 1994), 40–56.

16. Japanese terms refer to *giri* (obligation) and *ninjō* (personal inclination). See Keiko Iwai McDonald's "The Yakuza Film: An Introduction," *Reframing Japanese Cinema: Authorship, Genre, History*, eds. Arthur Noletti, Jr. and David Desser (Bloomington: Indiana University Press, 1992), 165.

17. Tadao Sato, "Change in the Image of Mother in Japanese Cinema and Television," *Cinema and Cultural Identity: Reflections on Films From Japan, India, and China*, ed. Wimal Dissanayake (Lanham, MD: University Press of America, 1988), 63–69.

18. Ma Ning points to the record earnings of *The In-Laws* (Xiyingmen, Shanghai Studio, 1982), which symbolically reenact the effect of decollectivized farming. See his "Symbolic representation and symbolic violence: Chinese family melodrama of the early 1980s," *Melodrama and Asian Cinema* ed. Wimal Dissanayake (New York: Cambridge University Press, 1993), 32.

19. Ann Kaplan, citing Chris Berry, calls this an "anti-individual aesthetic" in Chinese melodrama. See her "Problematising Cross-Cultural Analysis: The Case of Women in Recent Chinese Cinema," *Perspectives on Chinese Cinema* 145 and "Melodrama / subjectivity / ideology: Western melodrama theories and their relevance to recent Chinese cinema," in Dissanayake, *Melodrama and Asian Cinema*, 25.

20. For priorities of hyperbole and valuation see Wimal Dissanayake "Introduction," in his *Melodrama and Asian Cinema*, 2 & 4; and for inadmissible codes, Ann Kaplan citing Christine Glendhill, *Home Is Where the Heart Is* (London: BFI, 1987), 38 in Dissanayake, *Melodrama and Asian Cinema*, 10.

21. Thomas Schatz points out that social comedy is the inverse of melodrama. "Whereas the characters of romantic or screwball comedies scoff at social decorum or propriety, in melodrama they are at the mercy of social conventions." See his "The Family Melodrama," in Landy, *Imitations of Life*, 149.

22. Vijay Sharma's *Jai Santoshi Maa* (Hail Mother Santoshi, 1975) also had tremendous appeal for women viewers. Reminiscent of the 1930s religio-mythological films, it acquired a cult status among the urban lower class and was a bigger success than *Seeta aur Geeta*. This film too is a saga of a woman's ill treatment by her in-laws and her ultimate rescue by the goddess Santoshi in whom she places abiding faith.

23. Jeffrey and Jeffrey, "Killing My Heart's Desire: Education and Female Autonomy in Rural North India," in *Women As Subjects: South Asian Histories*, ed. Nita Kumar (Charlottesville: University Press of Virginia, 1994), 125–171.

24. Noël Carroll, "Notes on the Sight Gag," *Comedy/Cinema/Theory*, ed. Andrew Horton (Berkeley: University of California Press, 1991), 39–40.

25. Patricia Mellencamp, "Situation Comedy, Feminism and Freud: Discourses of Gracie and Lucy," *Studies in Entertainment*, ed. Tania Modleski (Bloomington: Indian University Press, 1986), 93.

26. Hindi cinema caricatures women organizing—especially westernized women acting as saviors of their subaltern sisters (see chapter 2).

27. Ella Shohat and Robert Stam, *Unthinking Eurocentrism: Multiculturalism and the Media* (New York: Routledge, 1994), 302.

28. Ibid., 305.

29. Ibid., 302–303.

30. James Scott, *Domination and the Art of Resistance* (New Haven: Yale University Press, 1990), 80, cited in Shohat and Stam, *Unthinking Eurocentrism*, 304.

31. Teresa L. Ebert, "The Romance of Patriarchy: Ideology, Subjectivity, and Femi-

nist Cultural Theory," *Cultural Critique, Special Issue: Popular Narratives/Popular Image* 10 (1988): 38.

32. Ibid., 41, and Janet Dailey, *Dangerous Masquerade* (London: Mills and Boon, 1976), 135, qtd in Ebert, 41.

33. Barbara Ehrenreich's phrase to describe women's enthusiastic support for Lorena Bobbitt in her "Feminism Confronts Bobbittry," *The Snarling Citizen* (New York: Harper Collins, 1995), 85.

34. The "rape bill"—the upshot of public shock and women's rage—became the Anti-Rape Act in 1986 despite its shortcomings. For more details see Radha Kumar, "The Agitation Against Rape," *A History of Doing* (New York: Verso, 1994), 127–142; and Kalpana Kannabiran, "Rape and the Construction of Communal Identity," *Embodied Violence: Communalising Women's Identity in South Asia,* eds. Kumari Jayawardena and Malathi de Alwis (New Delhi: Kali for Women, 1996), 32–41.

35. *Bharati* derives from the word *Bharat,* the Hindi name for India.

36. Star currency is crucial in viewer expectations. Ramesh Gupta played by Raj Babbar, not conventionally a villain, added to the quotidian nature of acquaintance rape.

37. "Conduct" was critical to the Supreme Court's verdict in the Mathura rape trial. According to the judges, Mathura's "boyfriends" and sexual liaisons prior to her rape pointed to her "loose" conduct. It was therefore difficult, the argument went, to establish whether she had consented to sex with the constables or not. In 1989 the courts again ruled against Rameeza Bee on the same grounds. See Kannabiran, "Rape and the Construction," 32–41; and Vimal Balasubrahmanyan, *In Search of Justice: Women, Law, Landmark Judgements and Media* (Bombay: Shubhada Saraswat Prakashan, 1990), 107–153.

38. *Anjaam* (Consequence, 1994) is held exemplary in this respect, though several other films, *Pratighaat* (Retribution, 1987), *Zakhmi Aurat* (Wounded Woman, 1988), *Haq* (Rights, 1991), and *Damini* (Lightning, 1994) fit this avenging woman category.

39. Carol J. Clover, "High and Low: The Transformation of the Rape-Revenge Movie," in *Women and Film: A Sight and Sound Reader,* ed. Pam Cook and Philip Dodd (Philadelphia: Temple University Press, 1993), 76–85.

40. Ibid., 76.

41. Inevitably a woman's body registers violation or injury of one kind or another. In *Pratighaat* and *Damini* neither protagonist is raped. The protagonist in *Pratighaat* is disrobed in public (see chapter 1) and in *Damini* a working-class woman is raped by members of the upper-class protagonist's family. In *Haq* the protagonist has a miscarriage and the public and private conflicts coalesce when she takes on her politician husband who is responsible for this.

42. Rosie Thomas refers to Radha's leveling a gun to kill her own son in *Mother India's* denouement as "the most powerfully horrifying image." See her "Sanctity and Scandal: The Mythologization of Mother India," *Quarterly Review of Film and Video* 11 (1989): 11–30 (and also chapter 3). In *Mamta,* a Madame X style variant of *Aradhana,* the protagonist/mother kills her extortionist husband and is defended in court by her long-lost daughter. The mother dies moments after learning that her daughter recognizes her maternal sacrifice after all.

43. Other films in the thriller genre include *C.I.D.* (1956) (C.I.D. stands for "central investigating detective"), in which a police officer tackles the mafia (see chapter 3), *Jewel Thief* (1967) about an international spy ring, and *Intikaam* (The Test, 1968), the story of an escaped convict.

44. Rules governing rape trials are based on Sir Mathew Hale's opinion written to the King's Bench in 1671: since "rape is a charge 'so easily made and so difficult for a man to defend against' . . . it must be examined with greater caution than any other crime." See Susan Brownmiller's seminal *Against Our Will: Men, Women and Rape* (New York: Bantam, 1976).

45. Lynn Higgins and Brenda A. Silver, "Introduction," *Rape and Representation*, eds. Lynn Higgins and Brenda Silver (New York: Columbia University Press, 1991), 2–3.

46. Brenda A. Silver, "Periphrasis, Power and Rape in *A Passage to India*," in *Rape and Representation*, 115–137.

47. Carol J. Clover, *Men, Women, and Chainsaws* (New Jersey: Princeton University Press, 1992), 20.

48. Ibid., 137.

49. In "Life After Rape: Narrative, Rape and Feminism," *Real and Imagined Women: Gender, Culture and Postcolonialism* (New York: Routledge, 1993), 64–82, Rajeswari Sunder Rajan refers to the "almost mandatory" rape scene in Hindi films (82), while Lalitha Gopalan reads it as an excuse for violent sex—though ultimately necessitating the woman's revenge ("Avenging Women in Indian Cinema," *Screen* 38.1 [1997]: 51). I am suggesting we closely examine the variations in staging rape.

50. Speaking of another context—female masochistic role-play in sadomasochistic pornography—Linda Williams points to the double standard in patriarchy which distinguishes the sexually passive "good girl" from the sexually active "bad girl." The masochistic role play allows the "bad girl" pleasure while demonstrating she has "paid for" it—while of course keeping the cultural laws dividing good/bad girls intact. See her "Film Bodies: Gender, Genre, and Excess," *Film Genre Reader II*, ed. Barry Keith Grant (Austin: University of Texas Press, 1995), 150.

51. *Shringaar rasa* connotes the mood of love, romance, and sensual pleasure—one of the nine *rasas* in classical Indian drama theory.

52. Pandit Indra, "Pandit Indra Advocates Vulgarity!" *Film India* June 1947: 47–48. Opposing the editor's condemnation of the film *Panihari* (1947), he says, "First of all I should warn the puritan editor that he is doing the greatest injustice to the industry by exciting the Government against our pictures. . . . Does he want to turn our 'Romantic industry' into [a] heartless business institution? If romance[,] which he alleges [is] . . . vulgarity[,] is squeezed away[,] what will remain? Preaching sermons? Then why go to the pictures at all? We can attend temples, mosques and churches for sermons."

53. This shift might lend credibility to the feminist charge that the rape scene substitutes for the vamp. My own preferred reading, however, is that the vamp figure is at odds with a populist feminist discourse, which has increasingly become Hindi film's cachet.

54. Three recent essays address this question: Shohini Ghosh, "Deviant Pleasures and Disorderly Women," *Feminist Terrains and Legal Domains: Interdisciplinary Essays on Women and Law in India*, ed. Ratna Kapur (New Delhi: Kali for Women, 1996), 150–183; Priyamvada Gopal, "Of Victims and Vigilantes: The *Bandit Queen* Controversy," *Thamyris* Special Issue: Gender in the Making: Indian Contexts 4.1 (1997): 73–102; and Gopalan, "Avenging Women," 42–59.

55. This recapitulation is based on my participation as an activist in the women's movement through the 1980s. Ashish Rajadhyaksha echoes this sentiment in his write up on *Insaaf ka Taraazu*: "The three rape sequences staged with

voyeuristic relish, no doubt contributed to its commercial success." Ashish Rajadhyaksha and Paul Willemen, *The Encyclopedia of Indian Cinema* (New Delhi: Oxford University Press, 1995), 416. Also see Susie Tharu, "On Subverting a Rhetoric: a Study of the Media Versions of Rape," *Olympus* 8, no. 9 (August 1981): 1–5.

56. See Mary Ann Doane's "Woman's Stake: Filming the Female Body," in *Feminism and Film Theory*, ed. Constance Penley (New York: Routledge, 1988), 216, 225, and 226 for quotations in this and the next paragraph.

57. Gopal's sensitive iteration of the confusion unleashed by competing claims between Phoolan Devi's pain, the invasion of her privacy, and the commodification of her narrative in *Bandit Queen* point to the profound contradiction wherein rape is experienced as a private trauma despite the women's movement's effort to view it as a public issue, a manifestation of quotidian power structures and relations. Gopal, "Of Victims and Vigilantes," 96–97.

58. Jonathan Dollimore, "The Cultural Politics of Perversion: Augustine, Shakespeare, Freud, Foucault," *Genders* 8 (1990): 2–16, qtd. in Williams, "Film Bodies," 148.

59. Ghosh, "Deviant Pleasures," 176; Gopalan, "Avenging Women," 53. Additionally, Gopalan points to the "unresolved problems attending representational struggles, around femininity, violence and the State (59)." In Hindi cinema's rape revenge narratives, she argues, on the one hand the rape is occasioned by the state's absence, its lapses in convicting past rapists, and on the other the state's presence is felt in filmic representations of rape via censorship. In contrast, in a regional Telegu film like *Police Lock Up* (1992), rape is not required to stage a woman's heroic revenge in drama inflected by the political genre. Here the female protagonist is a police officer, a law enforcement official, and the film's text and subtext offer suggestions for lesbian fantasies—even though Gopalan concedes that it is ultimately uneasily implicated in state power.

60. Anupama Chopra and Farah Baria, "The Beauty Craze," *India Today*, 15 Nov. 1996: 20–29.

61. On melodrama see Glendhill, *Home Is Where the Heart Is*, and Landy, *Imitations of Life*.

62. As Clover argues, in "popular cinema's redefinition . . . rape [is] less an act of sex than an act of power." In *Men, Women, and Chainsaws*, 153.

63. Hindi cinema is wont to represent feminist discourses as well as participate in the backlash against such discourses.

Chapter 6 *Re-reading Romance*

1. Among other nineteenth-century reform measures child marriage was outlawed. Although the "enlightened" population does not practice child marriage today, it is not uncommon for powerful businessmen or politicians to flout this law.

2. Hindi films use stereotypes, generally caricatures, to represent minority ethnic communities—Marwaris, Sikhs, Parsis, Christians, and so on. Christians, since Nadia (alias Mary Evans) in the 1930s and Helen in the 1950s and 1960s, were coded the eroticized hybrid Indian in westernized clothing (see chapter 5).

3. *Kabari* is a traditional occupation, dealing in recycling used household products.

4. A *kabarigaar* is a person who runs a *kabari* operation.

5. In *Trishul* for instance, the Amitabh Bachchan character at war with his fa-

ther combines themes of avenging his mother's suffering and class conflict (see chapter 3)—not generalized irreverence.

6. Personal interview in June 1992 with a Hindi film fan, Mr. V. Sodhi, a fifty-year-old bank employee. Another interviewee, Nanda Saadh, a housewife with two teenage daughters, vehemently disapproved of love stories portraying harsh parents; I couldn't help noting her vehemence was in part a message to her fifteen-year-old daughter, who sat in sullenly on the interview.

7. The practice of dowry, originally conceived as *stree-dhan* (woman's wealth), took the form of gold and jewelry a woman received when she married, ensuring her financial security. The practice is now transformed to include anything from consumer durables to start up capital for the bridegroom.

8. Paternal authority has long obstructed young love. K. Asif's grand "historical" film, *Mughal-e-Azam* (The Grand Mughal, 1960) tells a similar story: Prince Salim's legendary affair with a commoner, Anarkali, is thwarted by his father, Akbar, the Mughal emperor.

9. Tanika Sarkar, "The Woman as Communal Subject: Rashtriya Sevika Samiti and the Ram Janambhoomi Movement," *Economic and Political Weekly* vol.xxvi (1991): 2057–2062.

10. Teesta Setalvaad, "Sisterhood in Saffron," *Communalism Combat*, March 1995: 12–13, excerpted from *Women and the Hindu Right*, eds. Tanika Sarkar and Urvashi Butalia (New Delhi: Kali for Women, 1997). Setalvaad argues that engagement in the feminist movement induces difficult choices and crises in women's personal lives. These are skirted altogether by the Hindu Right's ideology, which ignores conflict in traditional patriarchal man-woman relationships.

11. An *anthakshari* session is a game, a singing contest between two teams. Opposing teams alternately sing film songs in which the first word must begin with the last letter of the alphabet from the previous song.

12. Gayatri Gopinath argues that the cross-dressed woman transgresses accepted social boundaries and temporarily displaces the hero, who the film reassuringly reinstates (as is typical) in the end. See her "Nostalgia, Desire, Diaspora: South Asian Sexualities in Motion," *Positions* 5.2 (1997): note 39, p. 489. Also, Mary E. John cites Giti Thadani, who points out that the hero has access to women's space denied to the "butch-looking woman." Giti Thadani, *Sakhiyani: Lesbian Desire in Ancient and Modern India* (London: Cassell, 1996), 100, cited in Mary E. John "A Question of Silence? An Introduction," *A Question of Silence? The Sexual Economies of Modern India*, eds. Mary E. John and Janaki Nair (New Delhi: Kali for Women, 1998), 35.

13. Lisa A. Lewis, "Emergence of Female Address on MTV," *Sound and Vision: The Music Video Reader*, eds. Simon Frith, Andrew Goodwin, and Lawrence Grossberg (New York: Routledge, 1993), 136–137.

14. Since the mid–1980s women's groups all over the country have produced and popularized feminist songs and plays that appropriate folk music in lyrics propagating feminist ideas.

15. Lewis, "Emergence of Female Address," 139.

16. The Non-Resident Indian is a person of Indian origin recognized by the Indian state (in The Foreign Exchange Regulations Act of 1973) as residing outside India, and on whom it bestows special financial privileges with expectation of foreign exchange investments in India. See Purnima Mankekar, "Brides Who Travel: Gender, Transnationalism, and Nationalism in Hindi Film," *Positions* 7.3 (1999): 731–761 and Arvind Rajagopal, *Politics after Television: Hindu*

Nationalism and the Reshaping of the Public in India (New York: Cambridge University Press, 2001), 241–242.

17. Comparing the film to the earlier *Purab aur Paschim* (East and West, 1970; see chapter 2), Mankekar finds the male's role changed—from going west for knowledge to returning as an investor. Arguably, the two still fit together paradigmatically—both belonging to the material sphere, the world, which as Partha Chatterjee delineates, is deemed the Indian male's domain. Mankekar, "Brides Who Travel," 750–751.

18. Patricia Uberoi, "The Diaspora Comes Home: Disciplining Desire in *DDLJ*," *Contributions to Indian Sociology* 32.2 (1998): 332.

19. Jagori Collective, *Nukkad-Nukkad, Aangan-Aangan: Mahila Aandolan ke Dauraan Ubhre Nukkad Naatakon ka Sankalan* (*Every Corner, Every Courtyard: A Collection of Street-Plays Emerging from the Women's Movement*) (New Delhi: Jagori, 1988).

20. Eva Illouz, *Consuming the Romantic Utopia: Love and the Cultural Contradiction of Capitalism* (Berkeley: University of California Press, 1997), 146, 152.

21. Television serials in the 1980s and 1990s, starting with *Buniyaad* (Foundation), abound with female protagonists of all classes heroically overcoming sexism at home or in the work place. Not infrequently, episodes include a middle-class women's group helping a woman in distress. For more details see Purnima Mankekar, *Screening Culture, Viewing Politics: An Ethnography of Television, Womanhood, and Nation in Postcolonial India* (Durham: Duke University Press, 1999), especially chapter 3, "'Women-Oriented' Narratives and the New Indian Woman," 104–162.

22. Mankekar, "Brides Who Travel"; Uberoi, "Diaspora Comes Home"; and Rachel Dwyer, *All You Want Is Money, All You Need is Love: Sex and Romance in Modern India* (London: Cassell, 2000), 141.

23. In the scene in question Simran awakes after a night of drunken revelry, distraught by the tell-tale signs, until Raj assures her that the signs are fabricated—a prank. The ellipsis in the events rather deftly leaves it open to an equivocal, even opposite reading—by second generation NRIs, for instance. Some of my conversations with south Asian undergraduates in North America suggest that they prefer obfuscation around their own sexual encounters and are even comfortable with their subcontinental parents' deliberate "naivete," their confidence in their own children's distance from a sexually permissive milieu.

24. David Bordwell, Kristin Thompson, and Janet Staiger, *The Classical Hollywood Cinema: Film Style and Mode of Production* (New York: Columbia University Press, 1985).

25. Illouz, *Consuming the Romantic*, 9–10.

26. Ibid., chapter 1, note 1, p. 321.

27. Ibid., 30, this and the next quote in this paragraph.

28. Ibid., 32.

29. Gurcharan Das, *India Unbound* (New York: Knopf, 2001), esp. 287. Also see Rachel Dwyer's excellent description of Bombay's middle classes, relevant for the rest of India (Dwyer, *All You Want Is Money*, 58–95).

30. Arif Dirlik, "Is There History after Eurocentricism? Globalisation, Postcolonialism, and the Disavowal of History," *Cultural Critique* 42 Spring (1999): 11.

31. Dwyer, *All You Want Is Money*, 102.

32. Illouz, *Consuming the Romantic*, 14.

33. Ibid., 26.

34. Ibid., 82.
35. Ibid., 56.
36. Ibid., 110.
37. Ibid., 81.
38. B. R. Tomlinson argues that with the end of colonial rule, nationalist rhetoric for internal self-reliance became the model for economic planning. However, it caved to foreign aid—in practically every decade since independence—due to endemic problems of low food production, food imports, and the need for foreign exchange to support basic industries. See his *The New Cambridge History of India: The Economy of Modern India 1860–1970* (New York: Cambridge University Press, 1993), 156–218.
39. Akhil Gupta, "Song of the Nonaligned World: Transnational identities and the Reinscription of Space in Late Capitalism," *Cultural Anthropology* 7.1 (1992): 73.
40. Arjun Appaduari discusses "refiguring the nation" in *Modernity at Large: Cultural Dimensions of Globalization* (Minneapolis: University of Minnesota Press, 1997). Also see Gupta, "Song of the Nonaligned," 68–79.
41. In the 1960s transnational locations were not uncommon as in *Sangam* (Confluence, 1964), *Love in Tokyo* (1966), and *Evening in Paris* (1967).
42. In *Maine Pyar Kiya* and *Hum Aapke* more attention is paid to details of the mis-en-scène, departing from earlier films employing minimalist signifiers to indicate a wealthy or poor home. Maria Laplace observes a similar fetishization of "consumerist objects and a consumerist lifestyle" within the mise-en-scène of the 1930s' Hollywood films. See her "Producing and Consuming the Woman's Film: Discursive Struggle in *Now, Voyager,*" in *Home is Where the Heart Is*, ed. Christine Gledhill (London: BFI, 1987), 141. Ronald Inden observes the elites appropriated the films both on the screen and in the upscale refurbished theatres during the 1990s, displacing the "masses." See his "Transnational Class, Erotic Arcadia and Commercial Utopia in Hindi Films," *Image journeys: audio-visual media and cultural change*, eds. Christiane Brosius & Melissa Butcher (New Delhi: Sage Publications, 1999), 41–68.
43. Rustom Bharucha argues the film creates desires for both material and filial abundance where, under new material conditions, the latter is eroding and the former remains elusive for the majority. See his "Utopia in Bollywood: *Hum Aapke Hain Koun,*" *Economic and Political Weekly* 30.15 April 15 (1995): 801–804.
44. In contradistinction, Uberoi finds the denouement in *Dilwale* credibly motivated rather than miraculous. See her "The Diaspora Comes Home," 305–336.
45. M. S. Gore, *Urbanisation and Family Change* (Bombay: Popular Prakashan, 1968), 34–35, cited in Amrita Singh Tyagi and Patricia Uberoi, "Learning to Adjust: Conjugal Relations in Indian Popular Fiction," *Indian Journal of Gender Studies* 1.1 (1994): 93–120.
46. In Dwyer's view Aditya Chopra emulates his father Yash Chopra's style—incorporating spectacular visuals and music in films where ultimately social conservatism triumphs against any challenge, restores the status quo, and frees the experience from guilt (Dwyer, *All You Want Is Money*,140–142 and 162–165). However, for Inden "the idea that erotic love has displaced parental and filial love as the basis of social relations is little in evidence ("Transnational Class," 54–55)." Dwyer, too, finds the family is valued over romantic love (*All You Want Is Money*, 139).

Conclusion

1. Chuck Klienhans, "Melodrama and the Family Under Capitalism," in *Imitations of Life: A Reader on Film and Television Melodrama*, ed. Marcia Landy (Detroit: Wayne State University Press, 1991), 199.
2. Arjun Appadurai and Carol A. Beckenridge, "Introduction," *Consuming Modernity: Public Culture in a South Asian World*, ed. Carol A. Beckenridge (Minneapolis: University of Minnesota Press, 1995), 7–8.
3. Arvind Rajagopal, "Communalism and the Consuming Subject," *Economic and Political Weekly* 10 Feb. 1996: 341–348.
4. Wimal Dissanayake, "Critical Approaches to World Cinema," *The Oxford Guide to Film Studies*, eds. John Hill and Pamela Church Gibson (New York: Oxford University Press, 1998), 530.
5. Interview, *Movie Mahal*, a documentary series on the Hindi film industry produced for British Television's Channel 4, London, U.K.

Index

About the Author

Jyotika Virdi has a Ph.D. in film and telecommunications from the University of Oregon and is currently an assistant professor in the Department of Communication, University of Windsor, Windsor, Ontario. She has published essays on popular Hindi cinema in *Jump Cut*, *Film Quarterly*, *Screen*, and *Visual Anthropology*.